AMERICA'S MUSICAL HERITAGE

A COMPANION BOOK
TO
OUR DEVELOPING CIVILIZATION
SERIES

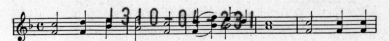

AMERICA'S
MUSICAL HERITAGE

CASSIE BURK, Ph.D.
Department of Education, State Teachers College
Fredonia, New York

VIRGINIA MEIERHOFFER, A.M.
Department of Music, State Teachers College
Fredonia, New York

CLAUDE ANDERSON PHILLIPS, Ph.D.
Professor of Education, University of Missouri
Columbia, Missouri

•

Illustrations by
MILO WINTER

LAIDLAW BROTHERS
Publishers

CHICAGO   NEW YORK   SAN FRANCISCO

DALLAS   ATLANTA

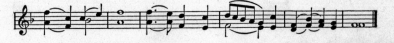

ACKNOWLEDGMENTS

The American Book Company for a selection from *Music in History* by Howard D. McKinney and W. R. Anderson, copyright 1940. D. Appleton-Century Company for a selection from *The Cowboy and His Interpreters* by Douglas Branch, copyright 1926. Church of the Latter Day Saints for "Come, Come, Ye Saints" by William Clayton. Thomas Y. Crowell Company for selections from *Men and Women Who Make Music* by David Ewen, copyright 1939; for selections from *Our American Music* by John Tasker Howard, copyright 1939. Oliver Ditson Company for selections from *History of Public School Music in the United States* by E. B. Birge, copyright 1937. *The Etude* for a selection from "Music Popular at the Time of Lincoln" by Pearl Brown Brands; for a selection from "The Saga of the Immortal Jenny Lind" by Kitty Cheatham; for a selection from "Thomas Jefferson's Musical Interests" by Charles Edward Gauss; for selections from "A Remarkable American Musical Tradition" by J. Media (James Francis Cooke). Farrar & Rinehart for a selection from *Old Gimlet Eye; Adventures* of Smedley D. Butler by Lowell Thomas, copyright 1933. Houghton Mifflin Company for "The Mission Bells of Monterey" by Bret Harte from *The Poetical Works of Bret Harte;* for "The Kansas Emigrants" by John Greenleaf Whittier from *The Complete Poetical Works of John Greenleaf Whittier.* The *Kansas City Star* for a selection from "An 1878 Prophecy of Radio"; for a selection from "This Whacky Thing Called Swing That Is Upsetting the Musicians." The La Grave Company for a selection from *The Autobiography of Charles Peters;* for a selection from *The Good Luck Era of the Placer Mining Days of the Fifties.* J. B. Lippincott Company for a selection from *Body, Boots & Britches* by Harold W. Thompson, copyright 1940. John A. Lomax for "A Cowboy Alone with His Conscience" from *Songs of the Cattle Trail and Cow Camp,* copyright 1931. The Macmillan Company for selections from *Child Life in Colonial Days* by Alice M. Earle, copyright 1927. The *New York Times* for a selection from "Higher Soars the Swing Fever" by Gama Gilbert; for a selection from "The Aims of Music for Films" by Aaron Copland. W. W. Norton & Company for a selection from *American Jazz Music* by Wilder Hobson, copyright 1939. RCA Manufacturing Company for a selection from *Music and Romance* by Hazel Gertrude Kinscella. Charles Scribner's Sons for a selection from *Spanish Explorations in the Southwest, 1542-1706;* Original Narratives of Early American History edited by Herbert Eugene Bolton, copyright 1916. *Time* for a selection from "Bravos" from "Radio," November 20, 1939. The Whittlesey House of McGraw-Hill Company for a selection from *Music for Fun* by Sigmund Spaeth, copyright 1939.

TEACHER PREFACE

America's Musical Heritage is not written to give a detailed history of music in America, but to magnify the importance of music in the development of the culture of the people in America. In order to help the reader understand and appreciate the significance of this contribution, the account is interwoven with vital experiences of the country from its beginning to the present time. Episodes and incidents of definite historical importance have been chosen purposefully, and around them stories of music have been centered. Moreover, these episodes have been chosen with a recognition of the fact that they offer infinite possibilities for colorful and dramatic experiences which are so challenging to young people.

OBJECTIVES. Undoubtedly the book may serve the following purposes:

1. The stories parallel the patterns used in the teaching of the social studies and music in the upper intermediate grades and junior high schools. Obviously, in the case of the social studies, the material will add numerous opportunities for dramatic and emotional experiences.

2. The book supplies a wide range of musical material for a modern integrated school program.

3. The book furnishes an unusual type of recreational reading.

4. Certainly the book provides elaborate source material to help stabilize our emotional life and deepen the appreciation of our American heritage in war-time tension.

ORGANIZATION. *America's Musical Heritage* consists of four parts which trace the development of our nation's music from early colonial days to the present time.

1. The vocabulary of the book is carefully chosen so as to be well within the understanding of the pupil in the upper intermediate and junior high school grades. Pronunciations of technical words and names, definitions, and biographical data are given in the footnotes. Pronunciations are also included in the index. The sentence structure is also carefully adapted to the ability of the pupils.

2. *Study Exercises* are given at the end of the four parts of the book. The *Questions and Problems* are based on the facts given in the preceding chapters and so should be the minimum requirements for all pupils. The *Suggested Activities* include additional interesting projects involving dramatics, music, the radio, reading, and oral reports which will provide for individual differences.

3. Many illustrations of various kinds are found throughout the book. Photographs illustrating the historical setting of the stories are supplemented by original drawings by a well-known artist. Many songs are given for class use.

4. In the appendix a considerable list of suggested songs, records, piano pieces, and readings for both pupils and teachers is included for reference and optional use.

CONTENTS

Part One. Music in the Colonial Period

Part Two. Music in the Struggle to Become a Nation

Part Three. Music in the Period of Expansion

Part Four. Music in a Full-Grown Nation

Appendixes

LIST OF SONGS AND POEMS

OUR MUSICAL HERITAGE

America's musical heritage is not a thing of time or place. It has come from many countries; it has also grown up within our boundaries. It consists of music of every kind and for every occasion. From north, south, east, and west, from mountain, plain, swamp, and river, the melodies of all people have been interwoven into one great symphony which we call American music. These melodies have become as much a part of our national life as our laws, our customs, or our religion.

Our musical heritage does not come from people as individuals, but from groups of people and their influence on other groups. On the other hand, each individual does contribute something to his group and in this way helps to make up the musical culture of our nation at any one time.

This culture is constantly growing and changing. During the lifetime of the boys and girls of today, there will come many changes which will influence the music of our country. Each person who shares in our musical heritage today has, in turn, an opportunity to contribute to the growth and development of the music of his community. That will be added to our present heritage to make America's musical heritage of tomorrow.

America has become a singing nation.

PART ONE

MUSIC IN THE COLONIAL PERIOD

It is impossible to imagine our country without music. We know, for example, that even before the white men came here, the American Indians used some kind of rhythmic activities for their tribal ceremonies. While there is little in written history about music during the time of the discoveries, it is likely that, in the days of the early exploration of America, the adventurous men who sailed with Leif Ericson, the Cabots, Columbus, Magellan, or other explorers, sang together to lighten tedious tasks or to keep up their courage.

The known story of music in our land began with some of the first permanent settlements. From that time, music became closely associated with the story of each epoch, indeed, with every important event in our history. In time of war or time of peace, in the older settlements or on the new frontier, music was a part of our nation and of our people. One cannot truly appreciate the story of the development of the United States without knowing something of the part which music has played in that development. Moreover, it is a fascinating story.

More than three hundred years ago, at least five European countries—Spain, England, France, Holland, and Sweden—sent ships across the Atlantic Ocean to make settlements in the land we know today as our United States. The ships of these nations brought the people who were to establish new settlements. Equally important, the people brought with them their customs, habits, and ideas which were to form the culture of the new nation.

Doubtless, on some ships sailors and adventurers hummed gay tunes which they had heard in their native countries. Later on, other ships carried a few musical instruments. Devoutly religious men, stepping for the first time upon the shore of a new land, sang the hymns of praise they had sung in their homelands. Mothers rocked their babies to sleep with the lullabies which their own mothers had sung to them. All of these tunes became a part of the culture of the nation which was just beginning.

Within a few years, new words were set to the old, familiar tunes. By that time, groups living in certain communities were giving more attention to music than other groups, and so music centers were started. In some of these places, religious music received the greatest attention; in others, concerts, operas, and dance music were enjoyed. Singing in the churches of the English settlers was gradually improved. In some communities, too, the organ was used in church services, and the profession of music gained some recognition. Towards the end of the colonial period, the piano was invented, and other musical instruments were improved. It became fashionable to know how to play one or more of these musical instruments. In these ways the foundation of America's musical heritage was established.

In Part One we shall try to discover the kind of music which the first settlers brought with them to the New World. We shall find out what part of their music we still sing or play now. And, finally, we shall learn how their customs relating to music were different from those which we have today.

CHAPTER I

EARLY MUSIC IN THE NEW ENGLAND COLONIES

Music of the Pilgrims and Puritans

Kind of Music Sung. Have you ever tried singing several songs to the same tune? Wouldn't it seem queer if we sang songs that way? In the early colonial days in New England, that is the way many songs were sung.

The only kind of music the early Pilgrims and Puritans brought with them to this country was religious music—psalms[1] which they had sung in England. There were only eight or nine tunes, and the ability to sing these tunes constituted the colonists' entire knowledge of music. There were no musical instruments. There was no part singing. One tune the colonists sang, "Old Hundred," is familiar to us today. This tune was called "Old Hundred" because it was set to the One Hundredth Psalm. It is the "Doxology"[2] which is sung today in many of our churches.

Music in a Sunday Church Service. Let us imagine a Sunday church service in New England in the early colonial days. At nine o'clock in the morning the people were called to the meetinghouse by a blast on a conch[3] shell, by a trumpet, or by the roll of a drum. The long service was broken by psalm singing. The hymns most often sung

1. psalms. Sacred songs or poems. 2. "Doxology" (dŏks·ŏl′ō·jĭ). A hymn praising God. 3. conch (kŏngk) shell. A large, spiral seashell.

Psalm. C.   353

a Preſt, or Sacrificer, is the name of the Kings cheif officer, as in 2. Sam. 8, 18. Davids ſonns were Cohens, (Cheif-rulers, Aularchai as the Greek termeth them,) which is expounded in 1.Chron.18. 17. to be the firſt (or Cheif) at the Kings hand. It hath the name of miniſtration, Iſa.61,6.10 and was a title ſpecially given to Aaron and his ſonns, that miniſtred unto God in the Sacctuarie. Exo.28.3.4.41. caled or were caling: that is, prayed for the people, as Exod.32, 11. &c. Num.14,17,19.& 16,22,46. 1.Sam.7,9. & 12:19.23. Hereupon Moſes & Samuel were noted for cheif interceſſors with God , Ier. 15,1.   v. 7. of a clowd] as Exo. 19.9.Num.16,42. and this noteth Gods favour, but with ſome obſcurity: and ſo is inferiour to the mediation of Chriſt, who hath without clowds or ſhadowes obteyned eternal redemption for us, that we may goe boldly to the throne of grace, for to receiv mercy and find grace to help in time of need. Heb. 4,14,16. & 7,25. & 9.11,12.   v. 8. a God forgiving] a mighty-God that pardonedſt, or tookeſt away , to weet, the puniſhment of their ſyn: ſee Pſ. 51,18. and taking] or though thou tookeſt vengeance.   on their practiſes] theirs that is the peoples, for whom Moſes prayed , as Num. 14, 20, 21, 23. Exod. 32, 14,34,35. or theirs , that is, Moſes and Aarons ſynns; which God puniſhed and would not be intreated, as Num. 20,12. Deut. 3,23,24,25,26.

Psalm. 100.

1. A psalm for confeſſion:
SHowt ye triumphantly to Iehovah, al the earth.

2. Serv ye Iehovah with gladnes: come before him, with ſinging-joy.

3. Know ye, that Iehovah he *is* God: he made us, and not we: his people, & ſheep of his paſture.

4. Enter ye his gates, with confeſſion; his courts with praiſe: confeſs ye to him, bleſs ye his name.

5. For Iehovah *is* good, his mercy *is* for ever: & his faith, unto generation & generation.

Psalm. 100.

1. *SHowt to Jehovah, al the earth.* 2. *Serv ye Jehovah with gladnes: before him come with ſing- ing-mirth.* 3. *Know, that Jehovah he God is:*

Its he that *made us, and not wee;* his ſilk, *and ſheep of his feeding.*

4. *O with confeſſion enter yee his gates, his courtyards with praiſing: confeſs to him, bleſs ye his name.*

5. *Becauſe Jehovah he good is: his mercy ever is the ſame: and his faith, unto al ages.*

Annotations.

Verſ. 1. for confeſſion] for the publick praiſe of God, with thanks for his mercies. v. 2. ſinging] or thrilling, ſhowting-mirth.   v. 3. made us] this word is uſed both for our firſt creation in nature, Gen..1,26. and for the making of us hye and excellent with graces and bleſſings, as 1.Sam.12,6. Deut.32,6. Iſa.43,7.& 29.23. Ephe.2,10. and not we] and his we are: as the Debru. in the margine readeth it. Both ſenſes are good. ſheep] or flock which he ſeedeth. See Ezek.34,30,31. Pſal.95.7.   v. 4. confeſſion] the ſacrifice of thanks was this punith, 2.Chron. 29,31. Ier.17.26,   v. 5. faith] or, faith- fulnes: truth, in performing his promiſes.

Ii 3   Psalm. CI.

The words of the One Hundredth Psalm were used as the words for the song "Old Hundred."

were "Old Hundred," "York," "Hackney," "Dundee,"
"Windsor," and "Martyr." Hats were worn in the meetinghouse, but during the singing they were removed and
the congregation stood.

A deacon, elder, or the minister acted as leader in the
singing. He probably got the pitch by rapping on a candle-
stick with his knuckles. There were few books or none at
all. Many of the congregation could not have read the
words had there been books. And so the psalms were sung
by a method called "lining." The leader would sing one
line and the congregation would repeat it. Then the leader
would sing another, the congregation would repeat that,
and so on they would go through the song.

If the leader had a good ear for music and a good sense
of pitch, the singing would be musical; but, if the leader
could not carry a tune or if he pitched the song too high or
too low, the sound which resulted resembled music very
little and was sometimes scarcely more than a loud noise.
Sometimes it took half an hour to finish the psalm. Such a
service is very different from the beautiful music service
which we hear in our churches today.

Music in England. The New England church service
seems strange when we think that at the same time in England such famous composers as William Byrd, the father of
English music, Thomas Morley, John Wilbye, and Thomas
Weelkes, writers of madrigals,[4] and John Bull and Orlando
Gibbons, composers of keyboard music, were living. England at that time was famous for her madrigals and church
music.

Hardships in Early New England. The early settlers
had little opportunity for music. They were planting a
new settlement in a wilderness. Their manner of living

4. madrigals (măd′rĭ·gălz). Songs with parts for several voices.

In the Pilgrim meetinghouse, the singing was done by the
lining-out method.

was exceedingly primitive and hard. They had to endure cold, hunger, and sickness. Moreover, they frequently had to fight the Indians. Then, too, their troubles with the English government were a serious handicap for them.

Objections to Music. The early New Englanders had religious scruples against music as a means of pleasure. When they lived in England they had objected to such pleasures as plays, dancing, and music—particularly instrumental music—enjoyed by people of the court. Musical instruments were considered instruments of the devil. The Pilgrims and Puritans had left England because they were dissatisfied with religious and political conditions there; so it was not strange that they would have none of the music which was popular in England at that time.

They found reasons in the Bible for many of their beliefs. For example, Amos 5:23 says: "For I will not hear the melody of thy viols." This was interpreted to mean that instrumental music was improper. Some of the colonists did not even believe in the singing of psalms. They declared that "a Christian should make melody only in his heart." One group of people organized an antisinging church because they opposed any kind of church singing.

Manner of Singing. There were heated discussions as to how singing should be carried on. Some of the questions most frequently raised were: (1) Should one person sing for all the congregation, the others joining only in singing "amen," or should the whole congregation sing? (2) Should women as well as men sing, or only the men? (3) Should "carnal[5] men" and pagans be permitted to sing, or only the Christians and church members? (4) Should it be lawful to sing psalms in tunes invented by men, or should the congregation sing as inspired?

5. carnal (kär′năl). Pertaining to the body and flesh; not spiritual.

One group held that singing was the sole right of Christians; the heathen Indians might be given only the privilege of saying "amen." This group said that women couldn't even say "amen." Others believed that to sing a melody composed or made by man was only a "vain show," that God would not be pleased with praise in which man had a hand in making the melody. The hymn tunes were considered by many to be as sacred as the words themselves.

Songbooks and Choirs

Collections of Psalms. The Pilgrims, who had first migrated to Holland and then had come to America and settled at Plymouth, were more strict than the Puritans, who came directly from England and founded the settlements at Salem and Boston. The Puritans were in closer touch with England and were more progressive than the Pilgrims. The Puritans soon outgrew the crude method of "lining out" their psalms and hymns. They began to make collections of their psalms to be placed in books and attempted to improve their singing.

The preface to a psalter,[6] published in England, from which many psalms were taken, gives us an idea of some of the directions our colonists followed in singing. They were advised:

1. That psalms of tribulation[7] be sung with a low voice and in long measure.

2. That psalms of Thanksgiving be sung with indifferent voice, neither too loud nor too slow.

3. That psalms of rejoicing be sung with a loud voice and in a swift and jocund measure.

6. psalter. A book of psalms. 7. tribulation (trĭb'ū·lā'shŭn). Distress or suffering resulting from oppression or affliction.

THE PSALMES
In Metre

PSALME I

O Blessed man, that in th'advice
of wicked doeth not walk:
nor stand in sinners way, nor sit
in chayre of scornfull folk.

2 But in the law of Iehovah,
is his longing delight:
aud in his law doth meditate,
by day and eke by night.

3 And he shall be like to a tree
planted by water-rivers:
that in his season yeilds his fruit,
and his leafe never withers.

4 And all he doth, shall prosper well,
the wicked are not so:
but they are like vnto the chaffe,
which winde drives to and fro.

5 Therefore shall not ungodly men,
rise to stand in the doome,
nor shall the sinners with the just,
in their assemblie come.

6 For of the righteous men, the Lord
acknowledgeth the way:
but the way ot vngodly men,
shall vtterly decay.

A   PSALM

The *Bay Psalm Book,* a page of which is shown above, was used by
the Puritans when they sang in church.

The First Song Book. The first song book printed in the colonies was the *Bay Psalm Book* which appeared in 1640, ten years after the settlement at Boston. The book was so named because of its origin in the Massachusetts Bay Colony. In the first edition only the words of the psalms were printed. However, a second edition published seven years later had a staff printed from wooden blocks. There were no measure lines except to divide the lines of the psalms. In its ninth revision, the tunes were added to the words of the psalms.

The Origin of the Choir. The desire to sing songs better brought about the establishment of the earliest singing schools in New England. Naturally those who attended singing schools became more skilled in singing. They would sit together in the church to obtain the best effects in singing. Soon these people were assigned special seats called "singers' seats." This was the beginning of our church choir.

Early Books of Instruction. There was very little good instruction in the singing schools. In answer to a need for instructional helps, the Reverend John Tufts published the first instruction book on singing, *A Very Plaine and Easy Introduction to the Art of Singing Psalm Tunes.* Letters instead of notes were placed on the staff, and time was marked by placing one or two dots on the right side of the letter. The Reverend Tufts also published a collection of harmonized tunes in three parts, the first collection of harmonized tunes in America.

Progress in Music

Accompaniment for Singing. After the first hundred years of colonization, the attitude toward music changed considerably. Life became more comfortable. Wealthier and better educated people came to the colonies. Colonists from Ireland and Scotland came with their folk tunes.

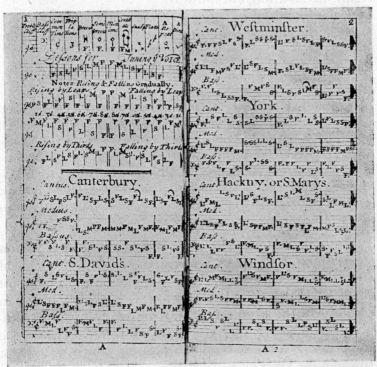

Courtesy Public Library of the City of Boston

In Reverend John Tufts' *A Very Plaine and Easy Introduction to the Art of Singing Psalm Tunes*, letters instead of notes were placed on the staff.

Musical instruments became more common as an accompaniment for singing. First the cello[8] was used, then the

8. cello (chĕl'ō). A stringed instrument with the same form as the violin but larger in size and with a deeper tone.

flute, and later the oboe.[9] These instruments could not
be properly tuned because of inadequate heating of the
churches. They often squeaked at the wrong time, and the
result was anything but musical.

Various kinds of instruments were available early in the
eighteenth century, as an interesting advertisement in the
Boston News Letter indicates:

> This is to give notice that there is lately sent over from London,
> a choice collection of musical instruments, consisting of flageolets,[10]
> flutes, haut-boys,[11] bass-viols, violins, bows, strings, reeds for haut-
> boys; books of instruction for all these instruments; books of ruled
> paper; to be sold at the Dancing School of Mr. Enstone in Sudbury
> Street, near the Orange Tree, Boston.
> Note: Any person may have all instruments of music mended, or
> virginals[12] and spinets[13] strung and tuned at a reasonable rate,
> and likewise may be taught to play on any of these instruments
> above mentioned.

Music in Boston. A public concert was held in Boston
soon after this time. A few years later the selectmen of
Boston allowed Faneuil[14] Hall to be used for "concerts of
Musick." Even before the Boston Tea Party, the Boston
public had the privilege of hearing really excellent programs of music. It was one of the few colonial cities to be
important as a music center—a position which it has kept
through the years.

9. oboe (ō'bō). A double reed, woodwind instrument. 10. flageolets (flăj'ō·
lĕts'). Small, flute-like instruments. 11. haut-boys or hautboys (hō'boiz). Early
French name for oboes. 12. virginals (vûr'jĭ·nălz). Early forerunners of the
piano. 13. spinets. Other forerunners of the piano. 14. Faneuil (făn''l) Hall.
A hall given to Boston by Peter Faneuil and made famous as a meeting place
of patriots during the Revolution.

CHAPTER II

MUSIC IN THE SOUTHERN COLONIES

Music in Early Virginia

Jamestown. The Jamestown colonists, who arrived in our country several years before the Pilgrims and Puritans, left no record of music. We know little of the music of any of the southern colonists who were in America during the first hundred years. It seems likely, however, that these early settlers must have whistled or hummed at their work and sung at their church services, for they did not have the religious objection to singing and to instruments which the New Englanders had. Many of them were of good families of social position in England; therefore, they probably knew and enjoyed music.

Williamsburg, a Gay Picture. Williamsburg, which became the capital of the Virginia colony after the burning of the statehouse at Jamestown in 1698, presented a gay contrast to New England towns. Concerts, plays, and dancing were enjoyed. Early in the eighteenth century, plays and ballad operas were given there. In the Apollo Room in the old Raleigh Tavern and in the ballroom in the governor's palace, gentlemen and their ladies in velvets and rich brocades danced to the stately minuet[1] or to the gayer Virginia reel.

---

1. minuet (mĭn′ṵ·ĕt′). A slow, graceful dance.

The recent restoration of the Williamsburg of colonial days, under the organization of John D. Rockefeller, Jr., gives us an accurate idea of the setting for those early activities.

Music, a Pleasant Pastime. Throughout the South, music was considered a gay and pleasant pastime. The younger children often played singing games such as "Here We Go Round the Mulberry Bush," "London Bridge," "Oats, Peas, Beans, and Barley Grow," and "Ring around Rosy." The older people considered music one of the social graces. It was quite as much the fashionable thing to be able to sing a new ballad[2] just brought from London as to wear a dress in the latest London fashion. All ladies were supposed to be able to play or sing. Men, too, could sing or play a little. There were many wealthy families and most of them owned musical instruments. As soon as room was found on the small vessels which came from England, organs, violins, and harpsichords[3] were imported. Later many fine pianos were brought to the southern colonies. The music, of a light and sentimental style, was usually written and printed in England.

Music in Rural Districts. Many English, Scotch, and Irish colonists settled in the country districts, particularly in the mountain sections. They brought with them their folk tunes. At their "play parties," fiddlers played by ear the dance tunes of the old country. The fiddlers were usually Negroes, although they were sometimes indentured servants.[4] Reels and jigs were the dance tunes most frequently played. Sometimes the dances or games were accompanied by singing. Our Virginia reel, "Stack of Barley," and "Geese in the Bay" were favorites. For their

2. ballad. A simple song. 3. harpsichords (härp′sĭ·kôrdz). Immediate fore-runners of the piano. 4. indentured servants. Servants bound by written contracts, usually for a limited number of years, to pay for passage to America.

Courtesy Colonial Williamsburg, restored by John D. Rockefeller, Jr.

The colonists in Williamsburg danced in the ballroom in the governor's palace.

religious music they had all-day singings, when families for miles around came to the courthouse or to the church to sing their songs of worship. Sometimes there was no sermon to hear, but a basket dinner and a visiting time at noon were always enjoyed.

A few years ago, the first Virginia State Choral Festival was held at the University of Virginia in Charlottesville. In the outdoor theater, twelve hundred people sat for over three hours listening to singing of folk songs and playing of folk tunes by fiddlers. These were the tunes which have been handed down from generation to generation since colonial times. A folk festival is held each year at White Top Mountain in southwest Virginia in order that this folk music may continue to be preserved.

Music Brought from England. In the southern colonies, the story of music is largely the story of the bringing of English musical culture into the new world. Many of the ballads and folk songs which we sing today were sung by the early colonists. Some of them are "Barbara Allen," "O No, John," "Drink to Me Only with Thine Eyes," "O, Dear, What Can the Matter Be," and "Frog Went A-Courting." Those songs, some of them ballads, some of them songs for dances and singing games, had been sung all over the countryside in the days of "Merrie England." They had been sung by parents to their children, and by these children when they grew up to their own children. It was only natural that the colonists should sing these same songs when they came to America. They made no attempt to create new melodies, but adapted the old tunes to their new surroundings. An example of this is "Sourwood Mountain," which is an old English folk tune adapted to Sourwood Mountain, one of the mountains in southwest Virginia. (See page 104.)

O NO, JOHN!

ENGLISH FOLK SONG

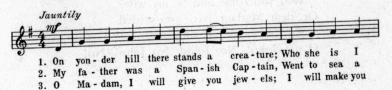

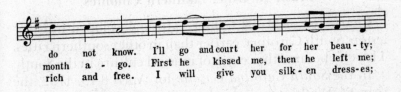

From the book KEEP ON SINGING, *published by the Paull-Pioneer Music Corporation, New York.*

4.

O Madam, since you are so cruel,
And that you do scorn me so,
If I may not be your lover,
Madam, will you let me go?
O no, John! No, John! No John! No!

5.

Then I will stay with you for ever,
If you will not be unkind.
Madam, I have vow'd to love you;
Would you have me change my mind?
O no, John! No, John! No John! No!

6.

O hark! I hear the church bells ringing;
  Will you come and be my wife?
Or, dear Madam, have you settled
  To live single all your life?
O no, John! No, John! No John! No!

Music in Other Southern Colonies

Charleston, a Music Center. Music developed in Charleston, South Carolina, earlier than in other southern cities. This city became the center of musical culture in the South.

In the *South Carolina Gazette* for April 8-15, 1732, the year of Washington's birth, this notice appeared: "On Wednesday next will be a Consort of Musick at the Council Chamber, for the Benefit of Mr. Salter."

John Salter was conducting a singing school at Charleston at the time. "For the benefit of Mr. Salter" meant that this gentleman was the business manager and promoter of the concert. Those who promoted concerts played one or more instruments and frequently played some of their own compositions.

The records reporting some of these concerts describe the beauty of the ladies, their costumes, their headdress, their quietness during the concert, and their gaiety when the concert was over. "Dances for the ladies" were customary after the concert.

The first song recital of America took place in Charleston a year later. Only English and Scotch songs were sung. There is considerable evidence to indicate that the first performance of an opera in America was one given at Charleston about twenty years later. It was the ballad opera, *Flora,* or the *Hob and the Well.*

DRINK TO ME ONLY WITH THINE EYES

BEN JONSON   ENGLISH AIR

1. Drink to me on - ly with thine eyes, And I will pledge with mine,
2. I sent thee late a ros - y wreath, Not so much hon - 'ring thee

Or leave a kiss with - in the cup, And I'll not ask for wine!
As giv-ing it a hope that there It could not with-ered be;

The thirst that from the soul doth rise Doth ask a drink di - vine;.
But thou there-on didst on - ly breathe And sends it it back to me;

But might I of Jove's nec - tar sip. I would not change for thine.
Since when it grows, and smells, I swear, Not of it - self but thee.

From Foresman's FIFTH BOOK OF SONGS. *published by the American Book Company.*

The St. Cecilia Society. An important musical organization was the St. Cecilia Society of Charleston. It had its beginning in the colonial period and continued in existence for nearly two hundred years. Its concerts were not open to the public. For this reason we find little mention of them in the newspapers of the day. The organization had a good orchestra made up of what were called "gentlemen performers" and of professionals—paid performers who were engaged by the season. The managers went to a great deal of effort to secure the best talent possible. A large number of the paid performers came from Europe.

An entry in the *Journal of a Voyage to South Carolina*, written by Josiah Quincy in 1772, gave this description of one of the concerts:

The concert-house is a large, inelegant building. . . . . The music was good—the two bass viols and French horns were grand. One Abercrombie, a Frenchman just arrived, played the first violin, and a solo incomparably better than any one I ever heard. He cannot speak a word of English, and has a salary of five hundred guineas a year from the St. Cecilia Society. There were upwards of two hundred and fifty ladies present.

Another item reported:

Dined with the Sons of St. Patrick. While at dinner six violins, two hautboys, etc. After dinner, six French horns in concert:— most surpassing music. Two solos on the French horn, by one who is said to blow the finest horn in the world. He has fifty guineas for the season from the St. Cecilia Society.

Religious Music of the Moravians. The funeral chorals[5] of a group of Moravians[6] in Salem, North Carolina, represented an unusual and interesting type of religious music.

---

5. chorals. Music sung by a choir. 6. Moravians (mô·rā′vĭ·ănz). People who came from Moravia, a former Austrian land, and settled in Pennsylvania.

PASSION CHORALE

From A Remarkable American Musical Tradition, *by J. Media (James Francis Cooke), in* The Etude, *September, 1933, published by Theodore Presser Company.*

The announcement of a death in the community was made by the choir which sang a song called "O Haupt voll Blut und Wunden" (O Sacred Head Now Wounded). Translated into English, the words are:

> A pilgrim, us preceding,
>   Departs unto his home,
> The final summons heeding
>   Which soon to all must come.
> O joy! the chains to sever
>   Which burden pilgrims here,
> To dwell with Christ forever,
>   Who to our souls is dear.

Negroes sang as they picked cotton in the field.

After this might come any one of ten different chorals which would inform those listening whether the deceased was a married brother or sister, a widow or a widower, a single brother or sister, an older boy or girl, a little boy or girl, or some other relative. Finally, as a closing announcement, the first choral was sung again.

Music in Georgia, Louisiana, and Maryland. We know little of early music in Georgia. Near the close of the eighteenth century the *Georgia Gazette* mentioned a benefit "concert of musick." When John and Charles Wesley were missionaries in Georgia, they published a collection of psalms and hymns. Catholic missions had been established there by the Franciscan and Jesuit fathers a century and a half before the arrival of Oglethorpe. Undoubtedly these missions used singing at religious services.

The music in Baltimore was similar to that in the other cities of the period. Concerts and ballad operas were held there. The religious music was, for the most part, that of the Catholic Church, although the religious freedom of Maryland would indicate that music used by followers of other religious beliefs was not frowned upon.

Negro Music. The story of music in the South would not be complete without mentioning the music of the Negroes. Negroes were first brought to North America a year before the Pilgrims landed. We can imagine a group of Negroes, some years later, singing at their work in the rice or cotton fields, singing as they gathered together in the evening after work was done, or singing at their religious services.

There not much evidence that the Negro brought much of his music with him from Africa. For the most part, his music was an adaptation of the folk songs learned from his white master.

CHAPTER III

EARLY MUSIC IN NEW YORK AND PENNSYLVANIA

Music in New York

The Dutch in New Netherland. Boys and girls in New Amsterdam sang and danced to the old dance song, "Rosa." Their parents settled New Netherland, that part of our country which we know as New York, almost as early as the Pilgrims landed at Plymouth. They left us fine, substantial manners and customs, but little in music except collections of Dutch songs. "Rosa," "Dutch Prayer of Thanksgiving," and "The Little Dustman" are those most familiar to us.

Sea Songs and Ballads. After the English took over the town of New York, formerly New Amsterdam, sailors went singing through the streets and sea songs became quite the fashion. In any one of the several leading coffee houses, one might expect to hear singing. Ballads also were popular. Local events were often featured in the ballads. An example is the "Ballad of Captain Kidd," which described the hanging of the notorious character who had been in New York Harbor a number of times. Some people believe that the composer got his idea for the ballad from the confusion of songs about the docks and coffee houses of Manhattan Island.

THANKSGIVING HYMN

TRADITIONAL NETHERLANDS TUNE

From MUSIC OF MANY LANDS AND PEOPLES, *by McConathy, Beattie, and Morgan, copyright, 1938, by special permission of the publishers, Silver Burdett Company, New York.*

Popularity of Open-Air Singing. Open-air singing was popular in New York as it was elsewhere in colonial America. Several gardens were opened where refreshments were served and music was heard. Sometimes "genteel" fireworks were displayed between the numbers of the more formal concerts which were given there. One of the gardens charged two shillings for admission. Those who paid the charge were entitled to listen to the music and also to enjoy a glass of ice-cream punch.

Ballad Operas. Ballad operas, popular in all the colonies, were performed in New York from 1732 on. They were little more than a group of ballads strung together with a thread of story running through. The best-known of the ballad operas was the *Beggar's Opera,* which was first given in New York about twenty years later. It was written by an Englishman named Gay. The theater in which it was given was an old building intended for another purpose. It had a platform and rough benches. The boxes were described as being like pens for pigs, with boards for seats and with other boards, shoulder high, for back rests. The lights were furnished by means of candles set in barrel hoops suspended from the ceiling or nailed to the wall. Several nails were driven through the hoops and the candles were stuck into these nails.

In England the music to the operas of that day was entirely under the Italian influence. It consisted either of original compositions or a medley of tunes from Italian opera strung together and fitted to the words. Gay, however, conceived the idea of using familiar English ballad tunes instead of the customary tunes from Italian music. One of the ballads used in the *Beggar's Opera* was the old English folk song, "Golden Slumbers Kiss Your Eyes." This use of ballad tunes became very popular in America.

GOLDEN SLUMBERS KISS YOUR EYES

Thomas Dekker   Old English Folk Song

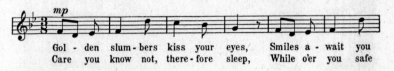

Gol - den slum - bers kiss your eyes,   Smiles a - wait you
Care you know not, there - fore sleep, While o'er you safe

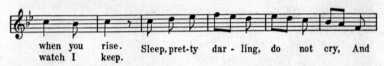

when you   rise.   Sleep, pret-ty dar - ling, do   not cry, And
watch I   keep.

I   will   sing you lul - la - bye,   Lul - la - bye,

Lul - la - bye,   Lul - - la - bye.

From Twice 55 Community Songs—New Green Book, *used by permission of C. C. Birchard & Company, publishers.*

The *Beggar's Opera* was a satire[1] on the evils of society in England. The story is concerned with the life of a gang of thieves in the pay of a man named Peachum, who received the stolen goods and then rescued the thieves from the arm of the law as long as they were successful. When they failed he gave them up to the authorities and claimed the forty pounds' reward.

Concerts. At about the same time, New York began having concerts. The first record of one is as follows:

A *Consort* of Music, Vocal and Instrumental, for the benefit of Mr. Pachelbel, the Harpsichord Part performed by himself. The songs, Violins, and German Flutes by private Hands.

1. satire (săt'īr). Ridicule.

The Beggar's Opera, by Gay, was a ballad opera about a gang of thieves.

Another announcement, which appeared in the New York *Weekly Post Boy* gave an interesting description of a concert of the time:

For the benefit of Messrs. Cobham and Tuckey, at the New Exchange on Monday the 29 instant; will be a Concert of Vocal and Instrumental musick. Among a variety of select pieces, both vocal and instrumental, will be performed, the celebrated dialogue between *Damon and Chloe,* compos'd by Mr. Arne. A two part song, in praise of a Soldier, by the late famous Mr. Henry Purcell.[2] *An Ode on Masonry* never perform'd in this country, nor ever in England, but once in publick. And a Solo on the German flute, by Mr. Cobham.

Tickets to be had of Mr. Cobham, in Hanover Square; of Mr. Tuckey near Mr. Willet's, at the New York Arms; and at the King's Arms; and at the new Printing Office in Beaver Street at 5s each.

To begin precisely at six o'clock. After the concert there will be a *Ball* for the ladies.

Influence of William Tuckey. The Mr. Tuckey mentioned in the announcement was a person who had considerable influence on music in New York. William Tuckey was an Englishman who came to New York in the early part of the eighteenth century and established himself as an organist, choirmaster, concert artist, and composer. He was appointed clerk of Trinity Church at a salary of twenty-five pounds per year. The clerk was an important official of the Episcopal Church. It was his duty to read out the hymns and psalms and to lead the singing. He made arrangements so that music could be taught to the pupils of the charity school which the church had established. Through the teaching of these pupils he developed a choir which sang for the church service. Soon the Trinity Choir became famous. Tuckey next wanted volunteer

2. Purcell (pûr'sĕl). An English composer (1658-1695).

singers for a chorus, and a group of considerable size
developed. One of his greatest contributions was the organization and direction of the first performance in America of music from Handel's[3] *Messiah*.[4]

Music in Pennsylvania

Attitude toward Music. The Quakers who settled in
Pennsylvania frowned upon music as they considered it
similar to other things they opposed—plays, games, lotter-
ies, and dancing. This attitude was in marked contrast to
that of the members of the Church of England who con-
sistently championed light amusements and favored music.

The Germans and Swedes who settled in the neighborhood of Philadelphia used much music, vocal as well as
instrumental. Good singing was required in the church.
One pastor of the Swedish church imposed a fine of six
shillings on certain members of his congregation for "un-
timely singing."

Music for the Church. The Gloria Dei Church, a Swedish church near Philadelphia, was one of the first American
churches to be equipped with an organ. An interesting
letter was written by the pastor of the church to a friend
in the old country, asking assistance in obtaining this organ. Apparently the letter brought results. Parts of the
letter are quoted because it pictures so accurately the feeling about music in the pastor's community at that time.

Many others besides myself, who know the ways of the land,
maintain that music would contribute much towards a good Christian service. It would not only attract and civilize the wild Indians,
but it would do much good in spreading the Gospel truths among

3. **Handel's** (hăn′d′lz). Handel was a German composer (1685-1759).   4. *Messiah*
(mĕ·sī′à). A famous oratorio composition by Handel dealing with the birth
and crucifixion of Jesus.

Gloria Dei Church had one of the first church organs in America.

the sects and others by attracting them. Instrumental music is especially serviceable here. Thus a well-sounding organ would perhaps prove of great profit, to say nothing of the fact that the Indians would come running from far and near to listen to such unknown melody, and upon that account might become willing to accept our language and teaching. . . . . Now as the melancholy, saturnine,[5] stingy Quaker spirit has abolished all such music, it would indeed be a novelty here, and tend to attract many of the young people away from the Quakers and sects to attend services where such music was found, even against the wishes of their parents. This would afford a good opportunity to show them the truth and their error. . . .

And it may be assumed that even a small organ-instrument and music in this place would be acceptable to God, and prove far more useful than many hundreds in Europe where there is already a superfluity[6] of such things.

There are in Europe masters enough who would build such instruments, and a fine one can be secured for 300 or 400 thalers. Then if an experienced organist and musician could be found, who would undertake so far a journey, he would be very welcome here. In case this could not be, if we only had an organ, some one or other might be found who had knowledge thereof.

Music of the Moravians. The Moravians who settled Bethlehem, Pennsylvania, furnished a musical center which few cities of its size in the United States today could rival. Music was exceedingly important in the lives of these people. They brought music and musical instruments with them when they came. A year after they arrived, they held their first Singstude (singing class). A few years later they founded the Collegium Musicum, a society of orchestra players and singers whose chief aim was to present music of a religious nature.

---

5. saturnine (săt'ēr·nĭn). Gloomy, grave. 6. superfluity (sū'pēr·flōō'ĭ·tĭ). A greater number than is needed.

A letter from a little girl attending a boarding school at Bethlehem indicates the part music had in the education of the children of these Moravian settlers. "I play the guitar twice a day; am taught the spinet and forte piano, and sometimes I play the organ." Another interesting account, taken from a description of one of their schools for girls, gives us an idea of the use of music in their schools at a slightly later time.

The first was merely a sewing school, little children and a pretty single sister about 30, with her white skirt, white short tight waistcoat, nice handkerchief pinned outside, a muslin apron and a close cap, of the most singular form you can imagine. . . . . The hair is all put out of sight, turned back, and no border to the cap, very unbecoming and very singular, tied under the chin with a pink ribbon—blue for the married, white for the widows. Here was a Piano forte and another sister teaching a little girl music. We went thro' all the different schoolrooms, some misses of sixteen, their teachers were very agreeable and easy, and in every room was a Piano.

The first copies of Haydn's quartettes and symphonies to reach this country were brought to Bethlehem. Two famous oratorios,[7] *The Creation* and *The Seasons,* had their premières[8] in this little Pennsylvania town. The famous Bethlehem Bach[9] Festival of today is an outgrowth of the early practice of singing the Bach chorales[10] in this community.

The Moravian settlement, however, was complete within itself. They did not mingle with others and their musical achievements were not carried into other colonies.

7. oratorios. Musical compositions based upon a Bible subject, usually with orchestral accompaniment. 8. premières (prē·myârz′). First performances. 9. Bach (bäк). A German composer (1685-1750). 10. chorales (kô·rälz′). Simple, sacred tunes.

The Pietists. A group of Germans called the Pietists,[11] who came to America for religious reasons, made a settlement near Philadelphia. They brought musical instruments with them. Some believe that Johann Kelpius, one of their leaders, brought with him from Europe an organ to be installed in their church. They sang hymns and accompanied their singing with instrumental music. Trumpets, the viol, hautboy, and kettle drums[12] were among the instruments used.

Settlers at Ephratah. Another group of Germans settled at Ephratah.[13] They are interesting because of the peculiar type of music devised by one of their leaders. In composing sacred music, this man took his ideas from nature and tried to represent the Aeolian harp[14] by means of harmony of voices. In singing this music, the voices of the choir imitated very soft instrumental music. The music was set in two, four, five, and seven parts. All the parts except the bass were sung by women's voices. The bass was set in two parts, the high and low bass, the latter resembling the deep tones of an organ. The melody was sung with falsetto[15] voice, the singers scarcely opening their mouths or moving their lips. It is said that the effect produced by this peculiar technique of singing was that of the music entering the room from above in some mysterious way and hovering over the heads of the audience.

Development of Music in Philadelphia. About the middle of the eighteenth century, musical life in Philadelphia began to develop rapidly. Music was enjoyed more

11. Pietists (pī′ĕ·tĭsts). A religious group in Germany in the seventeenth century. Some of them made settlements in America. 12. kettle drums. Drums made with a hollow hemisphere of brass or copper with a parchment head. They can be tuned to definite pitches. 13. Ephratah (ĕf′rà·tà). A town fifty miles west of Philadelphia. 14. Aeolian (ē·ō′lĭ·ăn) harp. A thin sounding box with strings, played by the wind. 15. falsetto (fŏl·sĕt′ō). Unnaturally high pitched.

and more in the home. Small groups of musicians began to meet in homes and play together. Church music improved. English opera became popular. One of the first important concerts given in America, in which the chorus had a prominent part, took place in Philadelphia. The chorus was composed chiefly of young men who were attending the College of Philadelphia, now the University of Pennslyvania.

Benjamin Franklin was an ardent lover of music. There is a story that he practiced his harmonica at night while his wife slept. When she was awakened by the sounds, she declared that she dreamed she was dead and was surrounded by angels singing heavenly music. The harmonica was not the French harp which we know, but an instrument Franklin himself had devised. It consisted of a group of "musical glasses" played like a xylophone.[16] He could also play the guitar and violin. He did much to further an interest in America among the musicians of France and England. Several European musicians came to the American colonies at his invitation.

16. xylophone (zī'lŏ·fōn). A musical instrument consisting of a row of wooden bars sounded by striking with wooden hammers.

CHAPTER IV

THE INFLUENCE OF THE FRENCH AND SPANISH COLONISTS

Music of the French

Familiar Songs from the French Colonists. You often hear the song "We Won't Go Home until Morning" or "For He's a Jolly Good Fellow." Sometimes the words of a school song are arranged to fit the same tune. Did you know that the tune came down to us from the early French colonists? This song, which was a favorite, was called "To War Has Gone the Duke of Marlborough." Other songs you may know are "At Pierrot's Door," "Alouette," "The Voyageur's[1] Song," and "Gai, la, la, gai le rosier" (Gay is the Rose).

A Singing People. Early French missionaries established churches in which there was singing. Records tell us that the St. Louis Cathedral, one of the oldest churches in New Orleans, had an organ and a choir from its earliest years. There were trading posts along the St. Lawrence and down the Mississippi River where groups of men probably sang together. Old records mention singing parties where sea chanteys[2] and folk songs were popular. Many of these gay songs may be heard today among the descendants of the

1. Voyageur's (vwä′yá′zhûrz′). Voyageurs were men employed to transport furs and other goods; trappers and boatmen. 2. chanteys (shán′tĭz). Songs sung by sailors at their work.

early settlers in Nova Scotia, in the northern peninsula of Michigan, in Vincennes, Indiana, in St. Louis and Ste.

TO WAR HAS GONE DUKE MARLBOROUGH

FRENCH FOLK SONG

From THE NEW AMERICAN SONG BOOK, *copyrighted by Hall & McCreary Company. Used by permission.*

Genevieve, Missouri, and in New Orleans. Sometimes they are sung in French dialect, but more often with English words.

Music of the Spanish

Spanish Songs in the Southwest. "Serene Is the Night" is one of the lovely songs left to us by the early Spanish people. In the southwestern part of the United States, particularly in California, New Mexico, and along the Rio Grande, one may still find much of the music which the Spanish colonists brought with them three centuries ago.

Earliest Music Instruction in North America. The settlements of the Spanish missionaries, their founding of missions, and the attempt to Christianize and to teach the Indians have left but little impression upon the music of our nation as a whole. However, the story of the old mission music is so interesting that it seems to have a place here. It is also interesting to know what was going on in the Southwest and on the Pacific coast at the time the English were colonizing the Atlantic coast.

Some of the earliest music schools of North America were the seventeenth-century monasteries of New Spain. There the making, as well as the playing, of instruments was a part of the curriculum. In fact, outside of the teaching of the "Doctrina,"[3] music received more attention than any of the other subjects taught at the missions. String and wind instruments were brought from Mexico City for use in instruction. Some of the more gifted Indians were taught to sing the elaborate chants and hymns as well as to play the flute and guitar. It is said that it was easy to teach music to Indians who had developed a civilization like that of the Pueblo Indians of New Mexico.

Some Early Music Teachers. Fray Garcia de Sanfrancisco[4] founded a mission in 1659 where the present city of El Paso, Texas, is now located. He taught the rudiments

3. "Doctrina" (dŏk′trĭ·nå). A religious creed. 4. Fray Garcia de Sanfrancisco (frī gär·thē′ä dā sän·frän·thēs′kō).

SERENE IS THE NIGHT

TRANSLATION   SPANISH SONG FROM CALIFORNIA

The night is fair and still dear, The winds are all a-sleep: Thy

lov-er stands and watch-es to guard thy slum ber deep: His

thoughts go out to tell to thee the love that's in his breast. He

sends his love out thro' the night To bring thee peace and rest. He

rit.

sends his love out thro' the night To bring thee peace and rest.

From THE NEW AMERICAN SONG BOOK, *copyrighted by Hall & McCreary Company. Used by permission.*

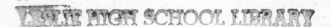

of music there and also gave religious instruction. Thus he may be called our first music teacher.

Another interesting character was Fray Antonio Margil,[5] the founder of a mission at San Antonio, Texas. He is said to have sung his way through the wilderness of the Southwest, through land which is now part of New Mexico, Louisiana, and Texas. A physical ailment prevented his riding on horseback; so he trudged along, followed by a small group of Indians, holding his crucifix and singing his favorite "Alabado" (Praise to God).

In the early part of the seventeenth century, an exploring party set out from Acapulco, Mexico, to California. Among the party was Fray Antonio de la Ascención,[6] who had a great desire to give musical education to the California Indians. You will learn his plans from a quotation from his own report:

And it would be well to bring from New Spain [to California] Indian minstrels, with their instruments and trumpets, that the divine services may be celebrated with solemnity and pomp, and to teach the Indians of the land to sing and play. Likewise it would be well and proper to choose from among the Indians some of the brightest, selecting among the young men and boys such as appear the most docile,[7] talented and capable; that they may learn to write and sing, and to play all the musical instruments.

Music in the Missions. The missions represented a type of community center. The daily life began at dawn by singing morning prayers set to simple melodies and to Indian chants. After a meager breakfast, the day's work in the fields began with morning hymns. The "Alabado" was always sung to a melody which was the same at all missions. The angelus bells announced the end of the day's work,

5. Fray Antonio Margil (än·tō′nēŏ mär·ghēl′).   6. Fray Antonio de la Ascencion (dä lä äs·thĕn′thê·ōn′).   7. docile (dŏs′ĭl). Easily managed and taught.

and the community—Indians, Mexicans, Spaniards—gathered in the church for religious instruction and devotions. These exercises always closed with the "Alabado."

San-to Dios San-to Fuerte Santo inmortal

Li-branos se-ñor de to-do mal

Courtesy The Musical Quarterly, *G. Schirmer, publisher*

The Indians in Texas still sing this old Spanish hymn:

"Holy God! Powerful God! Immortal God!
Deliver us, Lord, from all evil!"

Everyone learned the "Pater Noster," the "Salve Maria," and the "Ave Maria." Men and women sang alternately. A leader often sang the first line of the hymn, and the group repeated it and carried the song along. Singing in four parts seems to have been customary. There was a plain chant melody to which three parts were added. Colored notes were used to designate the parts. The top note was yellow, the next red, the third white outlined with black, and the lowest note was black.

The Tigua[8] Indians near El Paso, who are said to be the oldest permanent settlers within the borders of what is now Texas, have preserved and handed down many of the old mission songs. Gregorian[9] chants are still known to the descendants of the early people in New Mexico and neighboring regions. At the National Folk Festival, held in connection with the Texas Centennial Exposition in Dallas, the early Spanish and mission songs took their place with cowboy songs, Negro spirituals, and old fiddlers' tunes.

Mission Bells. One seldom thinks of an old Spanish mission without thinking of mission bells. Among the necessary things sent to California in the first Spanish ships were church bells, for these bells had a particular significance to those of the Catholic faith. A beautiful religious ceremony took place whenever bells were cast for use in a mission. Precious gifts of gold and silver were consecrated by prayer and thrown into the molten mass as a sacrifice. Sometimes, even today, the silver and gold may be plainly seen. The bells became a symbol of the mother church speaking to men and women in a foreign land.

The presence of a church bell was thought to bring success in journeys over land. Early exploring parties desired to have a priest and at least one of the holy bells with them on their expeditions.

The first thing done after the selection of a place for a mission was to hang the bells somewhere, perhaps on a branch of a tree, while the mission was being built. There was not always a special place provided for them in the construction of the buildings, and they were often hung in curious places. Sometimes they were attached to rafters or hung under the eaves or in a broad square window.

8. Tigua (tē′wä).   9. Gregorian (grĕ·gō′rĭ·ăn).   Pertaining to a pope named Gregory.

Mission bells were used to call people to the mission and to announce the events of the day.

There was no particular regard to tune or tone in the
arrangement of these bells, and no attempt was made to
play a melody on them. They were used chiefly to call the
members of the community to church or to announce the
events of the day.

THE MISSION BELLS OF MONTEREY
by Bret Harte

O bells that rang, O bells that sang
    Above the martyrs' wilderness,
Till from that reddened coast-line sprang
    The Gospel seed to cheer and bless,
What are your garnered sheaves today?
    O Mission bells! Eleison[10] bells!
O Mission bells of Monterey!

O bells that crash, O bells that clash
    Above the chimney-crowded plain,
On wall and tower your voices dash,
    But never with the old refrain;
In mart and temple gone astray!
    Ye dangle bells!   Ye jangle bells!
Ye wrangle bells of Monterey!

O bells that die, so far, so nigh,
    Come back once more across the sea;
Not with the zealot's[11] furious cry,
    Not with the creed's austerity;
Come with His love alone to stay,
    O Mission bells! Eleison bells!
O Mission bells of Monterey!
     (This poem was set to music by Charles Gounod.[12])

10. Eleison (ē·lī′sŏn). From the Greek, meaning "have mercy."   11. zealot's
(zĕl′ŭts). A zealot is a person who is an enthusiast, one who is absorbed in
devotion to some particular thing. 12. Gounod (goō′nō′). A French composer (1818-1893).

CHAPTER V

INSTRUMENTS AND INSTRUMENTAL MUSIC IN COLONIAL TIMES

First Instruments Used

Early Place of Instrumental Music. Instrumental music was at first used only as an accompaniment to singing or for dancing. In some sections, as in New England, where music was favored only as a means of expressing religious fervor, it was difficult to develop instrumental music beyond its place as an accompaniment for singing. It is probable that the first instrumental music along the Atlantic coast was heard among the Virginian settlers. They had dancing and dancing schools; so it is assumed there was some kind of instrumental accompaniment.

In the early days, there was strong prejudice against a man's devoting his entire time to music. Even after instrumental music became appreciated for its own sake, playing music as a profession was regarded as beneath the rank of a gentleman.

Organ Playing. This attitude was changed somewhat when the organ came into use. Organ playing called for more than ordinary musical skill and for serious preparation on the part of the player. Qualified organists had to be brought from England. As their salaries were small, many of them conducted dancing classes or shops where they kept music and musical instruments in order to make

Courtesy Colonial Williamsburg, restored by John D. Rockefeller, Jr.

The harpsichord, flute, hautboy, and bassoon were some of the musical instruments used by the colonists. Today, in the governor's palace in Williamsburg, concert artists give programs of music played in colonial days, using instruments popular at that time.

a living. They frequently played several other instruments as well as the organ. These men did much toward creating a taste for music at the time.

Colonial Instruments. The instruments which were familiar in colonial times were violins, viols, horns, flute, fife, flageolet, hautboy, jew's-harp, virginal, spinet, harpsichord, organ, and later the pianoforte. Most of the instruments were brought from England, although records and advertisements in newspapers indicate that a few instruments were made in the colonies.

The flute and violin were considered gentlemen's instruments. The German flute was as much a part of the colonial gentleman as his powdered wig and knee breeches. Ladies played the guitar and harpsichord or spinet. It was not ladylike to play the violin or flute.

Descriptions of Instruments. The names of some of these early instruments are still familiar to us today. A few of them have gone out of use and the rest are known by other names.

The hautboy is a wooden instrument with a high tone. It is what we know as the oboe. The name is from the French word "haut" meaning high and "bois" meaning wood. The word "hautboy" was used in Shakespeare's time. Now the term oboe is used.

The flageolet belongs to the flute family. It differs from the flute in that it has a mouthpiece and is played in a vertical instead of a horizontal position. Its tone is somewhat similar to that of the flute.

The fife also resembles a flute. It is a six-holed wind instrument pitched in various keys. It has a shrill sound produced by blowing in a hole near the closed end of a tube. It is often used with a drum to play military music.

The spinet was used in colonial days.

The spinet, virginal, and harpsichord all belong to the same family. Their mechanism is built on the same principle. The chief differences are in the size, in the number of strings to each note, and the manner in which the strings are arranged over the sound board. Instead of the hammers we have on modern pianos, they have wooden uprights called jacks. Each jack is provided with a little spur or quill of hard leather, which plucks the string as the note is played, almost as a mandolin player plucks the string with his pick. It produces a delicate, tinkling sound with a staccato[1] effect. All the notes have the same power and quality; so shading and varying the tone are impossible.

The harpsichord is the largest and most powerful instrument of the three. It has two keyboards. The keys are all of one color. The long keys play the naturals, the short ones the sharps and flats. It has two, three, or four strings to a note to increase the volume, and stops for varying effects. Usually the keyboard ranges from three to four octaves. Many are elaborately decorated with paintings, carvings, or printed mottoes. In the illustration on page 25 you can see the harpsichord in the governor's palace in Williamsburg, Virginia, and in the illustration on page 82 the harpsichord in the music room at Mount Vernon.

The virginal is said to have received its name from the fact that it was a favorite of Elizabeth, the virgin queen. It may have been given this name because its small range represents the range of a young girl's voice. It is a very light instrument and can be easily moved about. It is placed on a table for playing. It has only one string to a note, which gives it very little volume.

Usually the spinet is small. Each of its notes has a single string. A popular model is described as resembling a

1. staccato (stá·kä′tō). In quick, clear-cut manner.

harp laid in a horizontal position, with its longest string only a foot in length and with a compass of thirty-one notes.

The Piano and the Organ

A New Instrument. For many years, makers of harpsichords had experimented with keyboards, trying to build a stronger instrument with richer tone. Some hundred years after the founding of Jamestown in America, an Italian builder, Cristofori,[2] succeeded in making a keyboard which gave loud or soft tones. Pianoforte was the name given to the improved instrument because it could make soft (piano) or loud (forte) tones. The name was soon shortened to piano.

Pianos were made in this country in both Philadelphia and Boston during the eighteenth century. The pioneer in the piano-making industry was Jonas Chickering, and the Chickering piano has been one of the best-known makes ever since.

Harold W. Thompson, in his book, *Body, Boots, & Britches,* tells an amusing story of the first piano which was brought into a certain section of western New York.

The first instrument of its sort in the county, it attracted as much attention as the circus of a later era. . . . . One farmer left his oxen at the mill, and with his son at heel started afoot across country to satisfy his curiosity. When the visitors arrived at the kitchen door, Mrs. Sprague had just taken biscuits from another new contraption, a tin bake-oven whose fame was not yet abroad. As he entered, the boy pointed toward the oven and whispered hoarsely, "Paw, paw, what is that?" Not to be overawed by the grandeur of the Spragues, his father answered, "Piano, you . . . . fool."

The Organ. Organs in colonial times are associated with music in the churches, although there are some reports of

2. Cristofori (krĕs·tô′fô·rē). The inventor of the piano (1653-1731).

The Brattle organ, one of the famous early organs in America, is now the property of St. John's Church in Portsmouth, New Hampshire.

individuals who owned organs. These were pipe organs and are not to be confused with the small reed organ which became popular in later pioneer times. The bellows had to be pumped by hand, and the complete act of making organ music was truly physical labor.

It is believed that Johann Kelpius, the leader of the German Pietists who settled near Philadelphia, brought the first organ to America in 1694. Christopher Witt, an Englishman who had joined this group, was the first individual in America to own a pipe organ. He made it himself and could play upon it. The Episcopal church at Port Royal, Virginia, owned one of the first organs brought to this country from Europe.

One of the famous early organs was the Brattle organ. The story goes that Thomas Brattle, an amateur musician of Boston, imported an organ and had it installed in his home. Some years later he died. In his will he had left the organ to the Brattle Square Church on the condition that the offer be accepted within a year after his death. It was refused because of religious prejudice against instrumental music in the church. It remained on the porch of the church for several months and was finally given to King's Chapel in Boston. There it stayed for a time and later became the property of St. John's Church in Portsmouth, New Hampshire, where it may be seen today.

STUDY EXERCISES

Questions and Problems

1. In what ways was the New England church music service different from the music we hear in church today?

2. What discussions were there about the manner in which singing should be carried on in the early New England churches?

3. How did the choir originate? What were some of the peculiar traits of early choirs?

4. What attitude did southerners have toward music? How do you account for this attitude?

5. What influence did the English, Scotch, and Irish colonists have on music?

6. What was unusual about the religious music of the Moravians? Did the Moravians have much influence on music in other sections? Why?

7. What kind of songs were sung in New York after the English took the town? Why was this particular type of song popular?

8. What was the attitude of the Quakers toward music? of the Swedes in Pennsylvania?

9. In what way did Benjamin Franklin express an interest in music?

10. What reason do we have to believe the French influenced music in America?

11. In what ways did the Spaniards contribute to America's musical heritage?

12. How was the profession of music regarded in colonial days? Was this attitude changed?

13. Describe some of the musical instruments used in colonial days.

14. What instruments preceded the piano, and how was the piano finally developed?

15. How do you account for the peculiar fate of the Brattle organ?

Suggested Activities

1. Find in the Sunday issue of city papers the announcements of concerts to be given during the week. Compare them with the announcements of concerts published in colonial times.
2. Read in your history books accounts of the settlement in America of groups of people who came from Spain, France, Sweden, Holland, Germany, Ireland, and Scotland. What influence do you think these people had on music in this country?
3. Read descriptions of the customs, homes, and dress in various sections of the country during the colonial period. Alice Morse Earle's *Home Life in Colonial Days* is one book which will give you this interesting information.
4. Try singing several songs to the same tune. What difficulties do you have? Why do you think there should be different tunes for different words?
5. Make a collection of pictures of musical instruments used in colonial times and mount them for class use.
6. Compare the costs of early musical instruments used in the colonies with those of similar instruments used today. Compare the cost of admission to concerts with that of today.
7. Imagine you are living in Charleston in the eighteenth century. Write a letter to your cousin in England describing a concert you recently attended.
8. Find in old hymn books the words and music for "Martyr," "Hackney," or "York."
9. *Class exercise:* Paint a series of panels representing music in various sections of America in early colonial days.
10. *Class exercise:* Plan one of your school parties in the nature of a play-party of the Virginia colony. Dress in colonial costumes and play the games and sing the songs which you think would have been played and sung in colonial times.
11. *Class exercise:* Select a leader and, with the help of your teacher, try singing the "Doxology," "Dundee," or other old hymns by the lining-out method.

PART TWO

MUSIC IN THE STRUGGLE TO BECOME A NATION

The period beginning with the Revolutionary War and ending with the reconstruction after the War between the States was one in which a continuous struggle was carried on to make this country a strong and united nation. It is a dramatic story. The struggle of the English colonies to free themselves from the mother country, the problems attending the making of a new government, the acquisition and settlement of new territory, the efforts for recognition on the sea, and the War between the States are all like acts in a great drama.

What part did music play in this drama? Did it serve as an accompaniment and set the theme for the acts, as in our modern movies? Was it an integral part of the drama, weaving the action together? Or was it a motivating force? Undoubtedly, it was some of all three.

War songs were written to spur soldiers to action. Patriotic airs made people proud of their country. Between wars a peace-loving people, striving to build homes in a new country, responded to the need for emotional release, for intellectual stimulation, for spiritual uplift, and for the pure pleasure that comes from music. Far-seeing men and women began to realize that a common culture was as necessary as a common political organization, that "one nation, indivisable, with liberty and justice for all" could not exist without some common means of communication in literature, in art, and in music.

In Part Two we shall find what kind of music was enjoyed by the people of the time. We shall learn how events influenced the music of the period, how the music reflected the customs and interests of the people in different localities, and how music served to bring people together. And, finally, we shall see what progress was made in music during the period.

CHAPTER VI

MUSIC OF WAR AND PATRIOTISM

Songs of the Nation

Music in War. Have you ever noticed the expression of pride and reverence on the faces of a crowd of people when "America" or "The Star-Spangled Banner" is played? Haven't you, yourself, felt thrilled at Sousa's[1] stirring march, "Stars and Stripes Forever"? No doubt your feet have begun to mark time and you have felt as if you could go forth and conquer the world. Such patriotic music has always had a strong influence on the people of our country.

Someone has said that a singing army is never defeated. "If we had had your songs, you would never have beaten us," one of the officers of the southern army is quoted as saying to a northerner at the close of the War between the States. Army officers admit that songs and march music are almost as necessary to the soldier as his military equipment. They inspire him with the necessary courage on the march, on the battlefield, in camp, and even in prison. These same songs keep up the spirit of the men, women, and children at home.

Music of the Revolution. The songs of each of our wars have been typical of the times in which they were written. Many of them have been colored by particular incidents.

---

1. Sousa's (soō'sáz). Sousa was an American bandmaster and composer (1854-1932).

THE LIBERTY SONG

JOHN DICKINSON   WILLIAM BOYCE

Come join hand in hand brave A - mer - i - cans all, And
rouse your bold hearts at fair Lib-er-ty's call; No ty- ran-nous acts shall sup-
press your just claim, Or stain with dis-hon-or A - mer - i - ca's name. In
Free-dom we're born and in Free-dom we'll live; Our purs-es are read - y,
Stead-y, Friends, Stead-y, Not as Slaves but as Free-men our mon-ey we'll give.

For example, soon after the news of the passage of the Stamp Act was received, a ballad called "American Taxation" was written. The refusal of the Massachusetts legislature to cancel the circular letter relating to the imposing of duties and taxes upon the American colonies gave origin to the famous "Liberty Song." It was written by John Dickenson of Delaware and is said to be the first piece of separately printed sheet music issued in the colonies. The song immediately became popular. It so angered the Tories that they promptly made a parody[2] on it.

It was quite the usual thing at that time to compose words and fit them to a tune already known. The country then had few composers, and people saw no harm in appropriating for their own use the tunes of other countries. Naturally, they were familiar with many English songs, and so they used these tunes freely.

However, both the words and music of our first war song were composed by an American, William Billings. He was a fiery patriot. At the beginning of the Revolution he composed "Chester," which expressed the burning patriotism of the time.

CHESTER

Let tyrants shake their iron rod,
   And Slav'ry clank her galling chains,
We fear them not, we trust in God,
   New England's God forever reigns.

Howe and Burgoyne and Clinton, too,
   With Prescott and Cornwallis join'd,
Together plot our overthrow,
   In one Infernal league combin'd.

2. parody (păr'ŏ·dĭ). Humerous imitation of serious writing.

CHESTER

WILLIAM BILLINGS

1. Let ty-rants shake their i - ron rod And slav - 'ry
2. What grate - ful off - 'ring shall we bring, What shall we

clank her gall - ing chains; We'll fear them not; we
ren - der to the Lord? Loud Hal - le - lu - jahs

trust in God, New Eng - land's God for - ev - er reigns.
let us sing, And praise His name on ev - 'ry chord.

From THE NEW AMERICAN SONG BOOK, *copyrighted by Hall & McCreary Company. Used by permission.*

When God inspired us for the fight,
    Their ranks were broke, their lines were forc'd
Their Ships were Shatter'd in our sight,
    Or swiftly driven from our Coast.

The Foe comes on with haughty Stride,
    Our troops advance with martial noise,
Their Vet'rans flee before our Youth,
    And Gen'rals yield to beardless boys.

What grateful Off'ring shall we bring,
    What shall we render to the Lord?
Loud Hallelujahs let us Sing,
    And praise his name on ev'ry Chord.

Many of Billings' tunes, most of them religious songs, were sung around the campfires of American soldiers, but "Chester" was their favorite. The tune was often played by fifers in the Continental army. It has been called the "Over There" of the Revolution.

"Yankee Doodle." "Yankee Doodle" was the marching song most used by the Continental army. The tune had been familiar in the colonies for some time. Its origin is not clear, but here is one of the favorite stories which is claimed by some to be authentic. After the uprising against King Charles I of England, Oliver Cromwell is said to have appeared riding a small horse and wearing a hat with a single plume fastened to it with a knot jokingly called macaroni. The Cavaliers[3] laughed themselves sick over the amusing situation and made up the following words and set them to the melody of an old English nursery rhyme.

> Yankee Doodle came to town
> Upon a Kentish pony;
> He stuck a feather in his cap,
> Upon a macaroni.

During the French and Indian War, General Braddock of the British army was gathering colonial soldiers for an attack upon the French and Indians. When the Continentals appeared in their ragged clothes, the British thought it a huge joke and immediately recalled the traditional picture of Cromwell. Dr. Richard Shuckburgh, the regimental surgeon, then wrote the parody as we know it with its jolly tune and gave it to the band as the "latest martial music of Merry England."

It was immediately taken up by the Continentals, and twenty-five years later the same tune sounded in the ears

3. Cavaliers. Members of the court party opposed to Cromwell.

When Cromwell rode a small horse and wore a hat with a single plume, the Cavaliers laughed at him and made up the words of "Yankee Doodle."

of Cornwallis as he surrendered at Yorktown. "Yankee Doodle" became extremely popular. The story is told that in New York some musicians were bombarded with eggs and vegetables because they insisted on playing a movement of a Haydn[4] symphony when the audience demanded "Yankee Doodle" and "The President's March."

"Hail Columbia." It was the summer of 1798. The French Revolution was just beginning. There still were troubles in Europe between France and England. Some Americans favored the cause of France; others opposed it. The famous XYZ letters had been published by President Adams. The people of the United States were amazed. Another war seemed certain. In spite of all the political disturbance, the theater in Philadelphia was still open. Gilbert Fox, a young actor belonging to the theater, called one Saturday afternoon on his former classmate, Joseph Hopkinson. Fox was desperately in need of help. He was about to give a benefit performance on the following Monday. There were twenty boxes in the theater still unsold, and it looked as if the proposed benefit would be a failure. If he could only get a patriotic song adapted to the popular "President's March," he was sure it would save the day for him. Would Hopkinson help him? Hopkinson agreed and the next afternoon the song was ready. The object was to get a song which would arouse an American spirit, independent and above the interests and policies of both France and England.

It was advertised that after the performance of *"The Italian Monk,"* an entirely new song, written by a citizen of Philadelphia, would be performed to the tune of "The President's March" and accompanied by a full band as well as a grand chorus. The house was packed. The song was

4. Haydn (hā'd'n). A German composer (1732-1809).

encored in wild enthusiasm. At the seventh encore the audience rose as one man and joined with Mr. Fox in the chorus, "Firm united let us be."

The song, "Hail Columbia," has remained one of the most popular of our patriotic songs. Up to the time of the Spanish-American War it shared honors with "The Star-Spangled Banner" as a national anthem.[5] At that time Admiral Dewey designated "The Star-Spangled Banner" as the national anthem and "Hail Columbia" lost its place.

"The Star-Spangled Banner." It seems strange to us that the tune for "The Star-Spangled Banner" had its origin in England, and had been used there and in this country as the tune for a drinking song, "To Anacreon[6] in Heaven." Several years afterwards, Francis Scott Key wrote the words which we now associate with the tune. The tune had also been used about the time of the Revolution with the words of the song, "Adams and Liberty."

During the War of 1812, Francis Scott Key, a young lawyer, sailed down Chesapeake Bay to try to secure the release of a friend who was held prisoner aboard a British warship. The friend was released, but, as the British were planning a surprise attack on Baltimore, they detained both men until after the attack. Guarded by British marines, Key watched the attack from a small vessel anchored in Baltimore Harbor. All day the battle raged. All night he strained his eyes to see what was going on. Several times the firing stopped and he thought the fort had surrendered. Just as daylight came, he gradually saw the outlines of Fort McHenry and suddenly he saw his country's flag, the Stars and Stripes, still flying, and he knew the fort had not surrendered. Filled with joy and relief, he took a scrap of

5. anthem. A hymn of praise, devotion, or patriotism.   6. Anacreon (*à·năk′ rê·ŏn*). A Greek poet famous for his light and graceful lyrics.

paper from his pocket and wrote the words of "The Star-Spangled Banner," adapting them to the tune of the drinking song. While "The Star-Spangled Banner" has been exceedingly popular, it was not until March, 1931, that Congress officially recognized it as the national anthem of the United States.

While on a recent tour of South America, the National Broadcasting Company's symphony orchestra and their conductor, Arturo Toscanini,[7] spent the Fourth of July in Montevideo,[8] Uruguay. Toscanini called his men together for what they expected to be an early morning rehearsal. When they were assembled, however, he told them that since they were far from home on Independence Day, he had called them together to play "The Star-Spangled Banner." The men played as they had never played before, with no audience but the United States Minister to Uruguay. All were deeply moved by Toscanini's act.

"America." "America" is one of our patriotic songs which did not have its origin in any incident connected with war. The song dates back to 1832 and was written by the Reverend Samuel F. Smith.

Lowell Mason, a musician of whom you will read later, had become greatly interested in the method of teaching music to children which was then in use in Germany. A friend had lent him some books which contained songs and music especially adapted to children, but the songs were written in German and Mr. Mason could not translate them. He took them to Smith, who was then a young man studying to become a minister, and asked him either to translate the German words or to write new hymns and songs adapted to the German music.

7. Toscanini (tôs'kä·nē'nĕ). An Italian conductor in America (1867-   ).
    8. Montevideo, Uruguay (mŏn'tĕ·vĭd'ē·ō ū'rōō·gwā). The capital.

Courtesy National Park Service, Department of the Interior

After the attack, Francis Scott Key saw our flag still waving and wrote the words of "The Star-Spangled Banner."

As Smith was glancing over the book, his attention was attracted to one tune in particular. It was simple and natural in movement and seemed to be well-suited to children's voices. Looking at the German words, he saw they were patriotic. The Reverend Smith said later, "I was inspired to write a patriotic hymn of my own. Seizing a scrap of waste paper, I began to write, and in half an hour, I think, the words stood upon it, substantially as they are sung today. I did not know at the time that the tune was the British 'God Save the King.'" He put the song away and nearly forgot he had written it. Some weeks later he sent it to Mr. Mason. On the following Fourth of July it was sung by a chorus of children's voices. It is interesting to note that the Reverend Edward Everett Hale, author of *A Man without a Country,* at that time a boy of ten, was a member of the chorus.

The English, German, Swiss, and French claim the tune to which the words are sung. At any rate, it was another American song set to a borrowed tune.

"Columbia, the Gem of the Ocean." While there is some dispute as to the origin of "Columbia, the Gem of the Ocean," most people attribute the music to Thomas à Becket, an English actor, and the words to David T. Shaw.

The story as told by à Becket runs something like this: He was playing during an engagement at a theater in Philadelphia when David T. Shaw, who was at the time singing at the museum in the same city, called with some patriotic verses he had written. Not finding them satisfactory, à Becket rewrote them, composed a musical setting for them, and returned them to Mr. Shaw. A few weeks afterward, while playing in New Orleans, he was surprised to find a published copy of "Columbia, the Pride of the Ocean," in which David T. Shaw was credited with the authorship of both words and music, and Thomas à Becket with the arrangement. Mr. à Becket took the matter up with the publishers and convinced them that he was the author and composer. Later the song appeared under the proper title with Thomas à Becket as composer. This is frequently called the "army and navy" song because of the appearance of these words in it.

Songs of the North and South

Songs of the War between the States. It has been said that the greatest patriotic songs any nation ever produced were written during the War between the States. At that time people were much affected by music. Many popular songs had been written, musical instruments were more plentiful, gospel hymns had spread to every community— America had become a singing nation. Both the North and the South believed that appropriate songs were necessary to win the war. Both sides were eager to get songs which would inspire patriotism. One patriotic northern gentleman, at the beginning of the war, offered a prize of five hundred dollars or a medal of the same value for a song. The song which received the prize was little used and is now unknown.

It is strange that "Dixie," which became the great song of the southern army, was written and composed by a northerner, and that the North's best song, "The Battle Hymn of the Republic," was the work of a southerner.

"Dixie." Daniel Emmett was one of the most famous of early American minstrels. While he was a member of a band of minstrels several years before the war, his contract provided that he was to write a new "walk around" whenever called upon, and to sing it at the performance.

The "walk around" was the name given to the song and dance which came at the end of the first part of a minstrel show.

One rainy Sunday, the manager of the troupe told Emmett they must have a new song the next night. The following story of the composition of "Dixie" was told by one of Emmett's companions. Showmen used to say, "I wish I was in Dixie," because any showman who could get a job in the South in cold weather thought himself pretty lucky. The next day, Emmett, trying to think out the new song, remarked, "Well, I wish I was in Dixie." His wife replied, "Dan, that's the idea for a song." Emmett thought so, too, and wrote the song.

"Dixie" was a sensation. Other minstrels sang and danced it all over the country. Southerners loved it. It was used as a political song in the campaign of 1860, and, when the war broke out, southern troops immediately took it for their own, singing it in camp and on the march.

"The Battle Hymn of the Republic." This song was originally a Sunday school hymn tune written by William Steffe of Charleston, South Carolina.

> Say brothers, will you meet us?
> Say brothers, will you meet us?
> Say, brothers, will you meet us?
> Say brothers, will you meet us?
> On Canaan's happy shore?
> Chorus
> Glory, glory, hallelujah
> Glory, glory, hallelujah
> Glory, glory, hallalujah
> For ever, ever more.

It became very popular as a camp-meeting song with both Negroes and whites. It somehow found its way north, and at the beginning of the war became a northern camp song with verses about John Brown. The song became known as "John Brown's Body."

One day Mrs. Julia Ward Howe was a member of a party visiting a soldiers' camp outside of Washington. She heard the soldiers singing Steffe's tune and liked it. That night she wrote, to the tune of the camp song, the words which have become familiar as one of our national hymns.

"The Battle Cry of Freedom." George F. Root, one of America's foremost writers of war songs, wrote "The Battle Cry of Freedom," also "Tramp, Tramp, Tramp," "The Vacant Chair," and "Just before the Battle, Mother." President Lincoln had issued his second call for troops, but many felt that the reading of his proclamation would not be favorably received. Root wrote "The Battle Cry of Freedom" to be sung at a rally held in connection with the reading of the proclamation. President Lincoln later wrote a personal letter to Mr. Root, saying that he felt his song had aided greatly in winning the war.

"Tenting on the Old Camp Ground." This is one of the songs of the War between the States which is often sung today. It was written by Walter Kittredge, a young man from New Hampshire who was unable to join the army because of poor health. He gave his time to the cause of good music in the army camps of the North. He not only composed songs, but he made collections of songs. He published the first Union book of songs. "Tenting on the Old Camp Ground" became popular in the homes of the North as well as in camp.

"The Girl I Left Behind Me." This old Irish song, popular in colonial days, came into use at the time of the War between the States as the tune played when the boys marched away to war.

"When Johnny Comes Marching Home." This song was written to be played to welcome the boys when they came back. Roy Harris, a modern composer, has written a symphony based upon the tune.

"Maryland, My Maryland." In the beginning of the war, Maryland, although a slave-holding state and a southern sympathizer, did not actually leave the Union. One of her native sons, James Ryder Randall, was living in New Orleans when he heard that Massachusetts troops had been fired on as they passed through Baltimore. He hoped that this incident would swing Maryland to the cause of the South, and so he wrote his appeal in verses which were published in the New Orleans *Daily Delta*. They were copied into every southern newspaper and in less than two months became what someone aptly called the "Marseillaise"[9] of the Confederacy.

9. "Marseillaise" (mär'sĕ·lāz'). National song of republican France, 1792.

CHAPTER VII

AMERICAN STATESMEN AS PATRONS OF MUSIC

The Revolutionary Period

Music of Our Patriots. There are some interesting stories concerning the place of music in the lives of the leaders of our nation from the very earliest times. A few of these incidents will serve to show the influence of music on some of our patriots and, at the same time, will reflect some of the customs of the time relating to music.

Washington and Music. George Washington was always interested in music. At the age of fifteen he made an entry in his account book showing he had paid five shillings sixpence to attend a concert. His diaries and accounts from time to time show entries indicating his attendance at concerts and theatrical productions. He probably was familiar with the songs popular at the time—"The Girl I Left Behind Me," "Drink to Me Only with Thine Eyes," "O Dear, What Can the Matter Be"—for they were frequently heard at concerts and at the theater.

Washington also enjoyed the playing of music in his own home. While we do not know that he sang or played any instrument skillfully, we do know that he provided a musical education for his stepchildren and their children. Fifteen years before the Revolutionary War, Washington ordered a spinet from abroad. There are now several instruments at Mount Vernon which belonged to the Washington family—a flute, a guitar, and the harpsichord which Washington bought for Nellie Custis.

A guitar, a flute, and the harpsichord which Washington bought for Nellie Custis are in the music room at Mount Vernon.

Washington was particularly fond of dancing. The minuet and the gavotte[1] were the formal dances. Reels and country dances were popular. One of his favorite dance tunes was "Successful Campaign," which was also a popular march of the period.

When Washington was chosen first President of the United States, he traveled from his home at Mount Vernon to New York to be inaugurated. A triumphal arch had

---

1. gavotte (gȧ·vŏt′). An old, lively dance done by French peasants.

been erected on the bridge at Trenton, New Jersey, where he would pass. As he came beneath the arch, he was greeted by a chorus sung by a number of young girls dressed in white, holding baskets of flowers. As they sang they strewed flowers before the general, who halted until the chorus was finished.

"The President's March" may have been played at his inauguration. At any rate, it was written in his honor and became one of the most popular selections of the day. It was played on all occasions. The tune is what we know as "Hail Columbia."

During his presidency, Washington visited both the North and the South. On his tour through New England, he was greeted at Boston at a triumphal arch by the singing of an "Ode to Columbia's Favorite Son," performed by the Independent Musical Society. A concert was arranged in his honor, at which selections from the *Messiah*, an air from *Sampson*, and an organ concerto[2] by Handel were given.

On his southern tour, he visited the Moravian settlement at Salem, North Carolina, where he was a guest of Salem College, the oldest college in North Carolina for the higher education of women. He was entertained while there with a musical program at his temporary headquarters. In the museum at Salem is still shown the old spinet upon which a young lady played for Washington's entertainment. An amusing story gives us a hint that Washington did not always give his undivided attention to music. At the conclusion of the young lady's recital, she naturally expected that the great man would compliment her upon her playing, for he had been standing near by

---

2. concerto (kŏn·chĕr'tō). A piece of music played by one or more principal instruments with the accompaniment of an orchestra.

watching her performance closely. Imagine her disappointment when Washington, instead of mentioning her performance, gave her a formula for taking off a wart which he had noticed on her finger.

From the diary of one of the Moravians who lived in Salem at the time of Washington's visit, we find that:

> Six Brethren were then invited to dine with him, and during the meal there was again music. . . . . Toward evening the Governor of this State . . . . arrived from his plantation some forty miles from here. . . . . He, the President and Major Jackson attended a song service that evening, the singing being interspersed[3] with instrumental selections; and they expressed their pleasure in it. At the close of the day the wind instruments were heard sweetly beside the Tavern.

Washington's talents, his achievements, and the love and gratitude of the American people for him were expressed in song throughout his whole career. On the occasion of one of his birthdays, an "Ode on the Birthday of His Excellency, George Washington" was presented at the Pennsylvania Coffee House in Philadelphia. An "Ode in Honour of General Washington" was performed at a concert in Boston. Francis Hopkinson, America's first composer, dedicated a collection of eight of his songs to Washington. Twelve days after Washington's death, Benjamin Carr had ready for performance a "Dead March and Monody,"[4] which was performed at the memorial services held in the Lutheran church in Philadelphia. Van Hagen composed a "Funeral Dirge on the Death of General Washington." Oliver Holden was the composer of a "Collection of Sacred·Dirges, Hymns and Anthems Commemorative of the Death of General George Washington."

3. interspersed (ĭn'tĕr·spûrst'). Varied with something put here and there.
4. Monody (mŏn'ō·dĭ). A funeral song; also, music in which the melody is confined to a single part.

MY DAYS HAVE BEEN SO WONDROUS FREE

Francis Hopkinson

My days have been so won-drous free, The lit-tle birds that
fly With care-less ease from tree to tree Were but as
blest as I, Were but as blest as I Ask
glid-ing wa-ters if a tear Of mine in-creased their
stream, And ask the breath-ing gales if e'er I lent a
sigh to them. I lent a sigh to them.

From The New American Song Book, *copyrighted by Hall & McCreary Company. Used by permission.*

Francis Hopkinson. Francis Hopkinson was the only
musician of note to sign the Declaration of Independence.
He was not only a musician but was also Washington's
legal adviser, the first Secretary of the Navy, a satirist,[5]
poet, inventor, and painter. He was a member of the first
class to receive the bachelor's degree from the College of
Philadelphia, now the University of Pennsylvania. He
was active in the debates of the Constitutional convention.
According to some authorities, he was the designer of the
United States flag. When he was twenty-two he wrote his
first song, "My Days Have Been So Wondrous Free." This
was the first secular song written in America.

From his letters we can guess that Hopkinson was the
center of musical life in Philadelphia. He was a talented
harpsichordist, and a member of a group of amateur and
professional musicians who met at each others' houses and
who also gave subscription concerts in public. At one time
he was church organist and wrote some church music. He
trained choral groups in choral singing and taught singing
to the children in one of the churches in Philadelphia.

His interest in the harpsichord led him to invent a device for improving the method of quilling[6] for the harpsichord. He and his friend, Thomas Jefferson, while the
latter was in France, carried on an interesting correspond-
ence concerning his invention and concerning a plan for
adding keys to the harmonica.

The last of his collection of eight songs dedicated to
Washington was called "The Trav'ler Benighted[7] and
Lost, o'er the Mountains Pursues His Lone Way." Hop-
kinson thought if this selection were played very slowly

5. satirist (săt'ĭ·rĭst). A writer of articles ridiculing vice or folly. 6. quilling.
Plucking strings of an instrument by means of a quill. 7. Benighted (bē·nīt'ĕd).
Overtaken by night.

and sung with expression it would be "forcibly pathetic." This must have been true, for Thomas Jefferson, acknowledging receipt of the song, wrote to Hopkinson:

> I will not tell you how much they have pleased us, nor how well the last of them merits praise for its pathos, but relate a fact only, which is that while my elder daughter was playing it on the harpsichord, I happened to look toward the fire and saw the younger one all in tears. I asked her if she was sick. She said, "No; but the tune was so mournful."

Hopkinson's work was not original enough to exert great influence, but it is of interest historically. Francis Hopkinson was the father of Joseph Hopkinson, who wrote the words of "Hail Columbia."

Thomas Jefferson's Interest in Music. Thomas Jefferson at one time was described as a man "who is at once a musician, skilled in drawing, a geometrician, an astronomer, a natural philosopher, legislator, and statesman." He loved music deeply and deplored the lack of it in America. He was a skilled violinist and practiced faithfully from the time he was a child until an accident to his wrist made playing impossible. He is said to have practiced three hours a day for twelve years. He was fond of playing duets with Patrick Henry or with John Tyler. There is a story that Patrick Henry was considered the worst violinist in Virginia next to Thomas Jefferson. This is contradicted, however, by another statement that Jefferson, "an indefatigable[8] practicer, inheriting a touch of singular delicacy . . . has become a superior performer." Another story is that Jefferson caused wonderment by tucking the violin under his chin, instead of resting it on his knees when playing, as was the custom at that time.

8. indefatigable (ĭn′dē·făt′ĭ·gà·b'l). Tireless.

An interesting letter written from Williamsburg, Virginia, to a friend in France, told of a novel plan which Jefferson had for bringing good music to America.

If there is a gratification which I envy any people in this world, it is your country (France) its music. This is the favorite passion of my soul, and fortune has cast my lot in a country where it is in a state of deplorable barbarism. I shall ask your assistance in procuring a substitute who may be proficient in singing and on the Harpsichord. . . . .

The bounds of an American fortune will not admit the indulgence of a domestic band of musicans; yet I have thought that a passion for music might be reconciled with that economy which we are obliged to observe. I retain, for instance, among my domestic servants a gardener, a weaver, a cabinet maker, and a stone cutter to which I would add a vigneron.[9] In a country where, like yours, music is cultivated and practiced by every class of men, I suppose there might be found persons of these trades who could perform on the French horn, clarionet, or hautboy, and bassoon, so that one might have a band of two French horns, two clarionets, two hautboys, and a bassoon without enlarging his domestic expenses. A certainty of employment for a half dozen years, and at the end of that time to find them, if they chose, a conveyance to their own country might induce them to come here on reasonable wages.

The Period of the War between the States

The Music of Lincoln's Time. It was only natural that many of the popular songs of the War between the States were written about Abraham Lincoln because he was a national figure and because he was so intimately connected with all the events of the war. Thus, the music relating to Lincoln not only reflects the man but also forms an obbligato[10] to the history of the war. Lincoln music in-

9. vigneron (vě′nyē·rôn′). A grower of grapes and maker of wine. 10. obbligato
(ŏb′lĭ·gä′tō). An accompanying part.

cluded rail-splitting polkas and schottisches,[11] nomination and campaign songs, presidential hymns, emancipation songs, minstrel songs, funeral and memorial pieces.

Minstrel songs were popular during the war, and Lincoln figured in many of them. For instance, there were several versions of the well-known song, "Raw Recruits" or "Abraham's Daughter." Probably the most popular song written about Lincoln was "We Are Coming Father Abra'am, Three Hundred Thousand More," written after Lincoln issued a call in 1862 for three hundred thousand troops.

After the surrender of General Lee and his army, thousands of people crowded around the White House. Bands were playing and the cheering people called for President Lincoln. Finally he appeared and made a very brief speech. He concluded with:

I see you have a band. I propose closing up by requesting you to play a certain air or tune. I have always thought *Dixie* was one of the best tunes I ever heard. I have heard that our adversaries over the way have attempted to appropriate it as a national air. I insisted yesterday that we had fairly captured it. I presented the question to the Attorney-general, and he gave his opinion that it is our lawful prize. I ask the band to give us a good turn upon it.

As the incident is related, the musicians did give a good turn, not only to "Dixie," but to "Yankee Doodle" and "Hail Columbia" as well.

The largest number of Lincoln pieces written on any one occasion was composed soon after his assassination; there were nearly fifty funeral marches and more than thirty memorial songs.

11. schottisches (shŏt′ĭsh·ĕz). Old English dances.

WE ARE COMING, FATHER ABRA'AM

HUTCHINSON   L. O. EMERSON

1. We are com-ing, Fa-ther A-bra'am, three hun-dred thou-sand
2. If you look a-cross the hill-tops that meet the nor-thern

more, From Mis-sis-sip-pi's wind-ing stream and
sky, Long mov-ing lines of ris-ing dust your

from New Eng-land's shore; We leave our plows and
vis-ion may de-scry; And now the wind, an

work-shops, our wives and chil-dren dear, With
in-stant tears the cloud-y veil a-side, And

hearts too full for ut-ter-ance, with but a sil-ent tear; We
floats a-loft our span-gled flag in glo-ry and in pride; And

dare not look be - hind us, but stead - fast - ly be - fore. We are
bayo - nets in the sun - light gleam, and bands brave mu - sic pour, We are

com - ing, Fa - ther A - bra'am, three hun - dred thou - sand more.
com - ing, Fa - ther A - bra'am, three hun - dred thou - sand more.

CHORUS

We are com - ing, we are com - ing, Our Un - ion to re - store, We are

com - ing, Fa - ther A - bra'am, with three hun - dred thou - sand more, We are

com - ing, Fa - ther A - bra'am, with three hun - dred thou - sand more.

CHAPTER VIII

MUSIC OF THE FOLK

Development of Folk Music

A Rural Nation. During the period of time between the Revolution and the War between the States, the United States was a rural nation. At the time of Washington's inauguration, only a small percentage of the people lived in cities. At the close of the War between the States, more than three fourths of the people lived in the open country or in small towns and villages. If we consider the place of music in the culture of our people at that time, we must know what the music of the people who lived in the country was like.

Introducing Music to the People. Transportation and communication were difficult in those times. Travel, for the most part, was by stage, on horseback, or by walking. Letters and newspapers were scarce, and there were few books. Postage was high. There were no telephones, no free delivery of mail, and no radio. Practically none of the ways of spreading music which we have today existed then. Rich planters in the South often took their wives and daughters to the city in winter so that they might attend the theater, opera, and concerts. The majority of the people, however, sang the songs they had heard from their parents or neighbors in the small community in which they lived. These songs were the music of the folk—music of the people in general.

Meaning of Folk Music. The folk song is one known and sung by all the people. It lives for generations. The composer may or may not be known, for the song itself is more important than the person who wrote it. Folk songs reflect the character of the people who sing them by expressing their daily lives—what they do, what they think, how they feel. They are simple in form, usually being made of sixteen measures, with the first and third, the second and fourth alike; or with the first and second, and third and fourth the same. You may know this as A-B-A-B, or A-A-B-B forms.

American Folk Music. Some people claim there is no true American folk music. However, we are fortunate in having the folk music of many lands. Settlers of the United States brought here the folk songs of England, France, Holland, Spain, Germany, Russia, Italy, and all the other countries, and adapted them to conditions in the various sections of our country. It is quite natural that we should find the folk music of the English, Irish, and Scotch in the highlands of Virginia, the Carolinas, Kentucky, and Tennessee; the French characteristics of Creole music in Louisiana; and the influence of the Spanish in the Southwest.

There are some songs, such as war songs, hymns, and certain popular tunes, which are sung by nearly all the people of our country. On the other hand, there are some songs which represent life in particular parts of the country. The folk music of the Negroes, Indians, cowboys, mountaineers, and lumberjacks is usually considered American folk music. This is true because the peculiarities of each group may be traced to the conditions of life in its particular surroundings.

Let us see what music the people of the United States were singing and playing in their homes, at their work, and at their play during those years of our struggle to become a strong nation.

Folk Music of the South

Negro Music. Among the Negroes of the South during the time of slavery, a type of song developed which we speak of as Negro folk music. It is not the song of the African in his native land, but the product of the African in a new environment. The Negro brought with him from Africa a natural sense of rhythm, an almost monotonous expression of voice, and strong tendency to imitate. In his native home, the Negro made use of singing in his religious observances. It was but natural, when he came to this country, that he should cling to his voodooism,[1] the name given to his religion, and to the weird chants connected with it. Association with his white master gave him the English language. He soon began to imitate the songs the white men sang. Put all these ingredients together and you have the combination which made our Negro folk music.

Characteristics of Negro Singing. One must hear this music sung by Negroes to appreciate it fully, for they have a manner of singing as characteristic as their songs. The principle of the rhythm is syncopation;[2] that is, the accent is shifted to the unaccented beat of a measure. Peculiar sounds are put in. There is a slurring of voices, a sliding from one note to another with sudden emphasis on a syllable or word. When singing in chorus, the leader starts the

1. voodooism (vōō′dōō·ĭz′m). Superstitious belief of Negroes; magic among Negroes. 2. syncopation (sĭng′kŏ·pā′shŭn).

SWING LOW, SWEET CHARIOT

Negro Spiritual

Swing low, sweet char - i - ot, Com - in' for to car - ry me home,

Swing low, sweet char - i - ot, Com - in' for to car - ry me home.

Fine

I looked o - ver Jor - dan, an' what did I see,
If you get dar be - fo' I do,
I'm some - times up, and some - times down,

Com - in' for to car - ry me home? Tell all my friends I'm
But still my soul feels

A band of an - gels

D. C.

com - in' af - ter me,
com - in' too, Com - in' for to car - ry me home.
heab - en - ly bound,

From the Treasure Chest of Songs, *by Hesser and Dustman, published by the American Book Company.*

verse, the others joining as they choose. Sometimes they follow the melody; sometimes they improvise[3] parts. They keep perfect time and rarely produce discords. Frequent use of the minor form is another characteristic. Nearly all of the songs are in $\frac{2}{4}$ or $\frac{4}{4}$ time. There is much repetition of the words and tune. "Swing Low, Sweet Chariot" is a good example of a typical Negro folk song.

Negro Spirituals. The religious songs of the old southern Negroes included spirituals and "shout songs." The spiritual was their more formal type of song and it was sung "settin' down." Bodies swayed and heads waved, keeping time. The beating of drums, the shaking of a rattle, drawing a stick across the jaw bone of some animal, or the plunk of a banjo served as an accompaniment. Sometimes the spiritual was sad; sometimes it was happy. The sad spiritual is represented by "Nobody Knows the Trouble I've Seen"; the happy one by "All God's Chillun Got Wings."

The words often sound quite strange. The early Negroes could neither read nor write. Therefore their knowledge of Bible stories came only through hearing them read or told. They frequently failed to understand the meaning of the stories, and so made up their own interpretations. To them the people of the Bible were very real and they were made to seem so in the spirituals. Heaven, too, was a reality, a happy place where they would never have to work again.

The "Shouts." The "shouts" were called "running sper-'chals" to distinguish them from the more dignified "settin' sper'chals." They were sung under great religious excitement and were accompanied by a clapping of hands and a stamping and shuffling of feet as well as by a swaying of

3. improvise (ĭm'prŏ·vīz). Make up on the spur of the moment.

heads and shoulders. One might say they were spirituals "jazzed up." In some sections of the South, both the song and its accompanying dance are called "shouts"; in others, the dance alone is known as a "shout."

The following description is from an article published in the New York *Nation:*

The true "shout" takes place on Sundays or on "praise-nights" through the week, and either in the praise-house or in some cabin. . . . . The benches are pushed back to the wall when the formal meeting is over, and old and young, men and women . . . . stand up in the middle of the floor, and when the "sperchil" is struck up, begin first walking and by-and-by shuffling round, one after the other, in a ring. The foot is hardly taken from the floor. . . . . Sometimes they dance silently, sometimes as they shuffle they sing. . . . . More frequently a band composed of some of the best singers and of tired shouters stand at the side of the room to "base" the others, singing the body of the song and clapping their hands together or on the knees.

This was kept up hour after hour until late at night, and ended in complete exhaustion for those taking part. Shouts occurred frequently, for the Negroes were supposed to shout and sing when they got happy. They thought that if they didn't shout, they "squenched" the spirit. The shout was the only form of dancing permitted in some religious communities.

Funeral Songs. Closely related to the shouts were the funeral songs which accompanied the wakes and burial of Negroes. They were sung in a low, monotonous croon by those who sat up with the dead.

"Pattin' Juba." "Pattin' Juba" is a Negro expression for clapping of hands and stamping with feet at a Negro dance performed on the old southern plantations. Those who watched the dance stamped with their feet and fol-

LEVEE SONG

(*Wukkin' on de Railroad*)

I've been wuk-kin' on de rail-road All de live-long day;

I've been wuk-kin' on de rail-road, To pass de time a-way.

Doan yo' hyar de whis-tle blow-in', Rise up so ear-ly in de mawn;

Doan yo' hyar de cap-tain shout-in' Di-nah blow yo' hawn!

From THE NEW AMERICAN SONG BOOK, *copyrighted by Hall & McCreary Company. Used by permission.*

lowed that with two quick pats on their hands in $\frac{2}{4}$ measure. About one third of the crowd kept time in this way while the other two thirds danced. Sometimes this was done as a solo dance with all but the soloist keeping time. The music was furnished by a fiddler or banjo player.

Work Songs. Work on the plantations was often done
to the accompaniment of singing. Work was easier when
done to the rhythm of some work song. Black mammies
could be heard singing at their churning, keeping time to
the chug of the churn dash, or at their wash tubs. The
"Boll Weevil Song" is typical of the songs of the Negro
slaves in the cotton fields. Often the slaves who led the singing were given some special reward. During the building
of railroads in the South, bosses hired "singin' liners"
who did not work but who set the pace for the others.
Many a rail was laid to "Wukkin' on de Railroad" or other
railroad songs. Negroes on the river front sang as they
loaded bales of cotton.

Creole Negro Music. In Louisiana, the music of the
Negroes reflected the influence of their Creole masters.
This was noticeable in the words of French dialect in
the songs themselves and in the character of the music.
While the Louisiana Negroes, too, had spirituals, their
most characteristic songs were their love songs, called "mellows" for melodies, and their dance music. The "mellows,"
with their soft, crooning tunes and pretty words, took in all
sorts of subjects from the street cries of the fish peddlers
and flower sellers to love songs. A typical example of the
Creole Negro song is "Misieu' Banjo," in which the Negroes poked fun at a dandy in their midst.

The special charm of Creole music was first emphasized
by one of our first American composers of note, Louis
Moreau Gottschalk,[4] who was a native of New Orleans.
He used many of the Creole Negro melodies, including
"Bamboula,"[5] "Layotte,"[6] and "Le Bananier,"[7] in his com-

4. Gottschalk (gŏt′shälk). An American pianist and composer (1829-1869).
5. "Bamboula" (bäm·bōō′là). A primitive drum; the dance performed to the
beating of the drum. 6. "Layotte" (lä·yŏt′). 7. "Le Bananier" (lĕ bà·nà·nyāy′).
A banana tree.

MISIEU' BANJO

NEGRO-FRENCH FOLK SONG   ARRANGED BY
                                                                     HENRI WEHRMANN

Gar - dé mi - lat' là, O Mi - sieu Ban - jo, Com - men li in - sol - ent!
See that young dark-y Play-ing the ban-jo, Is - n't he in - so - lent!

Cha - po co - té,   O Mi - sieu Ban - jo,   Ba - dine à la
Hat on one side O Mi - sieu Ban - jo, Cane in right hand,

main, Mi - sieu Ban - jo, Sou - liers fé "crinc, crinc," O Mi - sieu Ban - jo,
O Mi - sieu Ban - jo, Boots that say "crink crank," O Mi - sieu Ban - jo,

Gar - dé mi - lat' là, O Mi - sieu Ban - jo, Com - men li in - sol - ent!
See that young dark-y Play-ing the ban-jo, Is - n't he in - so - lent!

positions. The bamboula was one of their best-known
dances. It was given that name because it was originally
danced to drumming on a bamboo log.

Other Louisiana Folk Songs. The Acadians, who came
from Nova Scotia in the middle of the eighteenth century
and settled in Louisiana and other southern states, brought
their own songs. These are called "Cajun" songs, for these
people are called "Cajuns." They are known chiefly for
their peculiar mixture of the English and French lan-
guages. This mixture is illustrated by an example which is

frequently given. A farmer's cow had strayed away. Seeing his neighbor coming up the levee, the farmer called, "Hè la bas Valsin! You see ma cow, you poosh 'eem 'ome."

Folk Music of the Appalachian Highlands

Mountain Music. In the mountainous regions of Virginia, Carolina, Kentucky, and Tennessee, there were settlers from the British Isles. Settlements were far apart and travel through the mountains was difficult. Everybody sang. It was one way to keep from being lonely. The only songs they knew were the folk tunes from the old country. These they sang again and again, substituting names of local people and places for the original words. Sometimes they added entirely new words to express the happenings of their everyday life.

Instruments. Few instruments were used. Some of those played were the guitar, the fiddle, and the dulcimer.[8] The dulcimer was something like a violin made longer. It was made of a shallow wooden box with four sound holes. Three strings were stretched over the box, one being used for the melody, the other two as drones.[9] It was laid upon the lap and plucked with a quill or hard leather. A short hickory limb strung with a single wire was sometimes twanged to provide rhythm.

Mountain children had few toys, and so at an early age they began to make their own. Frequently these toys took the form of musical instruments. They made cornstalk fiddles which consisted of two pieces of cornstalk twelve to fourteen inches long. Two slits were cut from one joint of the stalk to the other, and this portion of the stalk was

8. dulcimer (dŭl′sĭ·mēr). 9. drones. Continuous bass tones to melody played by another instrument.

raised by inserting a small block of cornstalk or light wood through the slits. One stalk was used as a bow on the other. Whistles were cut from a small stick of a willow or hickory tree. A long-necked gourd was often changed into a banjo by cutting off one side of the large portion, removing the seeds, and pasting a piece of heavy paper over the opening.

Kind of Songs Sung. The mountain songs, for the most part, were ballets (ballads), lonesome tunes and love songs, play-party and nonsense tunes, and religious songs.

The mountain people were deeply religious. "Singin' gatherin's" were held on Sunday at their crude little log churches. At these meetings, gospel and camp-meeting hymns, as well as other tunes, were sung. There were songs to please the "least 'uns" (children), lonesome tunes, and play-party pieces "without no harm in 'em." They wouldn't have thought of "stepping the tune" on the Lord's day.

Occasions for Merrymaking. The pioneers shared their work. Several families would come together to do the work of one household; then all of them would go to the home of another farmer on another day. Such work as corn huskin', hog killin', apple peelin', and the stir-off (sorghum[10] making) were usually followed in the evening by a frolic with play-party games and dancing. "The Miller Boy," "Skip to M' Lou," "Frog Went a Courting," "Liza Jane," "Cindy," "It Ain't Gonna Rain No More" were favorites on such an occasion.

Play-party songs and games were the delight of children and of courting couples in particular. They generally gave an opportunity for the boys and girls to choose the ones they liked best. There was a saying of the old folks, "It's the devil makes the foot pat"; but the young fellows and girls never thought of that when the fiddler began with

10. sorghum (sôr'gŭm). Sirup made from the juice of the sorghum plant.

ARKANSAS TRAVELER
Arranged by Robert T. Benford

From Dances of Our Pioneers, *by Grace Ryan. Copyright 1939 by A. S. Barnes and Company, Incorporated.*

such breakdowns[11] as "Zip Coon," "Arkansas Traveler," or "Sourwood Mountain."

Answering back or scolding ballads were favorites, too. A boy and a girl were seated side by side, the boy, perhaps, playing a simple accompaniment on a guitar or dulcimer.

11. breakdowns. Noisy, rapid, shuffling dances.

SOURWOOD MOUNTAIN

APPALACHIAN, U.S.A.

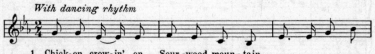

With dancing rhythm

1. Chick-en crow-in' on   Sour-wood moun-tain,
2. My true love's a   blue-eye'd dai - sy,   Hey de ing dang
3. My true love lives up   the   riv - er,

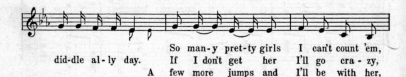

                          So man-y pret-ty girls   I can't count 'em,
did-dle al - ly day.   If I don't get her   I'll go   cra - zy,
                          A few more jumps and   I'll be with her,

                                               My true love she
Hey   de ing dang did-dle al - ly day.   Big dog'll bark and
                                               My true love lives

lives in Let - cher,
little one'll bite you,   Hey de ing dang did-dle al - ly day.
in   the hol - low,

She won't come and I won't fetch her,
Big girl'll court and little one'll slight you,, Hey de ing dang did-dle al-ly day.
She won't come and I won't fol - low,

From SINGING AMERICA, *used by permission of C. C. Birchard & Company,
Publishers.*

He would sing one verse and the girl would "answer back." Sometimes all the boys would sing the boys' part and all the girls would answer. Examples of these songs are "Paper of Pins" and "Bachelor's Song."

Love Songs. In pioneer days it was necessary for a young man to court the young woman of his choice in the presence of the whole family because there was but the one-room log cabin for all of them. Since he was often too shy to "speak his mind," he would sing as he rode up the valley toward the home of his loved one such tunes as "The Lonesome Dove," "Down in the Valley," "Lord Ullin's Daughter," or "Lord Lovell." Again, as he rode away, the expression of his love would echo back to her in song.

Folk Music of Other Sections

Songs of the Lumberjacks. In the forests of Michigan, Wisconsin, Minnesota, and Maine, there were many logging camps. The men who chopped, rolled, and hauled the logs were called lumberjacks or shanty boys. The term "shanty" came either from the name of the crude houses in which they lived or, as some believe, from the French word *chanter,* meaning "to sing." They did not sing to any great extent while they worked, for the rhythm of song did not serve to set the pace in logging as it did in other gang occupations, such as the work of sailors, stevedores,[12] and railroad workers. At night, however, in their shanties after a long, hard day's work, the shanty boys relaxed and became story tellers and singers. Men from all parts of the country were there and exchanged songs and stories.

There were many Irishmen who sang of ships, of pirates, and of battles. The French voyageurs brought songs such

12. stevedores (stē'vĕ·dōrz). Men who load and unload vessels.

LORD LOVELL

Mountain Song

1. Lord Lov - ell he stood at his cas - tle gate, A comb - ing his milk white steed, And by came La - dy Nan - cy Bell To wish her lov - er good speed, speed, speed, speed, To wish her lov - er good speed.

2. "Oh, where are you go - ing, Lord Lov - ell," she said, "Oh where are you go - ing," said she. "I'm go - ing my dear La - dy Nan - cy Bell, Strange coun - tries for to see, see, see, see, Strange coun - tries for to see."

3. La - dy Nan - cy she died as it might be today, Lord Lov - ell he died to - mor - row; And out of her bos - om there grew a red rose And out of Lord Lov - ell's a briar, briar, briar, briar, And out of Lord Lov - ell's a briar.

4. They grew and they grew, till they reached the church top, And then they couldn't grow any high'r; And there they en-twined in a true lov - er's knot, Which true lov - ers al - ways ad - mire, mire, mire, mire, Which true lov - ers al - ways ad - mire.

From The New American Song Book, *copyrighted by Hall & McCreary Company. Used by permission.*

as "Canadian Boat Song" and "Come, Good Winds," which were popular with the rivermen and lumbermen of Canada. Songs were brought from the Kentucky mountains and from the battlefields. The songs which particularly characterized the lumberjacks were those that told of accidents in log jams. "The Jam on Gerry's Rock" is a ballad of an accident in which a shanty boy was killed and his sweetheart died of grief; "James Whaland" also drowned in a log jam. "The Shanty Man's Life" describes the life of the lumberjack. "Driving Saw Logs on the Plover" is another characteristic song which shows the advantages of a farm boy over those of a lumberjack.

Cowboy Songs. Large forces of men were needed on the plains of the West and Southwest to take care of the cattle. They had to drive the cattle from one grazing place to another, and round them up in the spring and brand the calves. The cowboys also had to drive the cattle over long trails to market. In all this work the cowboys had to furnish their own entertainment. Sometimes the trails were long and tiresome. Sometimes the cowboys had to watch their herds all night. And so they sang. Sometimes they sang songs they had learned elsewhere, but often they sang songs composed by the cowboys themselves. Their songs told of their life in the wide, open spaces. These were ballads of desperadoes, sentimental songs such as "The Dying Cowboy" or "Home on the Range," or sometimes religious songs like "Rounded Up in Glory." "The Buffalo Skinners" told about the years when outfits of men went into the Great Plains and killed large numbers of buffaloes for their hides. "Poor Lonesome Cowboy," "Little Ah Sid," "Whoopee Ti Yi Yo," "Git Along Little Dogie," "When the Curtains of Night Are Pinned Back" are other examples of songs they sang.

Songs of Other Occupations. A number of short rail-roads, later to be joined into trunk lines, were constructed during the latter part of this period of the frontier and the cowboy. Many Irish workmen were employed in this work. An Irishman always likes to sing; so there were many railroad songs. Some of them were "Poor Paddy Works on the Railway," "The Railroad Cars Are Coming," "Casey Jones," and "She'll Be Comin' Round the Mountain."

The mule drivers of the canal boats sang to relieve the monotony of their work and to keep themselves awake at night, for their boats moved day and night. It is reported that the citizens of Albany, New York, filed a complaint against the singing at night by the boat drivers because the citizens were being disturbed at their rest. "The Erie Canal," "The Erie," "The Raging Can-all," "The Great Lakes" were familiar songs at the time. The flatboatmen, too, found many an occasion for enjoying music and dancing on board their boats. A good illustration of how these men entertained themselves with music will be found on page 109.

Boat captains knew the value of singing when pulling bow lines. Their sailors have given us the songs they sang on these occasions—"Blow the Man Down," "Rio Grande," and "Shenandoah." Pushing boats with long poles down shallower rivers gave origin to such songs as "Push Boat" and "Boatin' Up Sandy."

Composed Popular Music

The Popular Song. Singing many of these old folk songs probably led to the making of new songs. Some of these new songs were so appealing that people everywhere

THE JOLLY FLATBOATMEN, No. 2 by *George C. Bingham, courtesy of the Mercantile Library Association, St. Louis*

Men on river flatboats entertained themselves by singing, dancing, and playing musical instruments.

began to sing them. They became what we know as popular songs. Some of them so touched the hearts and lives of the people that the songs lived from generation to generation and became folk songs.

Early Popular Songs in America. America has produced much music of the popular kind. "Home, Sweet Home" is a good example of this type of music. John Howard Payne, an American actor and playwright, gave us the words. While in London at one time, he wrote and produced an opera, *Clari, Maid of Milan,* and used the song in that. The words were adapted to a tune already written called "Sicilian Air." Another early popular song is "Ben Bolt," written by Thomas Dunn English, a New Jersey physician. Several musical settings were written for the words. The air with which we are familiar now was composed by an actor, Nelson Kneass.

Songs of Stephen Collins Foster. The most successful popular song writer America has yet produced is Stephen Collins Foster. His success is measured by the fact that his songs have gained a wider and more lasting popularity than those of any other native writer in the same field. Although he composed over one hundred songs, only a few are as widely sung and enjoyed now as at the time they were written. These, "Old Folks at Home," "My Old Kentucky Home," "Old Black Joe," "Massa's in the Cold, Cold Ground," "O, Susanna," "Old Uncle Ned," "Jeannie with the Light Brown Hair," and "Camptown Races" are now classed as folk songs.

Foster was born near Pittsburgh, Pennsylvania, on July 4, 1826, and he died when still a comparatively young man at the age of thirty-eight. When he was a child, there were references in family letters to the boy's "strange talent for music." There was no mention of a thought of developing

D1EO/864

CAMPTOWN RACES

STEPHEN C. FOSTER   STEPHEN C. FOSTER

1. De Camp-town la - dies   sing dis song: Doo-dah, doo-dah;
2. De long-tail fil-ly an' de big black hoss.   Doo-dah, doo-dah;
3. Old mul-ey cow come   on de track.   Doo-dah, doo-dah;
4. Oh, see dem fly-ing on a ten-mile heat,   Doo-dah, doo-dah;

De Camp-town race track   five   miles long, Oh, doo-dah-day
Dey fly de   track an' dey both cut a-cross, Oh, doo-dah-day.
De bob-tail fling her   o-ber his   back,   Oh, doo-dah-day.
    Roun' de race-track, den re-peat,   Oh, doo-dah-day.

I   come down dar   wid my hat caved in.   Doo-dah,   doo-dah;
De blind hoss stick-en in a big mud hole, Doo-dah,   doo-dah;
Den fly a-long like a rail-road car,   Doo-dah,   doo-dah;
I win my mon-ey on a bob-tail nag, Doo-dah,   doo-dah;

I go   back home wid a pock-et full o' tin, Oh, doo-dah-day.
Can't touch bot-tem wid a ten-foot pole, Oh, doo-dah-day.
Run-nin' a race   wid a shoot-in' star, Oh, doo-dah-day.
I keep my mon-ey in an old   tow   bag, Oh, doo-dah-day.

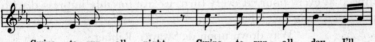

Gwine to run all night,   Gwine to run all day. I'll

bet my mon-ey on de bob-tail nag, Some-bod-y bet on de bay.

From SING!, *used by permission of C. C. Birchard & Company, Publishers.*

that talent. There were few music teachers near at hand; besides such an interest was not considered appropriate for an able-bodied man. The talent persisted, however, and the result was his songs with their simple and direct appeal. The illustration of "My Old Kentucky Home" on page 113 will give you an idea of the home life of some of the people who lived in the South when Foster was writing his songs.

"Old Folks at Home," his most popular song, was written for E. P. Christy, to be sung by the entertainers called Christy's minstrels. It was popular immediately. The Albany, New York, *State Register,* a year after the song had been written, had the following article concerning it:

Old Folks at Home, the *last* negro melody, is on everybody's tongue, and consequently in everybody's mouth. Pianos and guitars groan with it, night and day; sentimental young ladies sing it; sentimental young gentlemen warble it in midnight serenades; volatile[13] young "bucks" hum it in the midst of their business and their pleasures; boatmen roar it out stentorianly[14] at all times; all the bands play it; amateur flute players agonize over it at every spare moment; the street organs grind it out at every hour; the "singing stars" carol it on theatrical boards, and at concerts; the chamber maid sweeps and dusts to the measured cadence of *Old Folks at Home;* the butcher's boy treats you to a strain or two of it as he hands in the steaks for dinner; the milkman mixes it up strangely with the harsh ding-dong accompaniment of his tireless bell; there is not a "live darkey," young or old, but can whistle, sing, dance and play it, and throw in "Ben Bolt" for seasoning; indeed at every hour, at every turn, we are forcibly impressed with the interesting fact, that—

> "Way down upon de Swanee Ribber,
>   Far, far away,
>   Dere's whar my heart is turnin' ebber
>   Dere's whar de old folks stay."

13. volatile (vŏl'á·tĭl). Lively, airy; changeable in spirits. 14. stentorianly (stĕn·tō'rĭ·ăn·lĭ). In a loud manner.

MY OLD KENTUCKY HOME *by Eastman Johnson,*
courtesy of New York Public Library

In "My Old Kentucky Home" Stephen Collins Foster wrote about
people who "make merry all the day."

Recently a bronze portrait bust of Stephen Collins
Foster was placed in the Hall of Fame for Great Americans at New York University. He is the only musician who
has ever been so honored.

The Minstrel Show

How Music Was Popularized. A hundred years ago
there were no phonographs to bring records of the latest
popular songs into every home. One could not turn on the
radio and get any kind of music one wished. The only way

to hear new music was to hear it performed in person. An interesting kind of organization became the first means of popularizing songs and of spreading them through practically every community. This was the minstrel show.

The Beginning of the Minstrel. We are not sure of the exact origin of the Negro minstrel show. In the early days, guests at southern plantations were frequently entertained by groups of slaves who could sing or dance especially well. This may have been the beginning of the idea. At the close of the eighteenth century, a Boston newspaper announcement stated that in the performance of *Orinoko, or the Royal Slave,* a Mr. Graupner would sing a Negro song in character. The song was "The Gay Negro Boy" with a banjo accompaniment by the singer. This was Gottlieb Graupner, of whom we shall read about later in connection with quite another type of music.

W. D. Rice, afterward affectionately called "Daddy Rice," seems to deserve credit for popularizing the Negro character. When he was a young actor, he was walking down the street one day when his attention was called to an old darky who was humming a queer tune over and over, at the same time doing an odd shuffling step. This gave Rice an idea for a theater performance. He worked out a song with appropriate steps. That night he borrowed the clothes of an old Negro who hung about the theater, blacked his face, and gave the song, "Jump, Jim Crow." The audience was so delighted that Rice had to respond to several insistent encores. Finally, so the story goes, the forgotten Negro crept in through the stage door and, as the song came to an end, an audible whisper came from the wings, "Ah wants ma clo'es!"

The popularity of the blackface performers grew rapidly. In the early forties, the "Big Four," Dan Emmett who

JUMP, JIM CROW

Come lis-ten all you gals and boys, Ise just from Tuck-y-hoe, I'm goin' to sing a lit-tle song, My name's_ Jim_ Crow.

Weel a-bout and turn a-bout and do jis so,

Eb-'ry time I weel a-bout I jump Jim Crow.

wrote "Dixie," Dick Pelham, Frank Brower, and Billy Whitlock, organized with the idea of having a four-man how under the name of Virginia minstrels.

Edwin P. Christy's troupe was organized at about the ame time. This was one of the best-known troupes and he one for which several of Stephen Foster's songs were written. To Christy is due the credit for arranging the performance to provide for a whole evening's entertainment.

Scene from SWANEE RIVER, *Twentieth Century-Fox Motion Picture*

Minstrel shows were popular in the late nineteenth century.

Description of a Negro Minstrel Show. The performance was divided into three parts—the first part, the olio,[15]
and the afterpiece. In the first part the performers, varying in number from four to twenty, were seated in a single
row or in a semicircle. The interlocutor,[16] who usually
played whiteface and spoke painfully correct English, was
master of ceremonies. He carried on a running conversa-
tion and exchanged jokes with the two end men—Bones,
who played a set of bones (castanets),[17] and Tambo, who
played the tambourine.[18] The dialogue was interrupted

15. olio. The vaudeville part of a minstrel show. 16. interlocutor (ĭn'tēr·
lŏk'ū·tēr). 17. castanets (kăs'tá·nĕts'). Small shells of wood or ivory fastened to
thumb and beaten together. 18. tambourine (tăm'bŏō·rēn'). A small, shallow
one-headed drum with loose jingles on the side.

at regular intervals by songs announced by the interlocutor. The entire group often joined in the chorus. At the end of the first part the whole troupe joined in the "walk around," a walk or dance to lively music. The second part, or olio, was a variety of entertainment made up of banjo playing, clog dancing, and other specialities. The third part, or afterpiece, rarely touched upon anything in connection with Negro life. It was likely to be a short play.

The public parade, which always preceded the minstrel, was really an event. A child's shrill voice calling, "Hey, fellers! Minstrel's comin'!" was the signal for a crowd to gather. In front was a trumpet band. The minstrels marched four abreast or two by two. Each wore an elaborate, long-tailed coat with red silk lapels and a shiny plug hat. In front of the band marched the drum major in short red coat trimmed with gold braid, and with an immense imitation bearskin military cap on his head. He strutted along, juggling his brass-knobbed baton[19] continuously.

The minstrels in most instances were white men imitating the Negroes. They traveled from town to town playing a night or two nights in each place. Many songs of the South were given in these performances. Some of them were "Dixie," "Old Folks at Home," "Old Uncle Ned," "Susanna," "Hard Times Come Again No More," "Grandfather's Clock," "Listen to the Mocking Bird," "Going to the Silver Wedding," "Stop Dat Knockin' at My Door," "Root Hog or Die," "Old Dan Tucker," "Jump, Jim Crow," "Big Sunflower," and "Wake Nicodemus."

At a later date, the minstrel show took on a somewhat different character. The typical darky song became a "coon" song, and the performers frequently were Negroes instead of white men imitating the southern darky.

19. baton (bȧ·tôn'). A stick used by a band or orchestra leader for beating time.

CHAPTER IX

RELIGIOUS MUSIC

Early Church Music

Controversies about Church Music. The music of the church has always held an important place in the lives of the American people. In the early days, in those localities where the Catholic, Episcopal, or Lutheran churches represented the religious belief of the people, there was little or no disagreement regarding music in the church. The early settlers accepted and continued to use the music of the corresponding churches in Europe. Church music as it is known today, however, had its origin in the controversies concerning music in the church in New England.

The first controversy was over the question of whether any singing at all should be permitted in the church. The second concerned the manner of singing, that is, whether singing should be by rule and note (reading notes much as we do now), or according to the singer's own idea as to how the hymn should be sung. A third problem, an outgrowth of the second, was about the advisability of adopting the choir system. In this system, a choir took the lead and lining out of psalms and hymns was discontinued.

Singing by Note. It was difficult to reconcile the congregation to such a great change as learning to sing the psalms and hymns in time and in tune, "and above all by note.

As a general thing, the ministers took a stand for better music in the church, although one minister is said to have suspended seven or eight members for persisting in their singing by rule.

One minister expressed his opinion to his congregation in this way:

The beauty and harmony of singing consists very much in a just timing and tuning the notes; every singer keeping the exact pitch the tune is set in, according to the part he sings. Now you may remember, that in our congregation we us'd frequently to have some people singing a note or two, after the rest had done. And you commonly strike the notes not together, but one after another, one being half way thro' the second note, before his neighbor has done with the first.

From a history of one of the early churches, we find a statement that the congregation had voted that singing should be without reading the psalms line by line as had been done before. On the following Sunday, after the hymn had been announced by the minister, the old deacon, who had been accustomed to lining out the hymn, rose and proceeded to read the first line as usual. The singers continued to sing without pausing for a reading of the second line. The good old deacon raised his voice and read the second line. Finally his voice was overpowered by the joint voices of the choir and congregation, and he rushed from the meeting house, mortified at the triumph of the modern improvements. His conduct was criticized by the church and for a time he was deprived of the privilege of communion because he had been absent from public church service on the Sabbath.

Church Choirs. General adoption of the church choir system began about the latter part of the eighteenth century. In many churches those who had learned the art of singing were permitted to sit in the first gallery. In the beginning these groups of singers served merely as tune setters to lead the singing of the congregation. Later they frequently sang without having the congregation join them.

The choir leader was chosen either by the town or by the church. He was expected to sound the keynote and to give the pitch for each of the parts. At first this was done without the aid of any instrument, but soon the pitch pipe and later the tuning fork came into use. During the singing, the leader beat time in some conspicuous way and sang a part which is now known as the air or soprano part, but which was then called tenor.

The singers in the choir took liberties which to us would seem quite unusual and amusing. They would call attention to themselves and to their singing by straining the voice to an unnatural pitch, by singing flat or with a nasal twang, or by introducing continued drawls, holds, and other ridiculous things.

These efforts were apparently not always appreciated, for it is reported that on one occasion the minister turned to the choir and remarked, "You must try again, for it is impossible to preach after such singing."

Choirs were frequently criticized for their lack of devotion. This was indicated, as one minister remarked, "by smiling and whispering and looking over the tune book in the time of the sermon." A still greater lack of devotion is illustrated in an amusing story told of an incident which occurred in one of the churches in the South. The church was more elaborately furnished than many American churches of the time, and the choir loft was provided with thick crimson curtains which could be drawn, thus cutting off the choir from the view of the congregation. It was the custom that, when the singing was finished and the rec tor or minister gave his text, the singers would draw the curtain and read or sleep as they chose. On one very warm Sunday, the singers had brought along watermelon and lemonade for refreshments. In reaching across for a slice of watermelon, someone overturned the pitcher of lemonade. You can imagine the embarrassment of the rector and the surprise of the congregation when the lemonade began to trickle down through the cracks in the floor of the choir loft and to run down the main aisle of the church.

Need for Instruction in Music. The change in church singing from lining out to singing by the recall of notes led to the formation of singing schools or singing societies. Sometimes a singing school would change into a singing society, or a singing society would develop into a singing school. The chief difference in the two groups was that the singing schools gave not only practice in singing but also intensive study of music reading, while the singing societies were chiefly concerned with singing. Both organizations in the beginning used the same material, the psalm tunes of the church. There were few teachers of music, and frequently the task of giving instruction was undertaken by men of little or no training.

Fugue Tunes

William Billings and His Fugue Tunes. One teacher of music, William Billings, was an interesting and famous character born in Boston nearly two hundred years ago. He was an eccentric[1] person. He had a rasping voice, he was blind in one eye, one arm was withered, one leg was longer than the other, and he was slovenly in appearance—yet he is called America's first composer and first musician.

1. eccentric (ĕk·sĕn′trĭk). Odd, out of the ordinary.

Billings became a tanner's apprentice when a mere boy. He loved music, and it is said that he used to compose music as he worked, writing down the tunes on pieces of leather. Later, with only about three weeks of training in music received at a singing school, he decided to give up his trade as a tanner and to devote his whole time to teaching and composing music. There was not another professional musician in the country, but that did not bother him; he would be the first. He knew little about harmony or rules of composition, but he would not be cramped by rules. He would follow his own procedures. His mottoes were "every composer for himself" and "nature is the best dictator."

Up to this time all psalm singing had been in unison, with each singer singing the air. Billings disliked this kind of music and had little patience with the English psalm books that had been in use for more than a hundred years. At about this time, a quantity of so-called fugue[2] music from England had been introduced into the singing schools. There was not a very clear idea as to what constituted a fugue, and people began to call any composition written in contrapuntal[3] style a fugue. This type of music captured the imagination of Mr. Billings and he began to write his own fugue tunes. A collection of Billings' original fugue tunes appeared in his *New England Psalm Singer* or *American Chorister,* which is said to have marked the beginning of American music. At any rate, it was the first attempt at original composition. These fugue tunes resembled very little the true contrapuntal choral music of the lofty part writing of Handel or of Bach's fugues. In Bill-

2. fugue (fūg). A musical composition in which several themes follow one another at certain intervals. 3. contrapuntal (kŏn'trá·pŭn'tăl). According to rules of counterpoint, the art of plural melody.

ings' fugue tunes, one part came in after another, the one imitating the other. Someone described fuguing as "notes flying after each other although not always with the same sound. . . . Its beauties cannot be numbered. It is sufficient

---

To the PUBLICK.

A large Committee having been felected by the feveral Mufical Societies in Bofton and its vicinity, beg leave to folicit the attention of the publick to the following

PROPOSALS

For Publifhing a Volume of Original

AMERICAN MUSICK,

COMPOSED BY

WILLIAM BILLINGS, *of Bofton*.

THE intended Publication will confift of a number of Anthems, Fuges, and Pfalm Tunes, calculated for publick focial Worfhip, or private Mufical Societies. — A Dialogue between MASTER and SCHOLAR will preface the book, in which the Theory of Harmony, grounded on Queftion and Anfwer, is adapted to the moft moderate capacity. — Alfo an elegant FRONTISPIECE, reprefenting the ARETINIAN ARMS, engraved on Copperplate.

The publication of a volume of music by William Billings was announced in the *Massachusetts Magazine*, August, 1792.

---

to say that it is universally pleasing." Today we would say the music was confusing and a mere jargon[4] of sounds and words.

4. jargon (jär'gŏn). Chattering; confused language.

The fuguing music seems to have made a profound impression on the people of that time and it became very popular. A quotation from Billings himself gives his feeling about this type of music.

It has more than twenty times the power of the old slow tunes; each part straining for mastery and victory, the audience entertained and delighted, their minds surpassingly agitated and extremely fluctuated,[5] sometimes declaring for one part, and sometimes for another. Now the solemn bass demands their attention—next the manly tenor—now, the lofty counter—now, the volatile treble. Now here—now there, now here again. O ecstatic![6] Rush on, you sons of harmony!

This music was not deeply religious in character. In fact, much of its was definitely secular in its nature and was very much out of place in church services. "North Providence" was one of the many fugue tunes sung.

The air, called the tenor part then, and the bass were sung by men; the treble or true tenor part was sung by women; the alto, often called "counter," was sung by men, women, or boys. A selection was sung through from beginning to end without any attempt at expression, each part trying to outdo the other in vigor and volume.

A New Interest in Music. The music of Billings is not in use today. In fact, very few people have ever seen a copy of one of his fuguing tunes. Nevertheless, Billings and his music have had a great influence on the music of our country. His psalter, crude and imperfect as it was, awakened a new interest in music. Singing schools sprang up. The pupils of Billings founded the Stoughton Musical Society, which became one of the well-known musical societies of the United States. People began to study music seriously

5. fluctuated (flŭk′tū̇·āt′ĕd). Changed continually. 6. ecstatic (ĕk·stăt′ĭk). Joyful, filled with rapture; one who is subject to ecstasy.

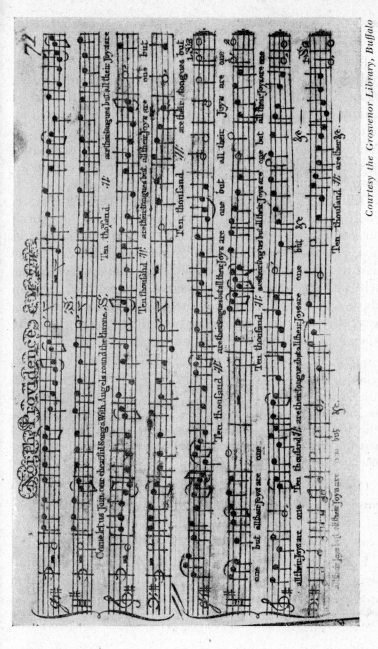

Courtesy the Grosvenor Library, Buffalo

"North Providence" is an example of a fugue tune.

and to practice on instruments. Billings is said to have introduced the pitch pipe which did away with faulty pitching of tunes. His use of the violoncello[7] led to the use of instruments as an accompaniment to church singing. The fugue tunes, however, led to an increase in singing by the choir in church and a corresponding decrease in singing by the congregation, for those who were unlearned in music were unable to participate in the singing.

Differences of Opinion concerning Church Music.
There were two distinct groups of composers of church music among the men who lived at the time of Billings and those who followed him. One group favored Billings' lively fuguing pieces; the other opposed this music, saying the style was trivial and undignified. A quotation from an address, given before one of the music societies just nine years after Billings' death, illustrates the feeling against the type of music Billings and his followers favored.

> The great part of those in our country who have undertaken to write music have been ignorant of its nature. Their pieces have little variety and little meaning. . . . . As they are written without meaning, they are performed without expression. . . . . Another very serious fault in the greater part of American music called sacred, is that its movements and air are calculated rather to provoke levity[8] than to kindle devotion.

Out of the controversy between the two groups came the music of the Protestant churches in America as it is today.

Hymns and Gospel Songs

Later Development of Church Music. American hymnology[9] began to develop in two directions. In one direction

---

7. violoncello (vē′ō·lŏn·chĕl′ō). A musical instrument like a violin but very much larger. 8. levity. Lack of gravity and earnestness. 9. hymnology (hĭm′nŏl′ō·jĭ). The composition of hymns; the study or science of hymns.

FROM GREENLAND'S ICY MOUNTAINS

REGINALD HEBER

LOWELL MASON

From Green-land's i - cy mount-ains, From In-dia's cor-al strand,

Where Af-ric's sun-ny fount-ains Roll down their gold - en sand;

From many an an-cient riv - er, From many a palm-y plain,

They call us to de - liv - er Their land from er-ror's chain. A - men.

1

From Greenland's icy mountains,
From India's coral strand,
Where Afric's sunny fountains
Roll down their golden sand;
From many an ancient river,
From many a palmy plain,
They call us to deliver
Their land from error's chain.

2

What though the spicy breezes
Blow soft o'er Ceylon's isle;
Though every prospect pleases,
And only man is vile?
In vain with lavish kindness
The gifts of God are strown;
The heathen in his blindness
Bows down to wood and stone.

3

Shall we, whose souls are lighted
With wisdom from on high,
Shall we to men benighted
The lamp of life deny?
Salvation! O Salvation!
The joyful sound proclaim,
Till earth's remotest nation
Has learned Messiah's name.

4

Waft, waft, ye winds, His story,
And you, ye waters, roll,
Till, like a sea of glory,
It spreads from pole to pole;
Till o'er our ransomed nature
The Lamb for sinners slain,
Redeemer, King, Creator,
In bliss returns to reign.

the dignified, stately type of hymns which we find in our hymnals today was developed; in the other, a type of music called gospel hymns. The latter was used chiefly in camp meetings, revival campaigns, and Sunday schools.

Work of Lowell Mason. Lowell Mason, about whom you will read more later, was one of the leaders in the movement for better church music. He is frequently called the father of church music. It is said that his name acts as the connecting link between the time of Billings and the present. He composed some original church music, including "My Faith Looks Up to Thee" and "Joy to the World," but probably his most important work was that of the arrangement, suitable for church music, of airs taken from the works of Haydn, Mozart,[10] Beethoven,[11] and other great masters. His first collection of hymns, the *Boston Handel and Haydn Society's Collection of Sacred Music,* was published in 1822. The collection was a success immediately and was used by churches and singing societies throughout the country. Mason's works are described as the first religious music in America which was respectable from a musical point of view. He did much toward improving the expression used in singing church music. He was especially interested in good music correctly harmonized and correctly sung. For this reason, in making arrangements his marks of expression were always natural and appropriate to the sentiment of the words.

The Bridgewater Collection. Ten years before the Handel and Haydn collection was made, another collection of songs was published called *Templi Carmina,* or *Songs of the Temple.* It was afterward called the Bridgewater collection and is frequently mentioned by the older people of today. It contained some three hundred and fifty pages of music taken from English sources. It was recommended by the Handel and Haydn Society.

Changes in Choir Singing. With better church music came an interesting change in part singing and in choir music. It was suggested by some of the singing masters

10. Mozart (mō'zärt). An Austrian composer (1756-1791). 11. Beethoven (bā'tō·vĕn). A German composer (1770-1827).

that the air, which had previously been sung by men, should be sung by women. There was serious objection to this as some people insisted that it interfered with the rights of man and was contrary to the scriptures (I Corinthians 14:34, "Let your women keep silence in the churches." I Timothy 2:11,12, "Let the woman learn in silence with all subjection. But I suffer not a woman to teach, nor to usurp authority over the man, but to be in silence.") The result, however, was the rearrangement of parts so that the women's voices sang the soprano or air and the alto (counter), while the men sang the bass and tenor parts.

The singing of solos and duets also came into use. At first those who dared to sing a solo part were often sneered at as being immodest. Soon, however, this came to be an accepted part of the song service.

The Hymn Tune. In speaking about the music of the early settlers, we sometimes say "psalm singing" and sometimes "hymn singing." The psalms were words of Hebrew songs found in the Bible. These were set to music, the same tune being used for a number of psalms. In the early days, many thought it was sacrilegious[12] to sing anything except psalms in church. Hymns are composed religious music. The hymn tune (melody for a hymn) is one of the smallest forms of musical composition. Since the sixteenth century, musicians have been composing these tunes.

How Hymn Tunes Get Their Names. If you glance through the hymnal of a Protestant church, you will notice that some of the songs have more than one title. You might find a hymn listed like the following:

O Love That Wilt Not Let Me Go

St. Margaret 8.8.8.6.6.

George Matheson 1842-1906   Albert L. Pearce 1844-1912

12. sacrilegious (săk′rĭ·lē′jŭs). Misusing something sacred.

"O Love That Wilt Not Let Me Go" is the title of the lyric or words to the hymn. "St. Margaret" is the title of the music for the hymn. The five numbers indicate that there are five phrases in the song. Each number represents the number of syllables in each phrase. These numbers were used in an earlier day when the music for a hymn was not always written in the hymn book. The singer used these numbers so that he would know where to pause for breath and where to break a word into syllables. The name at the left of the title above indicates the author of the words; the one at the right, that of the composer of the music.

In England, in the sixteenth century, the names of saints were often used as the names of hymn tunes; for example, "St. David" and "St. Edmund." Sometimes the composer's own name is used. "Weber" and "Webb" are examples of this. Frequently the titles were taken from the names of places, as "Bristol," "Birmingham," or "Dundee." An example of naming hymns from place names in more recent times is "Chautauqua"[13] ("Day Is Dying in the West"), which was written for a summer camp at Chautauqua, New York. Another is "Garden City" ("Our Day of Praise Is Done").

At a later date the names for hymns were most frequently chosen from the thought suggested in the words of the hymn. "Abide with Me" is called "Eventide." "All Hail the Power" is called "Coronation." Quite often the words for several different poems will be used for the same hymn tune.

American Hymns and Hymn Writers. During the nineteenth century, many of our familiar hymns were written by American composers. Sometimes the music for the

---

13. "Chautauqua" (shá·tô′kwá). The Chautauqua was an assembly held for educational purposes.

hymn was an original composition; sometimes it was an arrangement of a tune taken from the work of a well-known composer. The hymn "Mercy" was originally the theme of a piano solo, "The Last Hope," by Louis Gottschalk. Arne's "Arlington" was taken from the opera *Artaxerxes*.[14]

Among the more familiar American writers of words for hymns are Julia Ward Howe, James Russell Lowell, and John Greenleaf Whittier. Some of the familiar American hymns are "He Leadeth Me," "Bethany" ("Nearer My God to Thee"), "All Saints" ("The Son of God Goes Forth to War"), "Webb" ("Stand Up, Stand Up for Jesus"), "Coronation" ("All Hail the Power of Jesus' Name"), and "Beecher" ("Love Divine, All Love Excelling").

Many of our hymns have been published first in religious magazines or pamphlets and have gradually made their way into hymnals. Some of them have interesting stories in connection with their origin. For example, the Reverend Edward Hopper was serving as minister of the Church of Sea and Land in New York City. Thousands of sailors worshiped there, and the Reverend Hopper tried to reach them through illustrations of their life at sea. He wanted to picture Jesus Christ for them in their own language; so he wrote "Jesus, Savior, Pilot Me." The song first appeared anonymously in the *Sailor's Magazine*. It became very popular and is still one of our best-known hymns.

Gospel Songs. One of the most interesting forms of church music, and one that definitely characterizes certain sections of our country in the early nineteenth century, is the gospel hymn or gospel song. This music came into existence largely as a result of the Sunday school and revival meeting movements and of the trend in this country toward popular music. One might say that the gospel song

14. *Artaxerxes* (är'tăk·sûrk'sēz). An opera named after a king of Persia.

bears the same relation to church music that the jazz tune does to the classics of the masters. Because of their very careless musical form, and because they appeal purely to the emotions, they have been frequently criticized as trashy and unfit for religious service; nevertheless, they have become very popular among large numbers of people and some of them are now sung all over the world. "The Old Rugged Cross" is said to be the most popular and the most beloved song among English-speaking nations, and "Sweet Bye and Bye" is sung the world over.

The Sunday School and Gospel Songs. The first Sunday school was founded by Robert Raikes in England to teach reading and the church catechism to the poor children of a mill district. The idea spread to the United States, and the first Sunday school here was established in Virginia in 1786. Soon afterwards a Negro woman in New York City organized a Sunday school for children of the tenement districts. Other places rapidly took up the plan. The American Sunday School Union, organized early in the nineteenth century, was largely responsible for the spread of the Sunday school into every part of our country. Missonaries were sent into the West, and Sunday schools were formed all through the section from the Allegheny Mountains to the Rockies. In attempting to popularize these schools, it was quite natural that the leaders should choose songs which had a popular appeal and which would be simple enough to be sung by the children and adults who attended.

A number of gospel hymns were written especially for children in Sunday schools. "When He Cometh to Make Up His Jewels" is one of these hymns. The words were written by the Reverend William O. Cushing for use in his own Sunday school. The music as well as the words

WHEN HE COMETH

W. O. CUSHING   GEORGE F. ROOT

1. When He com-eth, when He com-eth To make up His
jew - els, All His jew - els, pre-cious jew - els, His
loved and His own.

2. He will gath - er, He will gath - er The gems for His
king - dom, All the pure ones, all the bright ones, His
loved and His own.

3. Lit - tle chil - dren, lit - tle chil - dren Who love their Re-
deem - er Are the jew - els, pre-cious jew - els, His
loved and His own.

CHORUS

Like the stars of the morn - ing, His bright crown a - dorn - ing, They shall shine in their beau - ty, Bright gems for His crown.

People came to camp meetings from miles around, listened to the preacher, and sang gospel hymns.

appealed to children, and it became a favorite in church schools everywhere. It was frequently sung at river baptizings, particularly at the baptism of children and young people. "Brighten the Corner" and "I'll Be a Sunbeam for Jesus" are other children's hymns which became universally popular.

Gospel Hymns in the Revival Meeting. Revival meetings were popular during the nineteenth century. The term refers to a special series of religious meetings held for the purpose of bringing more people into the church. These revivals were often spoken of as meetings for "saving sinners." For a period of two or three weeks or even longer, religious services were held every day and usually three times a day, with a morning, an afternoon, and an evening service. The largest meeting was held in the evening and consisted of a song service, prayers, testimonials,[15] a sermon, and an invitation to come into the church. The latter was usually accompanied by singing such favorites as "Rescue the Perishing," "Throw Out the Life Line," "Almost Persuaded," and "Come Sinner, Come."

Camp Meetings. The camp meeting was one form of the revival. These were especially popular in the South, where the warm climate made camping easy, or in the Middle West during the summer months after crops were "laid by." The first one is said to have been held in Logan County, Kentucky, nearly one hundred and fifty years ago. People came to these gatherings from miles around and camped for a week or two. A crude platform and benches were set up for the meetings. They were sometimes held in the open, sometimes on ground covered with a roof of brush or limbs from trees. Later, large tents were used. The sermons, as well as the music, were intended pri-

15. testimonials (tĕs'tĭ·mō'nĭ·ălz). Evidence, signs, or tokens.

BAPTISM IN KANSAS *by John Steuart Curry, from the collection of the Whitney Museum of American Art.*

Crowds gathered to witness country baptizings and sang while the ceremony was being performed.

marily to appeal to the emotions. They were filled with vivid descriptions of deathbed scenes and the horrors of hell. Under the influence of such strenuous religious services, people often showed their feelings in strange ways. Some fainted, others shouted, many had "jerks."

The Country Baptizing. A special feature of some of the revivals and camp meetings was the baptizing which came at the close. Large crowds gathered at a river, pond, or other shallow body of water. If the river was dry, a large tank might be filled with water and used for the baptizing, as the illustration, the "Baptism in Kansas," shows. The service opened by singing camp-meeting songs and gospel hymns. After this the preacher waded into the water until he found a place of suitable depth. Here he would place a long stick or pole to mark the spot. He would then walk to the edge of the river or pond, select a candidate for baptism, and lead him back to the designated spot. The minister grasped the crossed hands of the candidate with one hand, placed the other back of the head, and dipped him quickly into the water, repeating the usual ritual[16] for baptism. At the close of the procedure, other songs were sung. "When We Gather at the River" was a favorite. It is said that when revivals were held during the winter months, holes were cut in the ice to make a place for baptizing candidates for church membership.

White Spirituals. More than a century ago, the fasola[17] singers (See the story of singing schools.) began to include tunes of the camp meeting under the name of spirituals. These later became known as white spirituals to distinguish them from the Negro spirituals.

Moody and Sankey. Nearly every American of a generation ago knew of the evangelists[18] Dwight L. Moody and Ira D. Sankey. Mr. Moody was an outstanding revival preacher of the nineteenth century; associated with him was the remarkable singer, Mr. Sankey, who added greatly to the effectiveness of the meetings. Many of our well-known gospel hymns were composed by Sankey for use in the meetings. The tune for "Ninety and Nine" was improvised by him and sung in public at a few minutes' notice in one of Moody's meetings. A few days before he had clipped the words from a magazine.

---

16. ritual (rĭt′ů·ăl). Form of conducting worship. 17. fasola (fà·sō·là′). A name given to singers who used the fa sol la notation. 18. evangelists (ê·văn′jĕ·lĭsts). Men who preach at special services to awaken religious interest.

CHAPTER X

MUSIC EDUCATION

Singing Schools

Music in Education Today. Music today is considered an essential part of all education in America. The public or private school that does not have some form of music education is completely out of date. This position of music in education has not always been so strong. In the early periods of our country, only a privileged few had any musical training at all. Let us see how it came about that all the children in our country have been given an opportunity to learn something about music.

Development of Singing Schools. Can you imagine an evening scene in the kitchen of an early New England home? A group of men and women have gathered there to learn how to sing church music. The room is lighted by candles brought by the women. Seats have been provided by placing boards on chairs arranged around the room. In the center stands the singing master. He opens a book and reads a series of rules for singing. He then distributes books containing individual parts—the treble, counter, tenor, and bass. Directions for pitch are given. The singing master sounds a note and his pupils sound it. So on they go through the tune, some pupils learning to sing by imitation, others by reading notes. At the close of some two or three hours of instruction, the master agrees to take his pay of one shilling and sixpence in Indian corn. This is a description of a typical early singing school.

These singing schools were merely groups of persons who met more or less regularly, usually in the evening, for instruction in choral singing and the rudiments of music. The leader or singing master was frequently a member of the community who liked music. He probably had a good natural voice and had taught himself the elements of music. The singing masters conducted their singing schools in addition to their regular occupations.

The greater part of our information about the schools or classes comes from advertisements in the newspapers of the time. Two of these follow. The first appeared in a Salem newspaper in the late eighteenth century:

Samuel Wadsworth begs leave to inform the public, but the female sex in particular, that he has opened a singing-school for their use, at his Dwelling House near the Town House, to be kept on Tuesday and Friday evenings, from six to nine o'clock. If any of the sex are desirous of being instructed in this beautiful science, they shall be instructed in the newest method.

The other appeared in a Cincinnati paper early in the nineteenth century:

Those gentlemen and ladies who feel themselves disposed to organize a singing-school will please to convene at the court house tomorrow evening at candle light, as it is proposed to have a singing. Those who have books will please bring them.

Popularity of Singing Schools. The first singing school in the South was organized about 1730 at Charleston, South Carolina, where John Salter taught music in a boarding school which his wife conducted for young ladies. James Lyon was connected with a singing school in Philadelphia

Singing schools were first held in New England, where the singing master conducted his classes in the kitchen of an early colonial home.

about a generation later. Singing schools were established
about this time in Maryland and in Rhode Island. One of
the most important early New England singing schools was
formed by William Billings. A record of the membership
of this class is still preserved. There were forty-eight singers, eighteen of whom were women. They met at Stoughton, Massachusetts. This singing class became the Stoughton Singing Society.

When settlers from the East began to seek homes beyond
the Alleghenies in western New York, Ohio, Kentucky,
and even farther west, they took along the custom of the
singing school. Indeed, it was in these new settlements
in the Middle West and South that the singing school
reached its greatest popularity.

The Singing School as a Social Gathering. In the beginning, the moving force of the singing school was the desire
to improve church music. Later, however, these meetings
began to be valued as a means of recreation during the long
winter evenings. Before long, most groups included secular as well as sacred music in their singing. Frequently
those who attended were criticized because they spent too
much time in singing and staying out at night. One man,
in relating his experiences in an early singing school conducted by his father, said, "My father was . . . . unwaver-
ingly pious, yet he allowed us to fiddle anything from the
'Irish Washerwoman' to the 'Devil's Dream' except on
Sunday."

Another description of the singing school of the days
before the War between the States gives an excellent idea
of the social importance of such meetings.

It was the custom to have a singing-school every winter in different communities, and this naturally formed a gathering point
for the young people from villages and farms covering a consider

able radius. Snow on the ground, a sleigh, and a fine horse made a combination which brought the young people out to any gathering. . . . . The membership was not confined to the youth of the community. . . . . One would find in the class persons of various ages from boys and girls of nine and ten up to grandfathers and grandmothers.

Fasola Singers and Buckwheat Notes. Each singing teacher tried to make his method and material as simple and easy as possible. The most difficult part of the teaching was instructing pupils how to read notes, and so some teachers made use of shaped or buckwheat notes. The series of notes on the scale with which we are familiar— do, re, mi, fa, sol, la, ti, do—was sung fa, sol, la, fa, sol, la, with mi to fill out the seventh note of the octave, beginning again with fa. The shaped notes used by the fasola singers, as they were called, made reading notes very simple. The note fa was made in the shape of a triangle, sol was a round note, la was a square one. When one came to an occasional mi, one found the square set on end thus:

Another type of shaped notes was the seven-shape system which took the four-shape group and added three others. Their scale appeared like this:

The notes were often called buckwheat notes because of their appearance. Those who used the shaped notes were called "buckwheaters," and those who used our regular style of notation were called "roundheads." There was much argument and rivalry between the two groups. *Southern Harmony* and the *Sacred Harp* were two of the popular singing school song books using shaped notes.

Rudiments Taught. In the early singing schools the pupils were taught the clefs, syllables or notes, keys, and note lengths. In the latter, the old English terms were often used. These were semibreve[1] for whole notes, minim[2] for half notes, crotchet[3] for quarter, quaver[4] for eighth, semiquaver for sixteenth, and demisemiquaver for thirty-second notes. The entire group of singers sang a song through by note, part by part, again and again. The words were never sung until the tune was thoroughly learned. Everybody beat time with his right hand while singing. The beating generally was down and up. Three-part time, for example, was beat as follows: one—fingers on the table or book, two—hand flat on the table, three—hand raised.

The singing school usually lasted for about twenty-four sessions of three hours each. At the close of the school, an exhibition was commonly held at the local schoolhouse or church. The group of singers, as a rule, was arranged in a square with the leader in the center. The sopranos were in front of the leader, the tenors to his left, the basses at the right, and the altos at his back. The singers used books, even though the selections had been memorized.

Singing Conventions and Normals. Music conventions grew out of the singing schools. By the middle of the nineteenth century they had become well known in all parts

1. semibreve (sĕm′ĭ·brēv′). Having half the time value of the breve; a whole note. 2. minim (mĭn′ĭm). 3. crotchet (krŏch′ĕt). 4. quaver (kwā′vẽr).

of the country. The meetings were usually held in the spring or fall in some city or town. They lasted from three or four days to two weeks and were eagerly anticipated by all music lovers. Individuals or whole singing classes might attend. Distinguished leaders were usually in charge, and local teachers were given an opportunity to take part. Music of a higher quality than that in the singing school was used. One of the first conventions to be held was conducted in 1834 by Lowell Mason for the purpose of training teachers to teach music. Twelve persons are reported to have attended this convention. Four years later there were one hundred and thirty-four from ten states at Mason's convention. By the middle of the century, one thousand persons were in attendance.

Normals, which were somewhat similar to the singing conventions, were originated by George F. Root. They were organized for a term of a few weeks and usually were held in the summer. They were the means of bringing together earnest musicians who lived in isolated and distant communities.

Music conventions and normals had a short life, but their direct descendant may be found in the music festival of which you will read later.

Music in Public Schools

Teaching of Music before the Revolution. We have little evidence to show that music as an organized study was taught in schools until after the Revolution. By that time, girls' boarding schools had come into existence and some of them offered music. That the value of such a course was not accepted as one of the regular studies is indicated in the following letter written by a school girl:

Hon. Father:

I am again placed at school under the tuition of an amiable lady, so mild, so good, no one can help loving her; she treats all her scholars with such tenderness as would win the affection of the most savage brute. I learn embroidery and geography at present and wish your permission to learn music.

The Movement for Public School Music. The singing conventions which grew out of the singing schools made a great contribution to music education. As these conventions and normals became organized for the training of singing school teachers, the students who attended began to urge more and more that music be taught in the public schools.

At that time, our public school system was not well organized. Schools had little money for their care and support. Children studied only those subjects which were considered useful—reading, writing, spelling, arithmetic, grammar, and sometimes geography and history.

We have already seen that a hundred years ago or earlier there was little musical culture as we know it today. Except in a few cities, where an interest in serious music was just beginning, the musical resources of the average town or community consisted of the church choir, an occasional singing school or singing society, and now and then a private teacher of piano. People had to travel to the cities to hear good concerts. Travel was difficult and concerts few.

The leaders of the music conventions, music teachers, and other educational leaders in many parts of the country began to realize that, if all the people were to have an opportunity to enjoy music, it would be desirable to teach music in the public schools.

Finally, in 1837-1838, the Boston public schools tried the experiment of introducing vocal music into one of their schools. Within fifteen years Buffalo, Pittsburgh, Louisville, Cincinnati, and St. Louis had added music to the curriculums of their schools.

For a period of some forty years, music in the public schools was little more than a transfer of the private singing school into the public schools. The books in many cases were the same. The *Golden Wreath* was one of the popular books. The emphasis was almost entirely on reading notes. The teaching was done by a special music teacher. After the War between the States, grade teachers here and there began to teach music; but it was not until near the close of the nineteenth century that music teaching in the elementary school was placed directly in the hands of the regular grade teacher.

For a period of one hundred years it was a hard struggle to reach the place where practically every child who attended a public school had an opportunity to participate in all sorts of musical activities, vocal and instrumental, to learn the theory of music, and to hear and appreciate the best music of all times and all countries.

Lowell Mason. One man had so much to do with introducing music into the public schools that you will be interested in knowing something about him. The man was Lowell Mason. You have already read about his influence on religious music and on the training of teachers of music.

As a young man, Mason was a clerk in a banking house in Savannah, Georgia. He became interested in music at first only as a leisure-time activity. He studied music when he had time and soon began to write original compositions. He arranged a collection of sacred music, including some of his own compositions, which received favorable recognition from critics and secured for him an invitation to come to Boston and enter a musical career. He went to Boston about ten years before vocal music was introduced into the Boston schools, and the next year became president and conductor of the Handel and Haydn Society. This position he held for five years.

He conducted music classes and singing schools. In 1832 the Boston Academy of Music was established. This institution became the center for Mason's teaching. The first year he is reported to have taught fifteen hundred pupils, including both children and adults. Children were taught free of charge if they would promise to attend for the entire year. In addition to his teaching, Mason organized children's choirs. He traveled over New England and part of New York State, holding music conventions and teaching the theory of music to hundreds of teachers and singers.

He later moved to New York, where he was granted the honorary degree of Doctor of Music by New York University. This was the first degree of its kind ever granted in America.

Mason's Interest in Children's Music. It was Lowell Mason's interest in children's music which led to the introduction of music into the public schools of America. He was among the first to declare that every child has the right to receive elementary instruction in music at public expense. He became greatly interested in group singing by children, and on several occasions presented children's groups at public performances. At the first of these, a large group of children sang in Park Street Church, Boston, an "anthem composed and directed by Lowell Mason, 'Suffer Little Children to Come unto Me.'" A year later he is said to have led a chorus of children in the first performance of "America," the verses of which had been written early in that year by the Reverend Samuel Francis Smith.

Mason's book of songs for children, *The Juvenile Lyre,* was the first book of secular school songs for children to be published in America. A reproduction of it was published recently in commemoration of the one hundredth anniversary of the introduction of music into the schools of Boston.

Boston Tries an Experiment. The people of Boston were so enthusiastic about the public performances by Lowell Mason's pupils that the time seemed ripe to urge the matter of teaching music in the public schools. A special committee was appointed to prepare a report to the primary school board of Boston, urging the adoption of music and suggesting that "one school from each district be selected for the introduction of systematic instruction in vocal music." It was some time before the school board saw fit to take action on the suggestion.

It is interesting to note the objections to teaching music in the public schools. They were: (1) Singing is impractical; it depends upon a natural ear for music without which instruction will be useless. (2) Time spent would be inadequate to the end proposed; the labor of a life is needed to form the musician. (3) If one accomplishment is introduced into the schools, why not another; if instruction is given in vocal music why should it not be given in dancing? (4) Music would impair discipline.

The answer to these objections is equally interesting. Those who urged the teaching of music in public schools insisted that music must be examined by the following standards:

1. *Intellectually.* . . . . Memory, comparison, attention, intellectual faculties—all of them are quickened by a study of its [music's] principles. It may be made to some extent a mental discipline.

2. *Morally*. . . . . Happiness, contentment, cheerfulness, tranquility—these are the natural effects of music.

3. *Physically*. It appears self evident that exercise in vocal music, when not carried to an unreasonable excess, must expand the chest and thereby strengthen the lungs and vital organs.

They also maintained that oral reading would be helped by learning to sing, that vocal music would serve as a recreation, that it would "restore the jaded[5] energies, and send back the scholars with invigorated powers to other more laborious duties." Furthermore, since the school committee had provided that in all the public schools the day should open with "becoming exercises of devotion," it was thought that vocal music would add greatly to such exercises.

The school board finally agreed to try the experiment of introducing vocal music into the public schools of the city. The experiment was to be carried on by the Boston Academy of Music under the direction of the school board. Lowell Mason was selected to have charge of the teaching.

At first the experiment was tried in one school from each district. The board, however, did not appropriate any money for the experiment, and Mason taught without pay for an entire year and bought materials for pupils with his own money. During the year, exhibitions of the work in music were given from time to time. The final exhibition was a public performance. The program began with the song, "Flowers, Wildwood Flowers." This song has been called the Magna Carta of music education because the singing of this song convinced the people of Boston that vocal music in public schools was desirable.

Two weeks after this exhibition, the school board voted that a committee on music be instructed to employ

5. jaded. Dulled, worn out.

WILDWOOD FLOWERS

L. M.   LOWELL MASON

1. Flow - ers, wild-wood flow - ers in a shel - tered dell they grew,
2. Flow - ers, love - ly flow - ers in a gar - den we may see,

grew; I hur-ried a-long and I chanced to spy This small star flow'r with its
see; The rose is there with her ru - by lip, And pinks the hon-ey bee

sil - v'ry eye. Then this blue dai - sy peeped up its head;
loves to sip. Tu - lips gay as but - ter-fly's wing;

Sweet - ly this pur - ple or - chid spread, I gath-ered them all for
Mar - i - golds rich as the crown of a king, But none so fair to

you, I gath-ered them all for you, All these wild - wood flow - ers,
me, but none so fair to me As these wild - wood flow - ers,

Sweet wild-wood flow'rs; All these wild-wood flow-ers, sweet wild-wood flow'rs.
Sweet wild-wood flow'rs; As these wild-wood flow-ers, sweet wild-wood flow'rs.

teacher of vocal music in the several public schools of the city of Boston. Lowell Mason was placed in full charge of the music in the Boston schools and was given four assistants.

Early Public School Music in Other Cities. Music was introduced into the schools of Washington, D. C., about the middle of the nineteenth century. After the War between the States, when the returning armies of the Union marched past the capitol to be reviewed by President Lincoln, General Grant, and others, a chorus of twenty-five hundred school children sang "The Star-Spangled Banner," "The Battle Cry of Freedom," and other patriotic songs.

One of the pioneer music teachers in St. Louis was William A. Hodgdon. He studied with Lowell Mason and came from New Hampshire to St. Louis in 1854. His teaching there covered a period of more than fifty years. At that time there were no music books, instruments, or other materials for teaching music. Mr. Hodgdon would write the words of a song on the blackboard and sing them over, stanza by stanza, until the children had memorized both the words and the melody. Public school music teachers were poorly paid, some as low as $16 per month.

A copy of a letter from an early music teacher in the West gives an excellent picture of the activities of one of these teachers. The teacher was W. S. B. Matthews, who was for many years a leading teacher of music in the United States.

Perhaps some of your readers may like to know something of a music teacher's life "out west." For the edification[6] of such I subjoin[7] a memorandum of a week's work of a music teacher in regular standing.

6. edification (ĕd'ĭ·fĭ·kā'shŭn). Instruction.   7. subjoin. To add to something

Monday—Take the cars at ten o'clock and go to B., 13 miles, 10 by railroad and 3 by stage. In P.M. give private lessons from 2 to 4 on melodeon.[8] Eve., singing class numbering 75. They will sing the cantata *Daniel* at the close of the course as a concert.

Tuesday—9 to 10 A.M. singing lesson to public school. P.M. 2 private lessons. Eve., singing class at C., (3 miles from B.) numbering 50. The weekly singing-school is an event to most of them and the enthusiasm is proportionately great.

Wednesday—One private lesson. Eve., singing class, numbering 70, at D., (5 miles from C.). The enthusiasm is good, and they will sing *Esther,* by Bradbury, at close of the course.

Thursday—Take the cars at 3 A.M. and go to E., 17 miles from D., (we came back to D. after singing-school last eve.) and give private lessons on pianoforte all day, say ten lessons. Return to A. on the cars. This evening, for a wonder, we have to ourselves, and luxuriate in going to bed at 8 P.M.

Friday—Give 4 private lessons on piano. At 1 P.M. lesson to public school one hour. Eve., choir meeting; this is a Catholic choir, and sing Mozart's Masses and such like. This evening is a pleasure.

Saturday—Take the cars at 7 A.M., go to B., 7 miles, and walk to F., 3 miles further on. Give 6 piano lessons, return to A., and sing at the choir rehearsal (Baptist) from 7.30 to 8.30. At 8.30 go to Catholic choir, and return home at 11 P.M. thoroughly tired both in mind and body. You retire to rest with the comfortable consciousness of being able to sleep until 8 o'clock the next A.M.

Sunday—At 10.30 A.M. go to Baptist church and play and conduct for first 2 hymns, which being got along with, must be at Catholic mass at 11 A.M. This lasts until 1 o'clock, and then hurrah for freedom until 4 o'clock when Vespers require our attention. This is soon over, and we are free again until 5.30 P.M., when evening service at Baptist must be attended. Finally at 9 o'clock P.M., your week's work may be summed up at 28 private lessons, 3 singing classes, 2 public school lessons, 3 choir meetings, and 4 services on Sunday.

8. melodeon (mĕ·lō′dė·ŭn). A small reed organ.

CHAPTER XI

MUSIC ORGANIZATIONS AND THEIR STRUGGLE TO BRING MUSIC TO A NEW NATION

Singing Societies and Oratorios

The Beginning of Serious Music. Peoples everywhere express themselves by means of some kind of music. The manner of expression and the kind of music depend upon the life and surroundings of the people. We have seen how national airs are an outgrowth of a military struggle, and how gospel hymns originate as an accompaniment of a revival movement in religion. A still different type of music became a part of American life because groups of people began to make a serious study of music and to establish in this country some of the newer ideas in music found in Europe at that time. The first serious efforts were in the field of vocal and choral music. Later, attention was turned to instrumental, particularly orchestral, music.

Origin of Singing Societies. In New England, the desire for better singing in the churches led to singing schools and to singing by choirs. A singing school often led to the organization of a singing society. An example of this is the Stoughton Musical Society of Stoughton, Massachusetts, which was an outgrowth of the singing class William Billings had conducted in that town. This is said to be the oldest singing society now in existence in America.

The Handel and Haydn Society. Another famous singing society was the Handel and Haydn Society, probably
America's most famous choral society. The choir of Park
Street Church in Boston is said to have furnished several
early members of this organization. The church was
so conservative that at first it objected seriously to the
use of the organ in its church service. Its choir, however,
was the best in Boston. Among its members were General
H. K. Oliver, composer of the hymn "Federal Street," and
Mr. Jonas Chickering, founder of the piano house of
Chickering and Sons. These and many other members of
the choir were among the early members of the Handel
and Haydn Society.

The formation of the society came about in the following way. Boston held a great musical jubilee in honor of
the signing of the Peace of Ghent which concluded the
War of 1812. The people were so delighted with the program that within a few weeks a meeting was called of those
who were interested in forming a society for the purpose
of "cultivating and improving a correct taste in the performance of sacred music, and also to introduce into more
general practice the works of Handel and Haydn and other
eminent composers." The result of the meeting was the
formation of the Handel and Haydn Society.

The first concert was given on Christmas Day, 1815.
The concert began at six o'clock in the evening and must
have lasted until about ten o'clock or even later. All of
Boston was interested in the event, and nearly a thousand
people attended. The tickets were a dollar each, but an
advertisement in a Boston paper added:

N.B. Gentlemen who wish to take their families are informed
that on purchasing *four* tickets they will be presented with a fifth
gratis; and those purchasing *six* . . . with two additional ones.

There were one hundred voices, only ten of which were women's. An orchestra of twelve pieces and an organ furnished the accompaniments. The program was a very ambitious one. It began with seventeen numbers from Haydn's *Creation,* then came a number of Handel's selections, and, as a finale, the "Halleluja Chorus" was sung.

Several important musicians, among them Lowell Mason, have served as president of the Handel and Haydn Society. For more than thirty years the president of the society also served as its conductor. In the beginning, nearly all of the singers were native Americans, but European soloists were soon employed and more and more elaborate concerts were given.

An incident occurred a few years afterwards which showed the ambitious character of the organization. Members wrote to Beethoven, offering him a commission to write an oratorio especially for the society's use. Apparently Beethoven accepted the invitation, but never wrote the oratorio.

The society sponsored the publication of several oratorios and collections of music. The first one was the famous Bridgewater Collection. Later came the Handel and Haydn Collection, edited by Lowell Mason. This consisted of three volumes of miscellaneous anthems and several other works. The profits derived from the sale of these publications were used to pay the expenses of the organization. The society is still in existence, and the custom of giving an annual performance of the *Messiah* at Christmas has continued to the present time.

Growth of Interest in Sacred Music. The interest in sacred concerts and in oratorio music found its way west of the Alleghenies in a short time. The Haydn Society was organized in Cincinnati in 1819.

When Chicago was only about twenty-five years old, a society called the Musical Union was formed. This organization continued for about eight years and was followed by the Oratorio Society. It was a victim of the fire in 1871, when the library of the society was destroyed and the members were scattered. The Handel and Haydn Society of Boston came to the rescue by sending donations of books, including sets of oratories. The organization finally ceased to exist, and in its place came the Apollo Club which was organized the year after the fire. This became one of America's most famous musical organizations. Public oratorio performances have been given regularly since its beginning.

An Oratorio Society was organized in St. Louis, Missouri, nearly a century ago. Fourteen years later the Philharmonic[1] Society, with a chorus of about one hundred voices, was formed. The War between the States caused the discontinuance of the Philharmonic, but later the St. Louis Choral Society was organized. The state of Kansas has been strong in choral organizations for many years. The town of Lindsborg, Kansas, a small settlement of music-loving Swedish Americans, gave Handel's *Messiah* at an early date. The earliest oratorio society on the Pacific coast of which there is any mention was organized in San Francisco.

The Opera

Early Development in America. While the cities of New England were interested in the works of Handel and Haydn and were concerned with the development of choral

---

1. Philharmonic (fĭl'här·mŏn'ĭk). Loving harmony or music; often used in names of music societies and organizations.

The Apollo Club, organized in 1872, gave several public concerts each year.

societies and the singing of oratorios, cities in other sections, especially New York and New Orleans, were turning their attention toward opera. This movement came about largely as the result of an interest in the theater where plays and concerts were presented. In many of the concerts, selections from operas then popular in the countries of Europe were given. It is natural that the operas popular in England were the first to be received in this country. These were the ballad operas already mentioned.

The American Theater at the Time of the Revolution. During the Revolution there was little serious interest in musical affairs. The British army and navy officers and their Tory friends were subscribers to several regular concert series, and concerts were given on the king's birthday. They did not consider the rebellion of the colonists a serious matter, and took much pleasure in all lighter forms of entertainment. Groups composed principally of military persons gave plays and concerts. Howe's Thespians[2] were among these groups of entertainers. Major Andre, later hanged as a spy, was a moving spirit among the military players in New York and is said to have officiated as manager, actor, and scene painter.

Scudder, in *Men and Manners in America One Hundred Years Ago,* tells an amusing incident which occurred in the Faneuil Hall Theater in Boston.

The most elaborate effort at entertainment was in the theatrical representations given under the patronage of Gen. Howe. A number of officers and ladies formed a Society for Promoting Theatrical Amusements . . . . for their own amusement, and the benevolent purpose of contributing to the relief of distressed soldiers, their widows and children. . . . .

2. Thespians (thĕs′pĭ·ănz). Relating to the drama; named after Thespis, the reputed founder of Greek drama.

The most notable piece . . . . was the local farce of the "Block-ade of Boston," by Gen. Burgoyne, whose reputation as a wit and dramatist has kept quite even pace with his military fame. . . . . The comedy of the "Busybody" had been acted, and the curtain was about to be drawn for the farce, when the actors behind the scenes heard an exaggerated report of a raid made upon Charles-town [Mass.] by a small party of Americans. One of the actors, dressed for his part, that of a Yankee sergeant, came forward upon the stage, called silence, and informed the audience that the alarm guns had been fired, and a battle was going on in Charlestown. The audience, taking this for the first scene in the new farce, applauded obstreperously[3] . . . . when the order was suddenly given in dead earnest for the officers to return to their posts. The audience at this was thrown into dire confusion, the officers jump-ing over the orchestra, breaking the fiddles on the way, the actors rushing about to get rid of their paint and disguises, the ladies alternately fainting and screaming. . . . . Whether it [the farce] was ever given or not does not appear.

In Philadelphia and Boston there were antitheater laws. As a result, moral lectures and religious music were given to hide the plays. For example, Shakespeare's *Hamlet* was introduced between the parts of a concert. It was adver-tised as a "moral and instructive tale called 'Filial Piety, Exemplified in the History of the Prince of Denmark.'"

The Opera in New York. The interest in concerts, in plays, and in ballad operas turned toward Italian opera with the coming of the García family.

Manuel García brought to America the first opera troupe from across the Atlantic. The company opened its season in New York in 1825 with Rossini's[4] *The Barber of Seville*. It took the people of New York by storm. They loved opera. The orchestra which accompanied the opera was a

3. obstreperously (ŏb·strĕp′ẽr·ŭs·lĭ). Noisily. 4. Rossini's (rō·sē′nĕz). Rossini was an Italian composer (1792-1868).

The Barber of Seville was the first opera given in New York City.

most amazing thing at that time, for it consisted of seven violins, two violas, three violoncellos, two contrabasses,[5] two flutes, two clarinets,[6] one bassoon,[7] two horns, two trumpets, one pair of kettle drums, and a piano.

New York's interest in opera increased. A fine building, intended exclusively for opera, was opened. This was the first building of its kind in America.

The Opera in New Orleans. New Orleans was the original home of French opera in this country. The majority of families there were French, and music had a strong place in the everyday life of the people. A company of French comedians settled in New Orleans at the end of the eighteenth century and for twenty years gave regular entertainments, including opera.

Not long after that, the idea of establishing a special home for opera in the city was conceived, and the Théâtre d'Orléans was built. The theater was well built and was equipped with all the scenic and mechanical devices then in use in the best European theaters. Opera was performed three nights a week, and on alternate nights plays in the French language were given. This theater building burned four years later. It was replaced by a much more elaborate one. It is said this second building cost $180,000.

The Théâtre d'Orléans gave New Orleans a special distinction in opera circles here. Artists of real merit came from Paris every season. An excellent group of operas was given and, twenty-five years later, New Orleans sent a fully equipped French opera company to New York.

Opera in Other Cities. New York and New Orleans were the two cities most active in producing opera. Other

5. contrabasses (kŏn′trȧ·bās′·ĕz). Instruments sounding an octave lower than normal bass. 6. clarinets (klăr′ĭ·nĕts′). Wind instruments. 7. bassoon (bȧ-sōōn′). A wind instrument of the double-reed kind. It forms the natural bass to the oboe, clarinet, and others.

cities were interested in listening to opera but not in producing it. Philadelphia had its first regular opera a few years after New York heard the García troupe in the *Barber of Seville*. The performances were given in French and pleased Philadelphia so much that the French Opera Company continued to visit the city every season for many years. Soon Italian opera was produced in Philadelphia. Later, when the Academy of Music was opened in the city, it became known as the "temple of Italian opera" in America.

At the beginning of the eighteen hundreds, Charleston, South Carolina, and Baltimore, Maryland, became interested in opera. Traveling opera troupes frequently made a circuit of New York, Baltimore, and Charleston. By the middle of the century, Boston had decided that music was not to be limited to Handel, Haydn, Bach, and Beethoven, and permitted opera to be given there.

Lucia de Lammermoor was the first opera produced in Chicago in 1853. San Francisco first heard opera in that same year; Cincinnati a few years later.

American Composers of Opera. In the early days of our country there was little effort at composition of opera or other serious music by Americans. The name of William Henry Fry (1813-1864) is important as the composer of the first publicly performed grand opera by a native American. This opera was *Leonora*. His compositions were not very successful and have not lived. His more important contribution to serious music was his leadership in an effort to obtain recognition of American composers. Through newspapers and lectures he and a few of his contemporaries criticized the fact that only the works of foreign composers were played at concerts. What he said in one of his lectures is particularly interesting, as it indicates the efforts of this small group in the interest of musical composition in America. He was reported as saying:

Hitherto there has been too much servility[8] on the part of American artists. The American composer should not allow the name of Beethoven or Handel or Mozart to prove an eternal bugbear to him, nor should he pay them reverence. He should only reverence his Art, and strike out manfully and independently into untrodden realms, just as his nature and inspiration may incite him, else he can never achieve lasting renown.

Until this Declaration of Independence in Art shall be made—until American composers shall discard their foreign liveries and found an American school—and until the American public shall learn to support American artists, Art will not become indigenous[9] to this country, but will only exist as a feeble exotic,[10] and we shall continue to be provincial in Art.

We have some good musical societies and they should devote a portion of their rehearsals to American compositions.

Orchestras

Influence of Foreign Musicians. Foreign musicians were important in America before the Revolution and afterwards as well. After the war, many of them from various European countries came here to find a home in the newly established United States. Large numbers of them came to this country in the middle of last century, after a series of revolutions had taken place in Central Europe.

Orchestral Music in Boston. The man who has been called the father of American orchestra came to Boston at the close of the eighteenth century. He was Gottlieb Graupner, who had been an oboist in a regiment at Hanover in North Germany. When he came to Boston there

8. servility (sûr·vĭl′ĭ·tĭ). Attitude of a servant. 9. indigenous (ĭn·dĭj′ė·nŭs). Produced, growing, or living naturally in a country or climate. 10. exotic (ĕks·ŏt′ĭk). From a foreign country.

were only about a half dozen professional musicians there.
Graupner soon gathered these and a few amateurs about
him and a few years later formed an orchestra which was
called the Philharmonic.

This orchestra often played for performances of the
Handel and Haydn Society. While the Philharmonic
lasted only twenty-five years, the interest in group instrumental music did not die and it reached an unusual standard of excellence through the organization of the Boston
Symphony Orchestra in 1881.

The most important group of musicians who came from
Europe consisted of twenty-five German instrumental musicians who called themselves the Germania Society. The
group soon grew to fifty members. Their playing was better than Americans had ever heard before. They also
brought musical selections which Americans had never
heard. They gave the first performance of Wagner's[11]
Overture to *Tannhäuser* ever heard in this country. The
orchestra traveled throughout the country, but Boston
was the only city which gave adequate support to their
concerts. They had a hard time making expenses, and the
group held together for only six years. They are said to
have resorted to all sorts of devices to get people to listen
to them. For example, a toy locomotive was run across the
stage during the performance of a piece called the "Railway Gallop," fireworks accompanied the playing of another, and one of their selections represented a fight
between two fire companies.

The New York Philharmonic Orchestra. The New York
Philharmonic Orchestra was organized in 1842 and still
exists. At its very first concert, Beethoven's *Fifth Symphony,* Weber's Overture to *Oberon,* and a Mozart aria

11. Wagner's (väg'nĕrz). Wagner was a German composer (1813-1883).

were given. Members of the orchestra elected their own conductor, gave their concerts at their own risk, and the salaries of the musicians consisted of a division of whatever profits were realized from the performance. Undoubtedly this organization has influenced New York's orchestral music more than any other.

The New York Philharmonic Orchestra recently celebrated its hundredth anniversary. Some five hundred persons heard the Philharmonic orchestra's first three concerts in 1842; ten million listeners now enjoy the weekly Sunday afternoon concerts broadcast by the Columbia Broadcasting System. Sixty-three musicians constituted the orchestral personnel at the first concert given on December 7, 1842, and the total receipts for the season were $1854.50; today there are one hundred ten players, and the Philharmonic Orchestra operates on an annual budget of about $750,000.

STUDY EXERCISES

Questions and Problems

1. How did early American composers get the tunes they used?
2. What was the occasion for the writing of "America"?
3. In what ways was music used to honor Washington?
4. Who wrote "My Days Have Been So Wondrous Free"? Why was this song important, and what can you tell about the composer?
5. What was Jefferson's plan for bringing good music to America?
6. Give some characteristics of music during Lincoln's time.
7. In your opinion, do we have true folk music in America? Why?
8. What was unusual about the Negro's manner of singing?
9. What is the difference between a Negro spiritual and a "shout"?
10. Describe the musical instruments used by people who lived in the mountains of Virginia, the Carolinas, Kentucky, and Tennessee.
11. What occasions did the pioneers have for singing? What kinds of songs did they sing?
12. In what way did music help men who were working in the forests, on the rivers, or on the railroads?
13. What did the cowboys tell about in their songs?
14. What do you think there was about Stephen Collins Foster's songs that have made them so popular?
15. What contributions did William Billings make to music in America?
16. How did gospel hymns have their origin?
17. How do hymn tunes get their names?
18. What influence did the singing conventions and normals have?
19. What contribution to public school music did Lowell Mason make?

Suggested Activities

1. Make a picture map locating important places about which or at which patriotic songs have been written. Include in the map the names of typical folk songs of various sections of of the country.

2. Identify folk songs heard over the radio. Bring a list of those you hear to class.

3. Find and read articles or stories about William Billings in various books and magazines.

4. Try composing the words and music for a hymn.

5. Look in a church hymnal and make a list of hymns whose tunes were written by Beethoven, Haydn, Mendelssohn, Handel, and Weber.

6. Read the stories connected with some of our well-known hymns.

7. With the help of your teacher or librarian, select stories describing the ways in which our national songs were written and read some of these stories.

8. Find what material you can on American folk songs and read it; then make a report to the class on what you have read.

9. Select some dramatic incident in your own community and write a ballad about it.

10. *Class exercise:* Learn to sing "My Days Have Been So Wondrous Free" and other songs given in Part Two of this book.

11. *Class exercise:* Working with other members in your class, make a collection of all the folk songs you can find.

12. *Class exercise:* With the help of your teacher, plan and give a performance of a minstrel show like the early ones, using the songs which were popular at that time.

13. *Class exercise:* Arrange a Stephen Collins Foster collection, including pictures, stories, newspaper clippings, and songs.

14. *Class exercise:* With the help of your teacher, dramatize an early singing school.

15. *Class exercise:* Prepare a pageant, playlet, or pantomime based on the patriotic music of our nation, having each scene represent the event which gave rise to a song.

PART THREE

MUSIC IN THE PERIOD OF EXPANSION

The frontier of the United States again moved westward, this time across the plains and the Rocky Mountains to the Pacific Ocean. Vast areas of free land were opened to settlers, and population increased. Immigrants from Europe came by every boat to settle this new and rich country. Inventions changed the work of man to the work of machines, and immense fortunes were made. There was more time for leisure, and there was greater opportunity for travel and communication. State public school systems were established, and colleges and universities were opened to the youth of the nation. It was a time of expansion in territory, in population, in industry, and in education.

It was also a period of expansion in music. From people along the Mexican border on the southwest, from American Indians, from miners, from railroad workers, and from cowboys came songs typical of this great new land where the westward expansion of our country took place. The immigrants who came from Europe to take up free land in the West brought along the music of their countries. Many musicians from European countries sensed the opportunities in this new country and decided to try their fortunes here. Factories and machines were turned to making musical instruments as well as industrial equipment. Money was spent freely for all kinds of entertainment. Opera and theatrical companies soon followed the building of railroads and the discovery of gold and silver. People used some of their leisure time to take music lessons on piano, organ, or band instruments.

In Part Three we shall find out how music was affected by this period of expansion. We shall consider in what ways this could be called a period of expansion in music as well as in other aspects of life. We shall learn what new music activities there were. And, finally, we shall see what music did to the life of the people.

CHAPTER XII

MUSIC ON THE ADVANCING FRONTIER

The Westward Movement

The Advancing Frontier. The story of the United States from 1790 to 1890 is largely a story of advancing frontiers. A frontier may be defined as a line or boundary beyond which there are not more than two persons per square mile. When the first census was taken in the United States in 1790, there were nearly four million persons in this country. For the most part, they were distributed along the Atlantic coast. At that time, only a very small percentage of the population lived west of the Appalachian Mountains. It had taken nearly two hundred years for the English-speaking people here to make settlements along the eastern sea coast to a depth of approximately two hundred and fifty miles (about half a day's travel by automobile now). In a little more than a hundred years from that time, the entire country was settled and the constantly-moving frontier had reached the Pacific coast.

A movie news reel, which attempted to show the "march of time" from 1790 to 1890, would include scenes to illustrate the following events:

The Louisiana Purchase had been made. As the frontier line had moved westward, it became necessary to establish new settlements which were not along a natural water route. As a result, new means of transportation and communication, such as the turnpike, the canal, and later the railroads, had come into use. The territory around the Gulf of Mexico had been settled, and the Gulf states admitted into the Union. The Indians from several of the southern states, and also those in Illinois, Michigan, and Wisconsin, had been moved to the Indian Territory. Large areas of land had been obtained from Mexico. Gold had been discovered in California. Later, the riches of the Rockies, in terms of gold, silver, and other minerals, had become known. The War between the States had been fought. The first transcontinental railroad had been built. The buffalo of the Great Plains had been replaced by cattle, sheep, and horses. The Homestead Act had been passed by Congress, and people by the thousands had made permanent homes throughout the West.

These and many other events furnished the incidents in the story of the United States in its movement across the continent. They have furnished, too, an inspiration for the writing of songs of praise about the beauty and wealth of our homeland. One of these songs is the familiar "America, the Beautiful." The spirit of the great westward movement has been captured in a painting called "Westward Ho," which you will find reproduced on page 173.

Music and the Westward Movement. The story of the music of this period is as varied as the account of the territorial advancement. Since it would be impossible in these pages to tell the whole story, only a few of the more interesting incidents which represent different types of music and different occasions for development will be given.

Music in the Northwest. It is of interest to us today that the first opera to be written by a woman in America was

AMERICA, THE BEAUTIFUL

KATHERINE LEE BATES   SAMUEL A. WARD

1. O beau-ti-ful for spa-cious skies, For am-ber waves of grain, For
2. O beau-ti-ful for pil-grim feet Whose stern im-passion'd stress A
3. O beau-ti-ful for he-roes prov'd In lib-er-at-ing strife, Who
4. O beau-ti-ful for pa-triot dream That sees be-yond the years, Thine

1. pur-ple moun-tain maj-es-ties A-bove the fruit-ed plain. A-
2. thor-ough-fare of free-dom beat A-cross the wil-der-ness. A-
3. more than self their coun-try loved, And mer-cy more than life. A-
4. al-a-bas-ter cit-ies gleam Un-dimmed by hu-man tears. A-

1. mer-i-ca! A-mer-i-ca! God shed His grace on thee, And
2. mer-i-ca! A-mer-i-ca! God mend thine ev-'ry flaw, Con-
3. mer-i-ca! A-mer-i-ca! May God thy gold re-fine Till
4. mer-i-ca! A-mer-i-ca! God shed His grace on thee, And

1. crown thy good with bro-ther-hood From sea to shin-ing sea.
2. firm thy soul in self-con-trol, Thy lib-er-ty in law.
3. all suc-cess be no-ble-ness, And ev-'ry gain di-vine.
4. crown thy good with bro-ther-hood From sea to shin-ing sea.

From THE GRAY BOOK OF FAVORITE SONGS, *copyrighted by Hall & McCreary Company. Used by permission.*

WESTWARD HO by *Emanuel Leutze, courtesy of Handy Studios, Washington, D. C.*

Thousands of people moved across the plains and mountains to build new homes in the West.

based on the story of the Pacific Northwest. The opera is *Narcissa,* written by Mary Carr Moore. The leading characters are Marcus Whitman, an early missionary to Oregon, and his wife, Narcissa. Both of them were murdered by the Indians at their mission near Walla Walla.

The fur traders were the first to establish posts in the territory of Old Oregon (now the states of Washington, Oregon, and Idaho). Missionaries from various churches— Methodist, Presbyterian, Catholic—followed soon after. The year 1834 marked the first permanent settlement in Oregon. About ten years later, the Oregon Trail became familiar to many people, for thousands had taken the road to Oregon.

Contributions of the Mormons. A few years after the first permanent settlements were made in Oregon, a party of Mormons, or Latter Day Saints, arrived in the valley of the Great Salt Lake. This group of people had found themselves unwelcome in Missouri and Illinois and had decided to find a home outside of the territory of the United States. Their journey from northern Illinois to Utah was a long and tedious one. They encountered many hardships and were often discouraged. Elder William Clayton wrote a hymn to encourage them and to renew their faith. It is called "Come, Come, Ye Saints."

COME, COME, YE SAINTS

Come, Come, ye Saints, no toil nor labor fear,
　　But with joy wend your way;
Tho' hard to you this journey may appear,
　　Grace shall be as your day.
'Tis better far for us to strive
Our useless cares from us to drive;
Do this, and joy your hearts will swell—
All is well! all is well!

Why should we mourn, or think our lot is hard?
   'Tis not so; all is right;
Why should we think to earn a great reward,
   If we now shun the fight?
Gird up your loins, fresh courage take,
Our God will never us forsake;
And soon we'll have this tale to tell—
All is well! all is well!

We'll find the place which God for us prepared,
   Far away, in the West;
Where none shall come to hurt or make afraid;
   There the Saints will be blessed.
We'll make the air with music ring—
Shout praises to our God and King;
Above the rest each tongue will tell—
All is well! all is well!

And should we die before our journey's through,
   Happy day! all is well!
We then are free from toil and sorrow too;
   With the just we shall dwell!
But if our lives are spared again
To see the Saints, their rest obtain,
O how we'll make this chorus swell—
All is well! all is well!

The Mormons have contributed not only to the political and religious history of the United States but to its musical history as well. Shortly after the Mormons established a settlement at what is now Salt Lake City, they laid out a ten-acre tract which became known as Temple Square. This contains the famous tabernacle, temple, and assembly hall. The tabernacle seats ten thousand people and has in it a world-famous organ. Every day at noon (12:10 to

12:45), a free organ concert has been given. Here in the quiet of the tabernacle, one can listen to selections from the great masters played by skillful musicians.

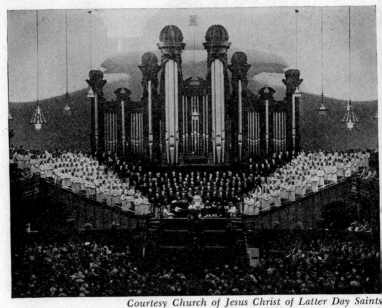

Courtesy Church of Jesus Christ of Latter Day Saints

The pipe organ and the choir in the Mormon tabernacle
are among the finest in the country.

The tabernacle choir is an unpaid organization of about three hundred voices. It furnishes music for religious services. No doubt many of you have listened to the Sunday morning radio broadcast by the tabernacle choir.

Music at the Time of the Gold Rush. Gold was discovered in California in 1848. The gold rush following the discovery was one of America's great adventures. Immediately people of all nationalities and from all stations in life began pouring into California to seek gold. Some went by boat around Cape Horn, some by wagon train, on horseback, or on foot across the plains, desert, and mountains. These were the days when gambling halls and saloons were open day and night. Miners are said to have tossed twenty-dollar gold pieces to children playing on the board sidewalks. Guns were carried and used with great recklessness. Extravagant statements, such as "lumps of gold set like raisins in a pudding" or "lumps of gold as big as rocks," were common.

The enthusiasm, recklessness, and freedom of the occasion naturally led to the singing of unusual songs. Tunes of folk songs, popular stage or vaudeville[1] hits, even religious songs were given new words to fit the occasion. The two melodies which seemed to be the favorites for parodies were Stephen C. Foster's "Camptown Races" and "Oh, Susannah." You will be interested in reading or singing the words to one or two of these parodies.

PARODY ON "OH, SUSANNAH"

I

I came from Salem City
    With my wash bowl on my knee;
I'm going to California
    The gold dust for to see.
I jumped aboard the Liza ship,
    And traveled on the sea
And every time I thought of home
    I wished it wasn't me!
Chorus:
Oh! California!
    That's the land for me.
I'm going to Sacramento
    With my wash bowl on my knee.

1. vaudeville (vōd'vĭl). Theatrical entertainment consisting of a variety of acts.

II

The vessel reared like any horse
    That had of oats a wealth,
It found it couldn't throw me,
    So I thought I'd throw myself.
I thought of all the pleasant times
    We've had together here;
I thought I ought to cry a bit,
    But couldn't find a tear.
Chorus:

III

I soon shall be in Francisco,
    And then I'll look around,
And when I see the gold lumps there,
    I'll pick them off the ground.
I'll scrape the mountains clean, my boys,
    I'll drain the rivers dry.
A pocket full of rocks bring home,
    So brothers don't you cry!
Chorus:

PARODY ON "YANKEE DOODLE"

I

Now's the time to change your clime,
    Give up work and tasking;
Yankee Doodle, all agog,
    With the golden mania[2]
California's precious earth
    Turns the whole world frantic;
Sell your traps and take a berth
    Across the wild Atlantic.

2. mania (mā′nĭ·à). Unreasonable excitement or desire; madness.

II

Gold is got in pan and pot,
  Soup tureen[3] and ladle,
Basket, birdcage, and what not,
  Even to the cradle—
Choose your able-bodied men,
  All whose arms are brawny,
Give them picks and spades and then
  Off for Californy.

Another popular song was "What Was Your Name in the States?" The first stanza ran like this:

Oh what was your name in the States?
Was it Thompson or Johnson or Bates?
  Did you murder your wife
  And fly for your life?
Say, what was your name in the States?

The familiar "Clementine" was still another favorite. Other titles which indicate the type of songs sung were "Sacramento," "The Fools of Forty-nine," "The Happy Miner," "Sweet Betsy from Pike," and "Sacramento Gals."

Some people say we have a modern reflection of the forty-niners and their songs in a recent westward movement to California by a group of people commonly spoken of as "Okies." These people are from the worn-out farm lands and dust bowl areas of the Southwest. Hearing of the riches in farming and fruit raising in California, they have traveled across country to try to find new homes. They, too, have a group of songs—some of them traditional folk ballads, some the more recent hillbilly or cowboy songs of the Ozarks and western grazing lands, and some their own

3. tureen (tṳ·rēn'). A large, deep, covered dish used for serving soup.

SACRAMENTO

Solo   American Sea Chanty

1. As   I   was walk-ing on the Quay, Hoo-dah to my hoo-dah. A
2. Her hair was brown, her eyes were blue, Hoo-dah to my hoo-dah. Her

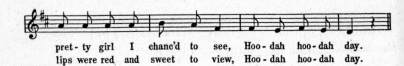

pret-ty girl   I   chanc'd to   see, Hoo-dah hoo-dah day.
lips were red   and   sweet   to   view, Hoo-dah hoo-dah day.

CHORUS

Blow, boys,   blow for Ca-li-for-ni-o. There's plen-ty of gold so

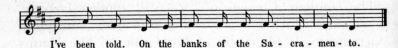

I've been told.   On the banks of the Sa-cra-men-to.

From Singing America, *copyrighted by C. C. Birchard & Company. Used by permission.*

"Sacramento" was a song of the "forty-niners" who sailed around
Cape Horn on their way to California.

1. As I was walking on the Quay,
    A pretty girl I chanc'd to see.

2. Her hair was brown, her eyes were blue,
    Her lips were red and sweet to view.

3. I raised my hat and said "How do?"
   She bowed and said, "Quite well, thank you."

4. I asked her then to come with me,
   Down to the docks my ship to see.

5. She quickly answered "Oh dear no."
   "I thank you, but I cannot go."

6. "I have a sweetheart young and true.
   And cannot give my love to you."

7. I said "Goodbye" and strode away,
   Although with her I longed to stay.

8. And as I bade this girl adieu,
   I said that girls like her were few.

songs which celebrate events of their migration, such as "Goin' Down the Road Feelin' Bad."

The Kansas Emigrants. One historian, in writing of Kansas, said that the musical history of the state began in 1854 when Forest Savage, a young man of twenty-two, came to Lawrence with the second company of settlers sent out by the New England Emigrant Aid Company. He and three other young men in the same company formed a band which consisted of two cornets, a bugle, and a fife. On their way out to Kansas they attracted attention from the time they left Boston until they reached Kansas by singing the song of "The Kansas Emigrants," which had been written for the occasion by John Greenleaf Whittier.

THE KANSAS EMIGRANTS

J. G. Whittier

We cross the prairie as of old
   The pilgrims crossed the sea,
To make the West, as they the East,
   The homestead of the free!

We go to rear a wall of men
   On Freedom's southern line,
And plant beside the cotton-tree
   The rugged Northern pine!

We're flowing from our native hills
   As our free rivers flow;
The blessing of our Mother-land
   Is on us as we go.

We go to plant her common schools
   On distant prairie swells,
And give the Sabbaths of the wild
   The music of her bells.

Upbearing, like the Ark of old,
   The Bible in our van,
We go to test the truth of God
   Against the fraud of man.

No pause, nor rest, save where the streams
   That feed the Kansas run,
Save where our Pilgrim gonfalon[4]
   Shall flout[5] the setting sun!

We'll tread the prairie as of old
   Our fathers sailed the sea
And make the West, as they the East
   The homestead of the free!

4. gonfalon (gŏn′fȧ·lŏn). A banner or standard.   5. flout. To mock or insult.

The Emigrant Aid Company was particularly significant in the settlement of Kansas. The company was originally formed for the purpose of aiding bands of people traveling across the Great Plains. By organizing into companies, the emigrants found the trip could be made more economically and safely. However, when the time came for Kansas to decide the problem of whether she should become a free or a slave state, the New England Emigrant Aid Company immediately sent into the territory large numbers of men who were sympathetic toward the abolition of slavery. These people were sent to offset the influence of hundreds of slave holders from Missouri who hurried across the border to vote for Kansas as a slave state. Savage and his company were members of the group from New England.

Kansas today is well known for its contributions to serious music. The Bethany Oratorio Society represents the interest shown in serious music in several Kansas communities. The little Kansas town of Lindsborg has become well known for the singing of Handel's *Messiah* each year at Easter time. The idea of having this annual performance seems to have originated with the founder of Lindsborg. On the occasion of one of his visits to London, he heard Handel's oratorio, the *Messiah,* and was thrilled by it. He had been eager to get singing started in Lindsborg; so, with the founding of Bethany College there, he thought his ideas could be carried out. The Bethany Oratorio Society was organized and began rehearsals in 1882. The chorus now has a membership of about six hundred. It is said to include almost one fourth of the entire population of Lindsborg. Music lovers from other near-by communities join the group.

Music in Denver and Central City, Colorado. Denver, Colorado, soon after its founding, became the center for

mining supplies and trade for a considerable area. For
many years the only available communication with the outside world was by means of stagecoach and ox team. Many
of the promoters of the Colorado mines were men of wealth
and culture. They desired to have music and musical instruments in their homes, and had many pianos brought to
Denver by ox team over the Santa Fe Trail from Kansas
City, Missouri.

Because of Denver's isolation and lack of transportation
facilities, the people of that city had to furnish their own
music for some time. Two events occurred, however, which
permanently put Denver in a position to enjoy music. One
was the building of railroads; the other was the opening of
the Tabor Grand Opera House. The theater was dedicated by Emma Abbott, a famous opera singer of that time,
and her opera company. The opera given was *Maritana*.
A wealthy man by the name of Tabor had donated much of
the money for the building of the theater, and so it was
named for him.

At the time of the dedication of the opera house, Eugene
Field was working on a Denver paper. He frequently
wrote a poem about some current happening and placed
it in his editorial column. As a joke, instead of signing the
poem himself, he would sign the name of some prominent
citizen. The following is the poem which appeared at the
time the new opera house was dedicated.

TABOR AND ABBOTT

The Opera House—a union grand
Of capital and labor—
Long will the stately structure stand,
A monument to Tabor.

And as to Emma, never will
Our citizens cease lovin' her,
While time lasts shall her name be linked
With that of the ex-Governor.

Because of its Grand Opera House,
Our city's much elated,
And happy is the time that Em
The structure dedicated.

For many a year and many a year
Our folks will have the habit
Of lauding that illustrious pair,
Tabor and Emma Abbott.

(Attributed to R. W. Woodbury)

Only a short distance from Denver was another early cultural center of the West. That was Central City, a small mining town from whose mines came millions of dollars in gold and silver during boom times. A splendid opera house was built there by popular subscription among the rich mining population. It was described as the "finest theater west of the river." The four-foot walls were of solid rock taken from the mountain back of the city. The interior was gay with crimson carpets, crystal chandeliers, and gold-leaf decorations. An annual season of opera, plays, and other entertainments became a part of the life of splendor in the little town. Among the list of entertainments were *She Stoops to Conquer, The Bohemian Girl, Ten Nights in a Bar Room, A Texas Steer,* and the *Passion Play.* Great opera singers and actors, among them Patti,[6] Jenny Lind,[7] Joseph Jefferson,[8] and Sarah Bernhardt,[9] traveled

6. Patti (păt′ė). An operatic soprano born in Madrid of Italian parentage (1843-1919). 7. Jenny Lind. A Swedish operatic and concert soprano (1820-1887). 8. Joseph Jefferson. A great American actor (1829-1905). 9. Sarah Bernhardt (bĕrn′härt). A great French actress (1844-1923).

The Central City Opera House has been restored and opera
has been presented there during the summer season.

up on the new narrow-gauge railway to make an appearance at the theater. They were entertained at the famous Teller House, the hotel where the entrance was paved with bricks of solid silver in honor of a visit by President Grant. Such was the glory of Central City in the seventies.

The boom days passed, however, and Central City became one of the ghost towns of the West. A short time ago the opera house was presented by descendants of the original builder to the University of Denver to be preserved as a memorial to Colorado pioneers. A society was formed to restore the building, and the Central City Opera House Association was incorporated. Since that time, Central City has again become a center for opera and drama. The season, under the sponsorship of the University of Denver, lasts for several weeks each summer. Among the productions given in recent seasons were Gilbert and Sullivan's *The Yeomen of the Guard,* or *The Merryman and His Maid,* and Smetana's[10] *The Bartered Bride.* The finest directors, opera singers, and actors of the day were obtained for the productions.

Music and the Building of Railroads. The bridging of the frontiers by means of railroads furnished one of the most romantic stories of our nation. Stories of early railroads in the Oregon region, where the rails were made of wood, covered with rawhide, and where trains were often delayed because hungry coyotes had chewed the hide from the rails, and accounts of driving the golden spike at the completion of the Union Pacific were filled with adventures of all kinds. The men who built the railways sang; so did those who guided the trains. They sang while at their work. They sang about their work. Someone has said the railroad songs were as varied as the men who worked

10. Smetana's (smĕ′tä·näz). Smetana was a Bohemian composer (1824-1884).

PAT ON THE RAILWAY

AMERICAN SONG

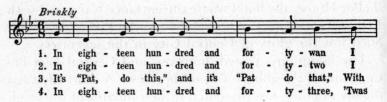

Briskly

1. In eigh - teen hun - dred and for - ty - wan I
2. In eigh - teen hun - dred and for - ty - two I
3. It's "Pat, do this," and it's "Pat do that," With
4. In eigh - teen hun - dred and for - ty - three, 'Twas

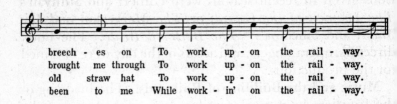

put me cord - 'roy breech - es on, I put me cord - 'roy
left the old world for the new, Bad cess to the luck that
out a stock - ing or crav - et, And noth - ing but an
then I met sweet Bid - dy Ma - gee, An il - e - gant wife she's

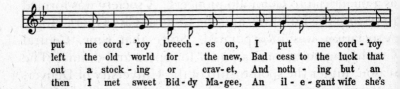

breech - es on To work up - on the rail - way.
brought me through To work up - on the rail - way.
old straw hat To work up - on the rail - way.
been to me While work - in' on the rail - way.

Fil - i - me - oo - re - i - re - ay, Fil - i - me - oo - re - i - re - ay,

Fil - i - me - oo - re - i - re - ay, To work up - on the rail - way.

From SINGING AMERICA, *copyrighted by C. C. Birchard & Company. Used b*
permission.

5. In eighteen hundred and forty-six,
   The gang pelted me with stones and bricks.
   Oh, I was in a terrible fix,
   While workin' on the railway.

6. In eighteen hundred and forty-seven,
   Sweet Biddy Magee, she went to heaven,
   If she left one child, she left eleven.
   To work upon the railway.

Union Pacific Railroad Photograph

The men who helped build the Union Pacific had many adventures.

in the roundhouse or sat in the cab. These men were frequently Irish, German, or Negro. The songs tell of brave engineers and train wrecks, of laying rails and driving spikes. Some of the best-known railroad songs are "Pat on the Railway," "Casey Jones," and "Red River Valley."

Music in the Southwest

Music in Texas. The history of the Southwest border and of that territory which now forms the state of Texas is so colorful and romantic that one naturally expects an interesting story of the music of the region. This territory, you will remember, was first claimed by Spain, then it became a Mexican province, afterwards the independent Republic of Texas, and, finally, one of the states of our country. Each period in the history of Texas left its impression on our American music, for the people of this section have always been musical.

The Southwest claims to have had the earliest music teachers in our country. (See page 50.) In the early Spanish missions, music was taught along with reading and writing. The natives were taught to play instruments which the Spaniards had brought from Europe, and they were also taught to play upon primitive instruments which they had made. Young men and boys were taught to sing, and here the first boy choirs in what is now the United States were formed. As early as the sixteenth century, much of the best music of Europe came to the region by way of Mexico City, which was a great center of culture. A relic of these very early days is found in *Los Pastores* (Shepherds' Play), a miracle play which was first given in the missions. It is now performed each Christmas in San Antonio, Texas.

The Mexican influence is best seen through the Mexican folk songs brought by the vaqueros,[11] the Spanish cattle herders. The typical Mexican folk song is a love song, and it is said that the vaqueros sang little else. One of the most popular of these songs is the "El Abandonado" (The Abandoned One). "La Paloma" (The Dove) is another which is

11. vaqueros (vä·kä′rōz). Spanish word for cowboys.

still heard. The melody of "La Paloma" has been transcribed and used as a popular instrumental number.

When the United States gained control of Texas, thousands of Americans began to settle this new country. There were also many Germans, Bohemians, Italians, Scandinavians, Russians, and Poles who moved into the new state. Each group brought its own music. Therefore, in Texas we may expect to find many types of music in the period of expansion.

With the folk songs of all of these groups, there were intermingled the songs of the Negroes who worked in the cotton fields, Creole love songs, white spirituals, the music of stately grand balls or of fandangoes,[12] and songs of the cattle herders (cowboys). German orchestras or bands and German and Scandinavian singing societies were common. Operatic music was heard in the theater of Houston, Texas, in the early eighteen hundreds.

Few musical instruments were brought along by the early settlers, and so many interesting and original instruments were devised by them for such occasions as weddings and dances. The music on one occasion is described as being furnished by one person beating on a clevis[13] of an iron plow, while his companion scraped on a cotton hoe with a case knife.

Tunes Sung along the Old Chisholm Trail. At the time when the grasslands of the Great Plains served as an open grazing land, cowboys drove herds of cattle back and forth from Texas to the grazing lands of Wyoming and Montana, and from Texas to the railroad shipping points in Kansas. Thousands of cattle were shipped from Kansas City, Dodge City, and other shipping centers. The ship-

12. fandangoes (făn·dăng′gōz). Lively Spanish dances performed with castanets and in triple measure. 13. clevis (klĕv′ĭs). A device used on the end of the tongue of a plow to attach it to a draft chain.

Santa Fe Railway Photograph

Cowboys sat around the camp fire in the evening and sang.

ping points were called "railroad corrals."[14] The trail,
over which the cattle were driven from Texas to the shipping points, became known as the Chisholm Trail. It was
as much a main highway for cattle as the Santa Fe Trail
was for travel and commerce.

Cowboys usually traveled in outfits. The typical outfit
was made up of some twenty or thirty cowboys, six or eight
horses to a man, chuck wagons, and supplies. A distance of
ten miles was considered a good day's travel. One can see
that the trip was long and tedious, especially when days
were lost when the half-wild Texas longhorns stampeded
and had to be rounded up. The cowboys relieved the

14. corrals (kŏ·rălz'). Enclosures for cattle and other animals.

THE OLD CHISHOLM TRAIL

Cowboy Song

From The New American Song Book, *copyrighted by Hall & McCreary Company. Used by permission.*

4. I'm up in the mornin' afore daylight,
   And afore I sleep the moon shines bright.

5. Old Ben Bolt was a blamed good boss,
   But he'd go to see the girls on a sore-backed hoss.

6. Oh, it's bacon and beans most every day;
   I'd as soon be a-eatin' prairie hay.

7. It's cloudy in the West, a-lookin' like rain,
   And my durned old slicker's in the wagon again.

8. I jumped in the saddle and I grabbed holt the horn;
   Best durned cowpuncher ever was born.

9. I went to the boss to draw my roll;
   He figured me out nine dollars in the hole.

10. So I'll sell my outfit as fast as I can,
    And I won't punch cows for no boss man.

11. Going back to town to draw my money,
    Going back home to see my honey.

12. With my knees in the saddle and my seat in the sky,
    I'll quit punching cows in the sweet by and by.

monotony of the trip by singing. Usually they sang old tunes, making up words to suit the occasion as they went along. The rhythm was fitted to the movement of the horses—jogging, loping, or cantering. Occasionally the song was broken by a cattle call, and "yippee-ti-yi's" became fitted into the song as naturally as the "amen's" and "Oh, Lawdy's" into the Negro spirituals. The free, gliding manner of singing became known as a "holler." Cowboys "hollered" at their cattle to keep them moving or to quiet them at night or after they had been turned back from a stampede. "The Old Chisholm Trail," "The Railroad Corral," and "Git Along Little Dogie" were among the familiar songs of the trail. The words of another typical song of the trail were as follows:

> Hoo-de-i-yea-e-ho, travel you Doe-gies
> Hoo-de-i-yea-e-ho, travel along—
> Hoo-de-i-yea-e-ho, step to it cattle,
> For old Wyoming will be your new home!

Leisure-Time Music of the Cowboy. In every outfit there usually were some men who could play a guitar, fiddle, banjo, or French harp. Seated before a fire near the chuck wagon in the evening, the cowboys had an ideal opportunity to spin yarns and sing. They sang stories of desperadoes, train robberies, and the like. Some of the songs were "Bad Man Jones," "Billy the Kid," "The Fightin' Booze Fighter," and "Denver Jim."

When the cowboys reached the railroad corral and disposed of their cattle, they frequently sought relaxation from the long monotonous trip in the town saloon or dance hall. The dance was about the only social affair in which they could participate. Many times they would engage in an all-night dance to which people came from miles around. They enjoyed most of all the old-fashioned square dances, with a fiddle and guitar or an accordian for accompaniment, and with a "caller" to give directions for the dances. They had entertainment in the form of dancing and singing on their ranches, too, and made up songs to tell about these festivities. Among these songs were some with the colorful and descriptive titles of "The Bunk-House Orchestra," and "The Cowboy's Dance Song."

Cowboys on the trail sang to entertain themselves and to quiet
their cattle.

Holidays were often celebrated in town where the cowboys could meet friends and strangers and exchange yarns and ballads. They took pleasure in bragging in song about their accomplishments or, if they were far from their home ranch or state, they might sing about their loneliness.

The Cowboy's Philosophy. The cowboys had their own peculiar philosophy about religion and justice and, although they might not be greatly concerned with church services and doctrines, they had a belief that their faults would be overlooked by a just God and that there might be a place for them in "the sweet by and by." These simple beliefs were expressed in many of their songs. "A Cowboy Alone with His Conscience" expresses the cowboy's philosophy very well.

A COWBOY ALONE WITH HIS CONSCIENCE

When I ride into the mountains on my little broncho bird,
Whar my ears are never pelted with the bawlin' o' the herd,
An' a sort o' dreamy quiet hangs upon the western air,
An' thar ain't no animation[15] to be noticed anywhere;
Then I sort o' feel oneasy, git a notion in my head
I'm the only livin' mortal—everybody else is dead—
An' I feel a queer sensation, rather skeery like, an' odd,
    When thar ain't nobody near me, 'ceptin' God.

Every rabbit that I startle from its shaded restin' place,
Seems a furry shaft o' silence shootin' into noiseless space,
An' a rattlesnake a crawlin' through the rocks so old an' gray
Helps along the ghostly feelin' in a rather startlin' way.
Every breeze that dares to whisper does it with a bated breath,
Every bush stands grim an' silent in a sort o' livin' death—
Tell you what, a feller's feelin's give him many an icy prod,
    When thar ain't nobody near him, 'ceptin' God.

15. animation. Life, spirit.

Somehow allus git to thinkin' o' the error o' my ways,
An' my memory goes wingin' back to childhood's happy days,
When a mother, now a restin' in the grave so dark an' deep,
Used to listen while I'd whisper, "Now I lay me down to sleep."
Then a sort o' guilty feelin' gits a surgin' in my breast,
An' I wonder how I'll stack up at the final judgment test,
Conscience allus welts[16] it to me with a mighty cuttin' rod,
    When thar ain't nobody near me, 'ceptin' God.

Take the very meanest sinner that the nation ever saw,
One that don't respect religion more'n he respects the law,
One that never does an action that's commendable or good,
An' immerse him fur a season out in Nature's solitude,
An' the cog-wheels o' his conscience 'll be rattled out o' gear,
More'n if he 'tended preachin' every Sunday in the year,
Fur his sins 'ill come a ridin' through his cranium rough shod,
    When thar ain't nobody near him, 'ceptin' God.
                        James Barton Adams.

Then, too, although they delighted in singing about the deeds of bad men, of the highway robbers and cattle thieves, their opinion about these bandits often was that they deserved the harsh fate which usually caught up with them. They give full accounts of the bad deeds of highwaymen in their songs, but at the same time they expressed no sympathy for an out-and-out bad man such as Billy the Kid.

John Lomax and David Guion. The real spirit of the music of the Southwest has been brought to us today largely through the work of two men, John Lomax and David Guion.[17] John Lomax has collected folk songs of the Southwest for more than thirty years and has published many of the songs of the cowboy.

16. welts. Striking a heavy blow; beating or lashing. 17. Guion (gī′ŭn).

David Guion has used the folk music of the region as themes for his serious compositions. The melodies of the cowboy songs sung around the campfire so fascinated David Guion, a young man born in a Texas cow town, that he began to write them down. He has used these tunes as the basis of serious compositions which have thrilled concert audiences all over the world.

Music as an Art and a Profession. While the folk music of Texas has been found to be a rich storehouse which has not yet been fully explored, the development of music as an art and a profession has kept pace with a similar development in other sections of the country.

Among the early settlers were many who had musical training. Player pianos, along with fine paintings and choice pieces of furniture, found their way by boat up the Red River and the Brazos. Among the cowboys of west Texas were cultured Englishmen who were trained in music. Ranch owners often gathered from miles around for a musicale, staying over night before returning home. There were singing schools, taught by traveling singing masters, and carried on as they had been from early New England days.

The younger generation of those early Texas settlers had musical training in the many colleges and schools that sprang up. Teachers came from eastern conservatories and from abroad to these schools and to the conservatories established in various parts of the state. Gradually young Texans began going to the great eastern schools and entering into the life of the country as professional musicians.

Early opera in Houston has already been mentioned. While there apparently was little opera given by local communities, Texas had her opera from traveling opera companies which came by boat to New Orleans and to Galveston, then the leading city of Texas. As railroads developed, opera companies came to Dallas, the rapidly growing railroad center, and from there traveled throughout the state. One city, San Antonio, has had its own opera company for years. The San Antonio Civic Opera Society has produced many light operas and musical comedies, and has featured Texas conductors and singers, offering scholarships throughout the state for gifted young singers. Only leading soloists have been imported.

Lack of local opera companies, however, does not prove a lack of interest in opera. In fact, the popularity of opera in Texas and the Southwest has resulted in the provision of a successful season of grand opera by the Metropolitan Opera Company, which is brought to Dallas each year. Capacity audiences are drawn from surrounding states and from as far away as Oregon.

Symphony orchestras also are a part of the history of this new land. A number of cities have their own symphony orchestras. In fact, Dallas had its symphony orchestra forty years ago, under the direction of Hans Kreissig, opera and orchestra conductor. Kreissig also gave music lessons to the young people in the city, arriving at their homes in an open buggy, with an umbrella to keep off the Texas sun.

Music clubs have had a long and influential history in Texas. Among the oldest was the St. Cecilians' Society which was active in Dallas thirty-five years ago. Soon after that the musical leaders organized the Dallas Federation of Music Clubs, which has sponsored opera and many other activities in the years since. Other professional organizations were formed throughout the state by music teachers, music educators in the public schools, and by music schools.

Along with all the interest in music as a profession carried on by specially trained individuals, training in music was made possible for everyone through the public schools at an early date. Again using Dallas as an example, one finds that music was included in school studies as early as 1885, and that the first of Dallas' three music supervisors was mentioned in the annual report of 1893-94. Out of those early beginnings in the state, there have developed fine bands, orchestras, and choruses which open the world of musical art to most of the young people of the state.

Throughout the broad acres of Texas, through all the musical activities of many kinds, and especially as brought through the radio, music has become a part of everyday living. And among those who have made musical life what it is, many have become known throughout the country as performers, composers, and arrangers. So Texas has taken of the best in music as in other phases of our American way of life, and has given of its best in return.

Indian Music

Folk Music. The removal of the Indians to special reservations set apart for them, and the trouble with the Indians of the plains in the settlement of the West are part of the story of the advancing frontier. In considering this part of our history and the music associated with it, our attention is drawn to the music of the Indians.

Some of the Indian tribes were found to lack musical ability; others were very musical. The Ojibways,[18] the Zuñis,[19] the Omahas, and the Moquis[20] had many songs. The songs of the Iroquois, Apaches,[21] and Comanches[22] were of a rather primitive nature. On the whole it may be the more warlike a tribe was, the less musical it was.

18. Ojibways (ò·jĭb′wāz). 19. Zunis (zōō′nyĕz). 20. Moquis (mō′kĕz). 21. Apaches (a·păch′ĕz). 22. Comanches (kò·măn′chĕz).

SENECA INDIAN WOMEN'S DANCE

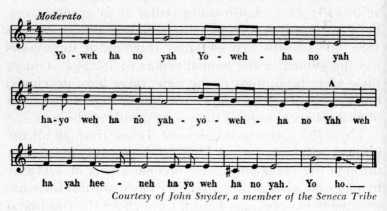

Yo - weh ha no yah   Yo - weh - ha no yah

ha-yo weh ha no yah - yo - weh - ha no Yah weh

ha yah hee - neh ha yo weh ha no yah. Yo ho.

Courtesy of John Snyder, a member of the Seneca Tribe

Melodies. Many Indian melodies were set in the ancient five-tone scale, and the direction of the melody was characteristically down the scale. Although the Indians used but five tones, they made use of many in-between tones so that a quavering[23] effect was produced. It has been found very difficult to record this effect. It has also been impossible for the voice of the white man to reproduce it. Indian melodies were usually short, expressing a single idea. The melody was repeated over and over again to the accompaniment of the drum and the rattle. The Indians knew nothing of harmony, but always sang in unison. Their sense of pitch was so true that every time they sang a particular song they began it on the same pitch. The words and melodies to their songs were not written, but were learned and repeated from memory.

Musical Instruments. The drum was their most important musical instrument. Other instruments were the rattle and the flute. It may seem difficult to understand the

23. quavering. Trembling, vibrating.

Indian's devotion to the drum, but if one should live among Indians for a time, one would soon learn its importance. The drum was important not only as a musical instrument, but also as a forecaster of the weather. If the drum made a dull sound, there was rain on the way. On the other hand, if the pounding brought forth a clear sound, then the weather would be fair. The drum was also used as a signal or means of communicating messages.

It is easy to see that the Indian drummer was a very important person in his tribe. In fact, he often ranked next to the chief in importance. He was not only the drummer but also the leader in singing. His drum might be made of a wooden frame across which was stretched the skin of some animal. It might be only a few inches across or as much as two feet. He beat his drum with a short stick much as we do. In a way, the drummer took the place of a historian for the Indians, for he knew all the songs of the tribe and taught them to others, thus passing on the history of the tribe.

Indian music often seems monotonous to the white man because of the way the drum is beat over and over. Sometimes it seems as if there is a race between the drum and the voices of the tribesmen. The drummer begins the beating slowly, while the voices of the Indians go faster. Then the drummer increases the tempo of his beating. Finally, in the course of the song, it seems that the drum and the voices are running neck and neck. In the end the drum wins out, for the drummer can beat faster than the Indians can sing.

The flute was also an instrument of much importance in the life of the Indian. It was used on many occasions, but was best known as a lover's instrument. If a young Indian brave was too bashful to speak to the young Indian

Drums and rattles were used to give rhythm to the ceremonial
dances of the Indians.

maiden of his choice, he got a flute and hid near her tepee or on the road to the spring where she went each day for water. He played to the Indian maiden. She might not appear to be noticing the music, but the chances were that she would inquire to find out who was playing. If she was favorable to the young man, then the next time she heard the music she let him know that she had heard. If he played on the flute and the Indian maiden made no sign to him, then he gave up and played no more to attract her.

Occasions for Music. Today we hear a great deal about Indian music in connection with the ceremonial dances which are still held by many tribes of American Indians. The Indian has a song for practically everything that influences his life. He may have a song about his canoe, his moccasins, or his tepee. He considers it unsuitable to sing a song at any time except when it has direct meaning for the situation. For example, he sings a song of the hunt only when he is going hunting. One would think it queer to teach a friend a song in payment for his bicycle; yet an Indian brave might teach another Indian, even one of another tribe than his own, the words and music of a song in payment for a pony.

Influence of Indian Music. The greatest influence of Indian music in America has been in the use of Indian themes and characteristics of Indian life as the basis for composition by American composers. Edward MacDowell's[24] *Indian Suite* and Charles Wakefield Cadman's[25] "The Land of the Sky Blue Water" are familiar examples of the use of Indian themes in American music.

24. MacDowell's (măk·dou'ĕlz). MacDowell was an American pianist and composer (1861-1908). 25. Cadman is an American composer (1881-   ).

CHAPTER XIII

MUSICAL ENTERTAINMENT

Concerts and Lyceums

The Period of Expansion. The United States was expanding in many other ways besides that of gaining more territory. Our public school system was being established. Horace Mann had seen the need for better-educated teachers, and the first teacher training institutions had been started. Industry was increasing because of new inventions, better means of transportation, and increased population. The work of American artists and writers was becoming recognized abroad. Longfellow, Emerson, Lowell, Whittier, and Hawthorne, through their writings and lectures, were forming what became known as "America's Golden Age of Literature."

As new homes were established in the West, parents became aware of the need for education. They desired culture for their families and their communities. New and improved methods of education were being tried in many schools in the East. Musical organizations, begun at an earlier period, were continuing and growing. All in all, the idea of "bigger and better" was carried out in practically every field of endeavor.

The expansion in musical interest and activities may be indicated through an account of a number of various kinds of musical entertainment.

Early Concerts. The early concerts were for a selected few. However, a great number of people attended the concerts of the latter nineteenth and early twentieth centuries. Transportation and communication had been improved, and people had more leisure time and more money to spend. The concerts sometimes consisted of instrumental numbers, sometimes of vocal selections, sometimes of both. A popular type of concert included a few vocal or instrumental numbers by a foreign artist of note, filled in with selections by the orchestra and solos by lesser artists. The grandparents of a generation ago could relate no more thrilling tale than that of the occasion when they heard Jenny Lind or Ole Bull.[1]

The Swedish Nightingale. Stories of Jenny Lind report that there had been nothing to compare with the furor that she created in the 1850's. She was a Swedish singer of whom Mendelssohn[2] had said, "She is as great an artist as ever lived and the greatest I have known." She was brought to America by the famous showman, Phineas Taylor Barnum. She spent some time here and gave concerts in all parts of the country. Perhaps no one but Barnum could have provided for the spectacular introduction of this young singer to America. When she arrived from Europe, he persuaded the whole fire department of New York City to serenade her. Her first concert was given at Castle Gardens in New York City in 1850. An excerpt[3] from a letter written by a Washington, D. C., attorney to his cousins in Missouri describes her concert which he attended, and will give you a picture of the manner in which Jenny Lind was received.

---

1. Ole Bull (ō′lĕ bōōl). A Norwegian violinist (1810-1880). 2. Mendelssohn (mĕn′dĕl·sŏn). A German composer (1809-1847). 3. excerpt (ĕk′sûrpt). A passage taken from a book, article, or other writing.

Jenny Lind, a famous Swedish singer, came to the United States in 1850 and gave concerts in all parts of the country. She was very popular with American audiences.

That vast assemblage waited with breathless silence until sweet "Jenny" came forward, each one desiring the first glimpse of the fairy songster. A little after eight, here she came tripping along, and never in this world was a mortal greeted with such an outburst of applause. The vast audience rose simultaneously to receive her and the scene which followed baffles all attempts at a description. Such shouts of *"Bravo," "Welcome Jenny," "Three cheers for Jenny,"* and the like intermingled with every mark of "welcome" and delight. Bouquets in showers and by thousands were thrown upon the stage and the waving of white handkerchiefs and the other demonstrations of applause was enough to make your humble servant cry out that he had already got the worth of his $6, the price of his ticket. She acknowledged the enthusiasm of her greeting in a manner peculiarly graceful and appropriate. Placing her sweet little hands to her heart, she bent before the storms of cheers with an evidence of deep feeling beyond the power of art to affect. . . . .

She was very plainly but becomingly dressed in white satin, with a short skirt of white lace over it, white flowers with green leaves in her head, a similar flower in her breast, and wore no jewels save diamonds at her bodice and a brilliant bracelet on her arms.

She began the first piece falteringly and tremblingly. Indeed "Jenny" was fairly overcome. I heard Mr. Barnum say, who boards at this house, that so alarmed was she that large drops of sweat fell from her face. She were more than human, indeed, if she could have mastered herself to do otherwise under such circumstances.

As she proceeded in the first piece she regained herself and gave to the *Casta diva* a most brilliant and startling effect. They made her come back and sing it over, and as she retreated behind the curtain from the scene of her conquest, she had to tread over a carpet literally covered with bouquets, which she endeavored to gather, but was obliged to relinquish the effort, from their profusion, some of which I have no doubt cost $10.

When something like quiet was restored she reappeared and sang the "Trio Concertante" and never did I ever dream that I should listen to such a miraculous execution of music. She accompanies two flutes, and as she motions her sweet little fingers, as tho' she was performing on a flute, you cannot distinguish the difference so greatly does her voice resemble the sweetest notes you ever heard upon that instrument.

She next gave us her famous Swedish *Herdsman's Song,* called *The Echo Song,* which has given her so much fame in England and on the Continent. This drove your *humble cousin* and the already excited audience into a frenzy of enthusiasm. In my wildest fancy, I had never imagined any thing like it. It was a new revelation of the capability of the human voice, and appeared to all a miracle. The instantaneous echo of her own voice by an inhalation of the breath, to a full gush of melody poured from the lips, and this produced many times in succession, was something beyond my anticipations however great they had been formed about Jenny Lind, and the result, whilst it bewildered, gave me such transports of pleasurable excitement, that, I fear, will for a long time unfit me for the ordinary avocations[4] of life. Why, W., to give you a better idea of this echo song, whilst I sat immediately in front of her with her voice she would give us the bellowing of the cow, the Herdsman calling his sheep, the cheerful laugh intermixed, and off yonder in the mountains we could hear the echo, which was of the sweetest and wildest melody that was ever listened to by the ears of man and it was such a perfection of art, and so closely resembled nature that you could not distinguish the difference. She next sung the celebrated *Welcome to America.* This was the only song sung in English and her pronunciation of the English was exceedingly beautiful. It called forth immense cheers and applause. But what a fool I am, endeavoring to give a description of "Jenny's" first concert. All that you may see or hear, every word that has been written and may be written cannot give you the faintest idea of the realities. It has to be seen to be realized.

I will only add that the singing does not constitute all the beauties of "Jenny." She is *noble, generous and benevolent; these are the qualities which will endear her to the American people.* To

4. avocations (ăv·ô·kā′shŭnz). Occupations, usually outside of ordinary business or profession.

think that a *Swede,* from that far distant land, should upon lighting upon the shores of America bestow $10,000 for charitable purposes is indeed noble and munificent.[5]

Such good acts she intends to keep doing. Her motto is, to "take from the rich and give to the poor." *I sometimes think that she has been sent on earth for some glorious end, and her field of labours are now about to commence in the land of Liberty.* The church pays her great homage. My apology for talking so much about the *Swede* is that I promised the girls on the Creek that as they could not be here to see Jenny I would represent them, and I have imposed upon you, as the medium, to impart the imperfect description given of the *sweet warbler.* I enjoyed the last concert more than the first from the fact that I was in company with Major C. of St. Louis, who had an opera glass which cost him $45, thro' which I had a fine view of the scene around me.

Ole Bull. Ole Bull, a brilliant Norwegian violinist, spent considerable time in America. He made five visits in all, giving concerts in all parts of the country. He not only thrilled audiences with his playing, but made a great effort toward encouraging the advancement of music in the United States. At one time he offered a prize of one thousand dollars for the best original grand opera by an American composer.

The Lyceum. The lyceum[6] movement was started early in the nineteenth century by Josiah Holbrook. Its purpose was the advancement of learning. The early lyceums consisted of a series of lectures or musical numbers or a combination of the two. The numbers of the series were not given on successive dates, but occurred at spaced intervals covering several weeks or months.

These series or courses were held in both large and small cities and towns. Individual soloists, opera companies, and

5. munificent (mū·nĭf′ĭ·sĕnt). Very liberal in giving. 6. lyceum (lī·sē′ŭm). An educational organization providing concerts and entertainment.

concert groups appeared on this type of public program. The musical numbers, while including good music, were mainly of a type that had a popular appeal.

Lyceum programs were extremely valuable because they carried the cultural advantages of music to the masses of the people. They were popular in this country until near the close of the First World War. Gradually, as public schools came to give more and more attention to music, and as centers for the cultural advancement of adults were established, the lyceum movement was absorbed.

Chautauquas

The First Chautauqua. The Chautauqua, which paralleled the lyceum, was a cultural movement in America that influenced the lives of millions of Americans. The first Chautauqua was held in 1874 on the banks of a beautiful lake at Chautauqua, New York, then called Fair Point. The movement had its beginning in a religious camp meeting, which grew into an assembly for the study of the Bible and Sunday school methods. Gradually the course of study was expanded until it included the whole field of education. Music was also a part of the cultural advantages offered to those who made the annual pilgrimage to Chautauqua for the ten-week offering of lectures and musical and dramatic series. The hymn "Day Is Dying in the West" ("Chautauqua") was written for these meetings.

The Circuit Chautauqua. It was not long before the spirit of the movement spread to nearly every city and village of the whole nation. The traveling or circuit Chautauquas, employing methods similar to those of the lyceum, sent lecturers, bands, orchestras, players, and others to appear on programs of Chautauquas up and down the land.

CHAUTAUQUA
Day Is Dying in the West

Mary A. Lathbury   William F. Sherwin

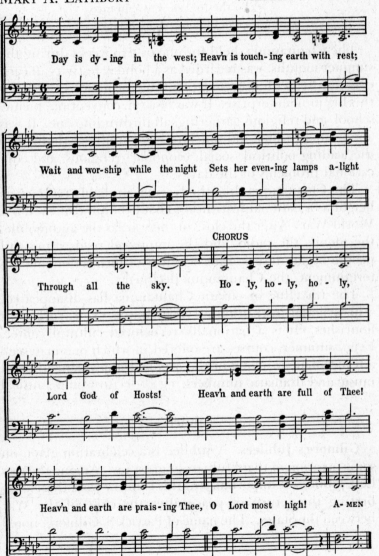

Day is dy-ing in the west; Heav'n is touch-ing earth with rest;

Wait and wor-ship while the night Sets her even-ing lamps a-light

Through all the sky.   **CHORUS**   Ho - ly, ho - ly, ho - ly,

Lord God of Hosts!   Heav'n and earth are full of Thee!

Heav'n and earth are prais-ing Thee, O Lord most high!   A - men

2. Lord of life, beneath the dome
    Of the Universe, Thy home,
    Gather us who seek Thy face
    To the fold of Thy embrace,
    For Thou art nigh.

The Chautauqua, held for one or two weeks during the summer months, was regarded as a holiday festivity in each community, with everyone planning for months ahead for this big joint enterprise. It was festival, convention, picnic, school, and religious gathering, all thrown into one. It was a movement which did much to give a unity of thought to the leading political, social, economic, religious, and educational problems of the day.

The Chautauqua, like the lyceum, probably reached its height as a national institution about the time of the First World War. After the close of the war, as the automobile, the movie, the radio, and the improved roads came and people began to seek other avenues of instruction and entertainment, the Chautauqua declined.

The traveling or circuit Chautauqua has disappeared. The original institution at Chautauqua, New York, still flourishes. It is a nationally recognized cultural center. Every summer, courses are offered in which one may seek advancement in many of the arts and enjoyment of good music and dramatic numbers.

Jubilees

Gilmore's Jubilees. A jubilee is a celebration given on some occasion of thankfulness or great joy. Among the earliest jubilees of importance in this country were those celebrating the return of peace after the close of the War between the States. The name of Patrick S. Gilmore, noted band leader and director, stands out in connection with these jubilees. He was not a musician of great ability, but

THE PROGRAM

ALBANY, MISSOURI
August 4 to August 10

JULIUS H. ROHDE—Superintendent

F. H. KOCH—Morning Hour Lecturer

Programs Begin Promptly

Children's Hour   -   9:00 A. M.   Morning Lecture   -   10:30 A. M.
Afternoon Music   -   2:30 P. M.   Afternoon Lecture   -   3:00 P. M.
Evening Music   -   7:30 P. M.   Evening Lecture   -   8:15 P. M.

MONDAY
AFTERNOON—Opening Exercises and Important Announcements
Popular Concert   THE SPANISH LADIES' ORCHESTRA
Don't Miss This Opening Concert As It Is Something Unusually Good
Admission 25 cents
4:00 P. M.—Organization of the Junior Department and Perfecting
Arrangements for the Many Interesting Journeys
EVENING—Concert by   THE SPANISH LADIES' ORCHESTRA
Popular Lecture
"A Lesson to the Nation"   JUDGE A. Z. BLAIR
Admission 25 cents

TUESDAY
Illustrated Travelogue for the Children
Morning Lecture—"A Midsummer Night's Dream"
AFTERNOON—Music by   JACOB REUTER COMPANY
Address   DR. FRANK W. GUNSAULUS
The Great Chicago Preacher
Admission 30 cents
EVENING—Concert by   JACOB REUTER COMPANY
Humorous Lecture   RALPH PARLETTE
Admission 35 cents

WEDNESDAY
Illustrated Travelogue for the Children
Morning Lecture—"Romeo and Juliet"
AFTERNOON—Music by   THE HARMONY CONCERT CO.
"Political Patriotism"   GOV. A. C. SHALLENBERGER
A Modern Live Wire
Admission 30 cents
EVENING—Concert by   THE HARMONY CONCERT COMPANY
Popular Lecture
"Popular Fallacies"   DR. ERNEST WRAY ONEAL
Admission 35 cents

THURSDAY
Illustrated Travelogue for the Children
Morning Lecture—"Macbeth"

AFTERNOON—   THAVIU'S INTERNATIONAL BAND
In Grand Musical Festival
Admission 30 cents
EVENING—"Lovely Galatea," by 12 GRAND OPERA SINGERS
and THAVIU'S GREAT BAND
Part I   Popular Band Concert. Selections from Grand
Opera
Part II Thaviu's Adaptation of the Opera, "Lovely Gal-
atea" by 12 GRAND OPERA SINGERS and
THAVIU'S INTERNATIONAL BAND
Admission 50 cents

FRIDAY
Illustrated Travelogue for the Children
Morning Lecture—"Twelfth Night"
AFTERNOON—Entertainment by THE RINER SISTERS CO.
Monologue Entertainment
"The Nest Egg"   MISS MARY AGNES DOYLE
Admission 25 cents
EVENING—Popular Entertainment   THE RINER SISTERS CO.
Illustrated Travelogue
"The Land of the Dragon"   DR. FREDERICK POOLE
Admission 35 cents

SATURDAY
Illustrated Travelogue for the Children
Morning Lecture—"Kipling's Ballads"
AFTERNOON—Music and Melody   EDWIN R. WEEKS CO.
Lecture
"Our Immediate Duty"   HON. VICTOR MURDOCK
Typical Kansas Orator
Admission 30 cents
EVENING—A Great Program of Fun and
Frolic by   EDWIN WEEKS Himself
Music   By the Company
Concluding with
"The Indian Mystery Man"   SHUNGOPAVI
Admission 35 cents

SUNDAY
AFTERNOON—Music by   THE DUNBAR QUARTET
and Bell Ringers
Lecture
"Business and Morals"   EDWARD F. TREFZ
If you can only hear one program, hear Trefz
Admission 30 cents
Vesper Service—4:20 P. M.
EVENING—Concert by   THE DUNBAR QUARTET
and Bell Ringers
Lecture
"Literary Adventures"   MARGUERITE CURTIS
Admission 35 cents

Chautauqua programs offered music and other forms of entertainment.

he took great delight in staging spectacular events on a gigantic scale.

A Great Peace Jubilee. A few years after the close of the
War between the States, Gilmore directed a great peace
jubilee in Boston which lasted for several days. Gilmore's
idea was to present an enormous and spectacular performance. There was a group of one thousand players, with
Ole Bull as first violinist. The great soprano, Parepa-Rosa,
was a soloist for the occasion. Oliver Wendell Holmes
wrote a "Hymn of Peace" in response to a need for a new
patriotic number. Edward Everett Hale, then an old man,
invoked the blessing at the first concert. Lowell Mason
attended as a guest of honor. President Grant and his cabinet, governors of states, and other notables of every kind
were present. Railroads arranged special excursions so that
people from all over the country might see and hear the
"grandest musical festival ever known in the history of the
world." Spectacular effects were produced, such as having
one hundred red-shirted firemen strike real anvils in the
"Anvil Chorus" from *Il Trovatore,* and firing cannons and
guns to emphasize patriotic selections.

A Second Peace Jubilee. Two years later Gilmore organized a second peace jubilee in Boston called the World's
Peace Jubilee. At this time Johann Strauss[7] was employed
at a fee of $20,000 to conduct the orchestra in the perform-
ance of his "Blue Danube" and other dance numbers. A
mammoth building was erected. Arrangements were made
for a chorus and orchestra twice the size of those of the
former jubilee. Foreign bands as well as the marine band
from Washington took part. People from all parts of the
country and from many large cities, including New York,
Chicago, Philadelphia, St. Louis, Omaha, and San Francisco, appeared in the chorus.

7. Johann Strauss (yō'hän shtrous). A Viennese composer (1825-1899); son of
   Johann Strauss, also an eminent composer of dance music.

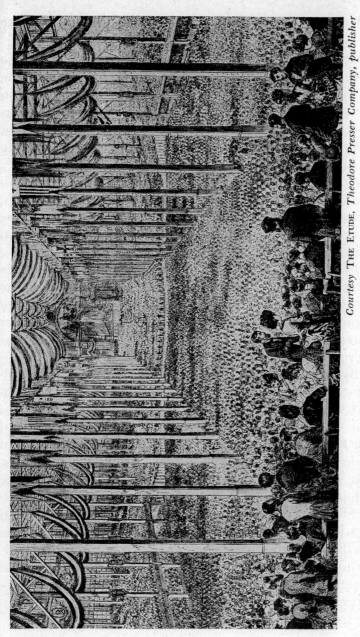

People from all parts of the country attended the World's Peace Jubilee.

Other Jubilees. A peace celebration was held at Chicago to celebrate the rebuilding of the city two years after the fire of 1871. The jubilee was held in the passenger station of the Lake Shore Railroad. When one considers that this structure was two blocks in length and could take care of forty thousand people, one gets an idea of the immense size of the jubilee.

Somewhat different types of jubilee, popular in Chicago and Cincinnati, were those led by Theodore Thomas. These festivals were not so large nor so magnificent as those staged by Gilmore, but nevertheless influenced music in the middle western United States to a great extent.

Fisk Jubilee Singers. The Fisk Jubilee Singers made their place in American music when they appeared in the World Peace Jubilee held in Boston. These singers were organized and sent out on tour by Fisk University in order to raise money for the school. They were so successful that they raised $150,000 in three years.

Because they were Negroes, they were not always welcome at hotels and in railroad stations or even in concert halls. They had a hard time, but when their voices rose in singing Julia Ward Howe's "Battle Hymn of the Republic," audiences were inspired. The singing of "Glory, Glory, Hallelujah," with accompanying orchestras, brought the people to their feet in wild, enthusiastic admiration.

The tours of the Fisk singers furnished the first medium by which Negro spirituals were carried to the masses of the northern people. For many years, on Chautauqua platforms, on lyceum programs, and on other programs of entertainment, various groups of colored jubilee singers toured the country, singing old melodies, hymns, and popular songs.

Vaudeville

Entertainment for All the People. People like to laugh away their sorrows. Perhaps that is the reason for the development of a new type of entertainment in America in the depressing years after the close of the War between the States. This was known as vaudeville. It represented a type of entertainment produced in taverns, theaters, and other places, and consisted of songs, dances, slapstick comedy, individual and group sketches, and acts.

On the vaudeville programs appeared not only singers, dancers, comedians, and black-faced actors, but also trained animals, magicians, and spiritualists. So popular did vaudeville become that at one time during the gay nineties at least twelve hundred acts were touring the country. Vaudeville circuits were formed to supply talent for the play houses in cities and towns.

Vaudeville, during the 1890's and until the motion picture became popular, became the chief source of popular public entertainment. It was thoroughly democratic, for it brought into the theaters at one time all kinds of people to enjoy the same type of amusements. The matinee idol of vaudeville was adored by servant, housewife, and professional person alike.

Song Hits Introduced. Vaudeville acts provided a means of introducing song hits to the public. From the vaudeville theaters in New York and other cities, these songs spread to all the people of the nation. Sales of songs were boosted, and people all over the country were singing the same tunes at the same time. Some of the hits of vaudeville days were "In the Good Old Summer Time," "The Bird on Nellie's Hat," "Under the Bamboo Tree," and "Everybody Works but Father."

Many of our famous actors have appeared on the leading vaudeville stages of the country. Lillian Russell,[8] Ed Wynn, Fred Allen, W. C. Fields, the Irwin sisters, John and Harry Kernall, Marie Dressler, and others were there.

Tony Pastor. Even the shortest account of vaudeville in the United States would not be complete without mention of Tony Pastor in New York City. It was he who conceived the idea of a theatrical performance consisting of a variety of shows. Apparently many of the theaters of the time were not very suitable for attendance by women. Pastor thought a place of popular entertainment, free from smoking and drinking, might attract the patronage of women and thus increase the proceeds. Consequently, he opened a variety theater to which women were invited. In order to get their trade, he at first offered practical prizes, such as dress patterns and half tons of coal. He later built a popular theater on Fourteenth Street in New York. To be booked at Tony's was to achieve the heights of success in vaudeville. Lillian Russell, W. C. Fields, and George M. Cohan[9] all appeared there.

One particularly interesting feature at Tony Pastor's place was the development of the topical song. It became the custom to introduce one or two new songs every Monday night, dealing in a comical way with some topic of the times. News events, political situations, new discoveries, and inventions were greeted with song.

Music Festivals

A Serious Type of Entertainment. The music festival represents a more serious type of musical entertainment. It appears to be a direct outgrowth of the music convention

8. Lillian Russell. An American actress and singer (1861-1922). 9. George M. Cohan (kō·hăn′). An American actor-manager and playright (1878-1942).

introduced by Lowell Mason and others. One of the earliest of these festivals was held at Worcester, Massachusetts. After the War between the States, the festivals of the Handel and Haydn Society in Boston introduced music festivals much as we know them now. They were modeled after the English music festivals and proved a great success. At the first one of them, three oratorios, the *Creation, Elijah,* and the *Messiah,* were given on three successive days with a chorus of six to seven hundred singers and an orchestra of seventy-five members. Later, symphony concerts were included as a part of the festivals.

The first in a series of festivals was introduced in Cincinnati, with Theodore Thomas as organizer and conductor. This festival continues at the present time and has greatly influenced the development of serious music in the Middle-West.

Many types of musical festivals came into existence in the years that followed. A few of the more interesting ones will be mentioned.

The Bach Festival. At Bethlehem, Pennsylvania, the annual music festival is devoted to the performance of music by Bach. An interesting feature of the festival there is a prelude by the trombone choir which plays the chorals from the tower of the church located on the campus of Lehigh University.

The Easter Festival. It is no uncommon practice now for thousands of Americans to awaken early on Easter morning to attend a sunrise Easter service. It is believed that one of the annual Easter services held at Winston-Salem, North Carolina, some twenty-five years ago, served as the beginning of these sunrise services. The Moravian congregation there had asked the nationally-known sacred song leader, Homer Rodeheaver, to conduct a song service on the church steps on Easter morning. Rodeheaver was so impressed that he remarked, "Why cannot the whole world sing in a service like this each year?" Since then sunrise services on Easter are held all over the United States from the Atlantic to the Pacific. A picturesque service is

Courtesy Los Angeles County Chamber of Commerce

An annual sunrise Easter service has been held in Hollywood Bowl at Hollywood, California, for many years.

held on Mount Rubidoux in California, another in Hollywood Bowl at Hollywood, California.

A National Folk Festival. The idea of a national folk festival is a recent one. We are indebted to Sarah Gertrude Knott and her interest in folk music for the organization of the first one. As a Carolina teacher, she had a vision of the benefits which might be received from collecting and preserving folk music. It was in St. Louis, during the early nineteen thirties, that she organized the first group of players who went·strolling about the depression-bound city, amusing audiences wherever they might be found with folk songs and dances. Sometimes this was in a park, sometimes in a church, or sometimes on the wharf.

One night an old man asked permission to play his fiddle for the audience. She granted the permission. The next night he followed the band for their next performance. His number pleased the audience. On the following night others appeared, wanting to be on the program. Finally the program was thrown open to anyone who wished to perform.

From her experience of that summer, Miss Knott gained the vision for a great national folk festival, the first of which was held three years later in St. Louis. Talent had been selected from eighteen small festivals which Miss Knott had held. Each year since, the national folk festival has been held. It has given rise to local festivals and regional festivals in various states and sections of the country. The annual folk festival at White Top Mountain in southwest Virginia is one of the well-known ones.

Symphony Orchestras

Theodore Thomas and Orchestra Music. The symphony orchestra, as the type of musical organization we know today, did not exist until some time after the War between the States. Theodore Thomas is largely responsible for establishing the high standards of musicianship and interpretation which we associate with the modern symphony orchestra in America. Thomas was a man who belonged particularly to the period of expansion in the United States. He came here nearly a century ago and lived here until he died at the age of seventy. During those years, he gave pleasure through his orchestra to people all over the country, in cities from Boston and New York to San Francisco. The story of the organization of orchestras in many large cities is to a great extent the story of Theodore Thomas trying to develop fine orchestral music in America. He felt that what this country needed to make it musical was a good orchestra and plenty of concerts. These he endeavored to supply.

Thomas came here from Esens, Germany, when he was a boy of ten. Not many years afterwards he began playing in a New York orchestra. He was ambitious to become a great violinist and while he was still in his teens he made a concert tour as a violin soloist. Not only was he his own advance agent, tacking up the cards advertising his concerts, but he also was the man who took tickets at the door. When the audience had arrived, he left his post at the door and hurried around to the stage entrance to appear a few minutes later to give his concert.

He always watched the actions of the leaders of the orchestra during rehearsals. When he was twenty-five, because of the death of the leader of the orchestra in which he was playing, he got his chance to lead. He was thrilled by the experience; from that time his career was devoted to the development of orchestras in cities of America. A few years after this experience he organized his first permanent orchestra and made a concert tour, going at that time as far west as Chicago and St. Louis.

Thomas' work with orchestras is somewhat comparable to Gilmore's work with jubilees. Where others were satisfied with making a success of a single program, nothing less than creating a taste on the part of the American public for the best in music satisfied Thomas.

Among the great orchestras of the country which he conducted were the New York Philharmonic, the Brooklyn Philharmonic, and the Boston Symphony. One of the high points of his career came in 1891, when he was asked to organize a permanent orchestra in Chicago. He accepted the offer and worked in that city until his death. After his death, Frederick Stock was selected to conduct the Chicago orchestra. Stock held this position for thirty-seven years, until his death in 1942, and steadily raised still higher the standards of excellence set by Thomas.

The Damrosch Family. Seldom have there been three names in one family so intimately linked with a musical development as those of three members of the Damrosch family who are associated with orchestral and other serious music.

The father, Leopold Damrosch,[10] came to America as director of a male chorus. In 1874 he founded the New York Oratorio Society. He later spent a season with the New York Philharmonic Society and then became conductor of the newly formed New York Symphony Society in 1878.

The New York Symphony Society had been formed as a competitor to the Philharmonic Society which Theodore Thomas was then conducting. There was great rivalry between the two men who did so much in producing fine orchestral music. In fact this rivalry probably influenced Thomas to go to Chicago and organize his own orchestra.

When Leopold Damrosch died, his son Walter became his successor as conductor of both the Oratorio Society and

10. Leopold Damrosch (dăm'rŏsh). A German-American musician (1832-1885).

the New York Symphony. The New York Symphony and the New York Philharmonic finally merged into one organization, and Damrosch served as one of the conductors. The following year, however, he gave up his work there in order to give his full time to radio broadcasting.

It is in this connection that the name and voice of Walter Damrosch have become familiar to nearly every boy and girl in the land. He believes that the boys and girls of today are the music lovers of tomorrow. So he has given a considerable amount of his time over the radio, as well as in other ways, to give to the youth of this nation a deep appreciation of fine musical experiences. He has engaged in much educational work over the radio, conducting programs especially for school children of the nation for the purpose of helping them to become familiar with the masterpieces of symphonic music.

Frank Damrosch, the older son of Leopold, was also well known in music circles for his work in promoting young people's concerts and as founder of People's Choral Union, an organization in which working men and women had an opportunity to enjoy singing together.

Carnegie Hall. Closely connected with the work of the Damrosch family is the rise of Carnegie Hall as a music center. When Walter Damrosch was on a ship sailing to Europe to study, he met young Andrew Carnegie, who was then on his honeymoon trip. Carnegie had been successful in iron and oil investments and had accumulated much wealth. Damrosch told Carnegie about his concerts, about the work of the New York Oratorio Society, and about how little space for rehearsals and performances there was in the auditorium. Carnegie became interested, and, because of the friendship which developed between these two men, Carnegie Hall was built.

The hall was opened with a five-day festival in which the Symphony Society and the Oratorio Society had charge of the concerts. Tchaikovsky[11] and other artists were engaged for the opening programs. It is said that either music or the spoken word could be heard perfectly and distinctly in any part of the hall.

The Philharmonic Society of New York broadcasts from Carnegie Hall of Music every Sunday afternoon during the concert season. The concerts are given by the Columbia Broadcasting Company without a commercial sponsor as a contribution to America's musical enjoyment. Carnegie Hall has really become a cultural center of New York City for, in addition to the music halls, it has studios for actors, painters, dancers, and music teachers.

Light and Comic Opera

Interest in Light Opera. The American public is undoubtedly more interested in light opera than in any other kind of musical drama. This interest dates back to 1879 when Gilbert and Sullivan's English operetta, *Pinafore,* first captivated American audiences.

The two men whose names are most often linked with light opera in the United States are Victor Herbert[12] and Reginald De Koven.[13]

Victor Herbert. Herbert was born in Ireland and was educated in Germany. He was a fine cellist and a great conductor. It was Herbert who, after the death of Patrick Gilmore, became bandmaster of the Twenty-second Regimental Band which had played in Gilmore's jubilees. He

---

11. Tchaikovsky (chĭ·kôf′skĕ). A Russian orchestral composer (1840-1893).
12. Victor Herbert. An Irish-American orchestra conductor and composer (1859-1924). 13. Reginald De Koven (dĕ kō′vĕn). An American composer (1861-1920).

also conducted the Pittsburgh Symphony and was guest conductor of the New York Philharmonic. At one time he was first cellist in the Metropolitan Opera orchestra.

In spite of our changing times, Herbert's fame seems to grow greater with the passing of the years. His music is constantly sought by amateurs and is played and sung over the radio and in the movies. Some of his best-known songs are "I'm Falling in Love with Some One," "Kiss Me Again," "Toyland," "Sweethearts," and "Gypsy Sweetheart." His best-known operas are probably *Babes in Toyland* and *Naughty Marietta.*

De Koven's Works. Reginald De Koven was born a few years after Victor Herbert. He was to rival Herbert in fame as a writer of light opera. It was his *Robin Hood* that the Boston Ideal Pinafore Company gave for a thousand performances. It is said that over a million copies of "Oh, Promise Me," from this opera, have been sold.

The Highwayman is considered his best work. Other popular light operas he produced are *The Fencing Master, Foxy Quiller, Red Feather, Maid Marion, The Little Duchess, Rob Roy,* and *Nut Brown Ale.*

A Modern Group of Writers of Light Opera. The twentieth century ushered into the musical world a group of younger men whose productions have been popular with theatergoers. In this group may be found the names of Friml, Kern, Romberg, Berlin, and Gershwin.

Rudolph Friml stands out in the musical comedy field. His *Rose Marie* has also been popularized in pictures by Nelson Eddy and Jeanette MacDonald. His first light opera was *The Firefly.* Another light opera which has pleased the public is *The Vagabond King.*

We know Kern for his *Sally, Show Boat, Cat and the Fiddle,* and *Music in the Air.* Romberg has given us *My*

Maryland, The New Moon, and *Desert Song.* Irving Berlin belongs in the list of song writers rather than with the group of dramatic producers, yet he is of the group of those now influencing the standing of the stage. Gershwin has given us the big hit, *Of Thee I Sing,* which is certain to have its place in musical comedy history, and which won for Gershwin the Pulitzer prize.

The Metropolitan Opera

Grand Opera for the Wealthy. The interest of New York City in grand opera has been mentioned previously. Opera at first found a place for performances in the old Park Theater. Shortly before the War between the States it was moved to the Academy of Music. The interest in that form of entertainment had increased so greatly, and the audiences had grown to such an extent that, twenty-five years later, the Academy of Music had come to be regarded as inadequate for the needs of opera lovers.

In those days, showing an interest in opera and maintaining a box at the opera were considered indications of great wealth. Desirable boxes at the Academy were retained year after year by the wealthy. Holders of the boxes are said to have refused offers of $30,000 by rich people who wanted to buy a certain desirable location. Many of the newly rich became dissatisfied when they were unable to get boxes at the Academy, and some of them decided to build a larger opera house with far more boxes than the Academy had.

For this reason the Metropolitan Opera House was built and opened in 1883. The lot on which it was built cost $600,000. The building was modeled after the theaters of Europe and contained a triple row of boxes. Its estimated

The Metropolitan Opera House had its boxes arranged
in a "diamond horseshoe."

cost was more than a million and a half dollars, a large
sum at that time.

Since an outward show of interest in opera was one way
to make a display of wealth and build up social standing,
it is no wonder that on the opening night the jeweled
audience represented more of a social function than a sin-
cere appreciation of an artistic stage production. It was
often remarked that the appearance of the audience seated
in what was called the "gold horseshoe" of boxes was a
spectacle more grand than could be presented on the stage
itself.

In the building of the Metropolitan, more attention was paid to the number of boxes than was given to the acoustics[14] or to the vision of the audience; so when, some ten years later, a fire was started which made necessary a reconstruction and rearrangement of the building, the Metropolitan Opera was probably rendered a real service. The building was reopened with a great show of splendor. It was under a reorganized management known as the Metropolitan Opera and Real Estate Company. This time the array of boxes became known as the "diamond horseshoe." In order to obtain a title to a box in the opera house, one had to subscribe to three hundred and thirty shares of stock at a par value of one hundred dollars per share. Thus one can see that the directors of the company had to be men who were wealthy and socially prominent in New York City.

The period after the second opening of the opera house witnessed an array of vocal talent that perhaps has not been surpassed. The house rang time after time with applause for such artists as Nordica,[15] Gadski,[16] Schumann-Heink,[17] and a host of others.

Caruso. Enrico Caruso[18] became the outstanding singer of the season of 1903-1904. For that season he signed an agreement to sing in twenty-four performances. The following year he gave thirty performances which brought him more than one thousand dollars each.

Caruso's popularity as an opera singer has never yet been equalled in this country. He sang in America for a

14. acoustics (à·kōōs′tĭks). Qualities that determine the value of a room with respect to the ease with which sounds produced in it may be heard. 15. Nordica (nôr′dĭ·kà). An American operatic soprano (1859-1914). 16. Gadski (gät′skĭ). A German singer, famous for Wagnerian roles (1871-1932). 17. Schumann-Heink (shōō′män-hīngk′). A German-American contralto (1861-1936). 18. Enrico Caruso (kä rōō′zô). An Italian operatic tenor (1873-1921).

period of less than ten years, making about six hundred appearances. During that time he brought financial stability to the Victor Talking Machine Company through the sale of his records, and to the Metropolitan Opera Company through his singing of operatic roles.

Opera over the Radio. During the years which have followed, the Metropolitan Opera Company has experienced many changes. The building has been rebuilt for a third time and the expensive tiers of boxes removed. The development of radio and the depression of the 1930's appeared to be determining its end. Wealthy supporters of the Metropolitan, who had been assessed forty-five hundred dollars annually, declared they could no longer pay this amount. For a time the opera was financed largely through the sale of subscription tickets for a season composed of a series of operas, and by the sale of tickets for individual performances. Finally, one of the very forces which seemed to threaten its closing has placed the Metropolitan on a firm financial foundation.

In 1931, opera was first broadcast over the radio. Opera broadcasts became so popular that, when an appeal was made over the air for support by subscription for the organization, the response was exceedingly generous. Metropolitan Opera is now assured to American audiences for some time to come.

Bands

Popularity of Band Entertainment. Few if any types of music have given more genuine pleasure to the American people than that of the brass band. Band music is especially fitted for large outdoor gatherings. One cannot imagine a Fourth of July celebration, a Memorial Day parade, or a political gathering without a brass band. All over the country in the summer time, from the bandstand of the small crossroads town to large stadiums in city parks, one finds the American public enjoying band concerts. Band music has served as a great socializing force for adults and children in many communities. In more recent years the high school band has been a means of interesting many young people in a more serious study of music.

The Military Band. Bands are usually divided into two classes, military bands and concert bands. As soon as the United States had an army, a band was provided. The early army required two musicians for every company. Later, these musicians were organized into regimental bands known by number, for example, the Seventh Regimental Band, or the Twenty-second Regimental Band.

The most famous military band in the United States is the Marine Band. This was provided for by law almost as soon as the United States became a nation. In the beginning, the Marine Band consisted of thirty-two members, sixteen drummers and sixteen fife players. Shortly afterwards this drum corps was changed to a brass band. Near the beginning of the twentieth century the number of players was increased to sixty and it is now sixty-five. The members of the band are enlisted in the United States Marines. They are subject to army drill and military discipline. The leader has the rank of captain and receives the salary of a captain. There have been only fourteen regularly appointed leaders of the Marine Band since its beginning. The most famous of these was John Philip Sousa.

For nearly a century, the Marine Band has appeared regularly in concerts in Washington, usually at the Capitol or on the grounds of the White House. It plays for all functions of national importance in Washington. It has played at every New Year's reception at the White House since 1800 and at inaugural balls since the time of President Madison. It may be heard frequently in concerts over the radio.

The United States Marine Band is a very famous military band. It is the oldest American military band, founded in 1798.

The Concert Band. The name of Patrick S. Gilmore is the first one to be closely associated with concert bands. It was through his work that the military band became important as a concert band. Gilmore was for many years the leader of the Twenty-second Regimental Band. He had a passion for band music and strove constantly for perfect performance. The band music of his jubilees was the best ever heard in the United States up to that time. His greatest contribution was that of providing for a band with well-balanced instrumentation. He frequently argued with orchestra conductors that the music of one hundred band players, if they were properly chosen, was far superior to that of a symphony orchestra.

During the period of the '90's, many local bands were organized. Leaders were usually local men with little training. There was little music, and many members played from memory, each using his own version of the melody. The leader would announce the number and the key, and each player would give his own interpretation. The result might be interesting but not necessarily musical.

Today, bands are well organized and commonly have use of an adequate music library. A concert band usually plays lighter music with a large proportion of marches or music with a martial rhythm. Much symphony music is easily adapted to band arrangement, and many really good concerts are given. Today the concert band at its best is represented by the band of Edwin Franko Goldman, which plays regularly each summer in New York City. In one year Goldman's band gave sixty open-air concerts. The following list indicates the quality and variety of music played: three Wagner programs, two Bach programs, two grand opera programs, two Beethoven programs, one Victor Herbert program, two original band music programs, and one Tchaikovsky program.

John Philip Sousa. The one name which is almost synonymous with band music is that of John Philip Sousa. He was known as the "march king," and his "Stars and Stripes Forever" has been called the trade-mark of American music, for if that selection is played in any part of the world, people recognize it as readily as they do our national anthem.

Sousa was leader of the Marine Band for twelve years; then he resigned to organize his own band. Sousa's band became world famous. Concerts were given all over the United States and in Europe as well.

Sousa became famous as a composer of band music as well as a band leader. He has written marches, primarily. Many of them were composed for special occasions or for use by certain organizations. For example, "High School Cadets" was written for a high school in Washington, D. C., "King Cotton March" was written for the Louisiana Exposition, and "Semper Fidelis" was written for the United States Marines. "Stars and Stripes Forever" was written on Sousa's return from a trip to Europe. He said the march was a translation of his feelings at that time. His philosophy of music is expressed in his own quotation, "Music is the finest profession in the world because it is the only one that does not bring sorrow."

At his death, the John Philip Sousa library of music was bequeathed to the University of Illinois at Urbana. It is probably the most extensive library of band music in existence. When ready for shipment, the library filled forty-two trunks and included nine tons of compositions.

CHAPTER XIV

POPULAR MUSIC

Songs

Fashion in Popular Songs. A light type of music which, because of its appeal to a large number of people, is called popular music, reflects the nature of the period in which it exists. In the period of expansion, a variety of popular music appeared. After the War between the States, popular music was largely of the sentimental ballad type. These songs were followed in the gay nineties by songs of a livelier, happier mood. In the early nineteen hundreds came the "coon songs" and "rag tunes" and so on. Only a few of the popular selections ever live very long, except to be used as an example of their time, just as a hoop skirt or a "merry widow" hat is used to illustrate a period of fashion in women's dress. These songs pass out of existence because they are no longer timely. Popular music includes those selections which people enjoy hearing in their homes, and which people whistle or sing at their work, or dance to in the evening. Songs and dance music are the two groups under which popular music is usually considered.

Three types of songs represent those popular from the middle to the close of the nineteenth century—the sentimental, the romantic, and the gay or ragtime tunes. The sentimental type of song may be illustrated by such songs as "Silver Threads among the Gold," "When You and I Were Young, Maggie," "Grandfather's Clock," "Little Lost Child," "Carry Me Back to Old Virginny," "The Picture That Is Turned to the Wall," and "Listen to the Mocking Bird."

The first popular song to sweep the country was "After the Ball." It was established as a hit when it was played by Sousa's recently organized band at the Columbian Exposition in Chicago. The song was composed by Charles K. Harris, who also wrote other popular sentimental songs, among them being "Always in the Way" and "Hello, Central, Give Me Heaven." The "Bird in a Gilded Cage" was sung by thousands and wept over by many. A somewhat gayer type of sentimental popular song is represented by "The Good Old Summer Time," "In the Shade of the Old Apple Tree," "Put on Your Old Gray Bonnet," and "By the Light of the Silvery Moon."

The romantic type of popular song was represented at one time by Indian songs, which bore no resemblance to Indian music except in name. "Red Wing" and "Hiawatha" will be remembered by many of the older people today. Then came a group of Negro songs such as "Ma Picanniny Babe," "Shortnin' Bread," and "Kentucky Babe." Irish songs, including "Little Annie Rooney" and "Maggie Murphy," were the fashion at another time. Oriental titles, such as "The Streets of Cairo," were popular with some. Hawaiian songs had an appeal for a considerable time. A whole group of state songs were in vogue at one time. These included "My Little Georgia Rose," "On the Banks of the Wabash," and "Missouri Waltz." Songs such as "The Man on the Flying Trapeze" were designed to emphasize the romance of certain occupations. The era of the waltz song enjoyed a longer period of popularity

LISTEN TO THE MOCKING-BIRD

A. H.

ALICE HAWTHORNE

1. I'm dream-ing now of Hal - ly, sweet Hal - ly, sweet
2. Ah! well I yet re - mem-ber, re - mem-ber, re -

Hal - ly, I'm dream - ing now of Hal - ly, For the
mem - ber, Ah! well I yet re - mem-ber, When we

thought of her is one that nev - er dies; She's
gath - er'd in the cot - ton side by side; 'Twas

sleep - ing in the val - ley, the val - ley, the
in the mild Sep - tem - ber, Sep - tem - ber, Sep -

val - ley, She's sleep - ing in the val - ley, And the
tem - ber, 'Twas in the mild Sep - tem - ber, And the

mock - ing - bird is sing - ing where she lies.
mock - ing - bird was sing - ing far and wide.

CHORUS

Lis - ten to the mock - ing - bird, Lis - ten to the

mock - ing - bird, The mock - ing - bird still sing - ing o'er her

grave, Lis - ten to the mock - ing - bird, Lis - ten to the

mock - ing - bird, Still sing - ing where the weep - ing wil - lows wave.

From THE NEW AMERICAN SONG BOOK, *copyrighted by Hall & McCreary Company. Used by permission.*

than most of the others. This is no doubt due to the fact that the waltz was the most popular form of dance for about twenty-five years. From "Two Little Girls in Blue" to "Beautiful Ohio," couples glided to the one-two-three rhythm.

The early "coon songs" and ragtime songs were generally introduced by Negro minstrel shows.

Music of the Spanish-American War. The Spanish-American War, unlike most of our other wars, produced little music worth remembering. The songs most associated with the war were not really written for it. Sousa's "Stars and Stripes Forever" answered the need for a patriotic march. "Just Break the News to Mother" was popular and expressed the homesickness of the boys who were away fighting. It is interesting to contrast the sentiment of this song with "Keep the Home Fires Burning" of the First World War. "My Sweetheart Went Down with the Maine" was another sentimental song written at the time of the Spanish-American War.

A more cheerful and extremely popular song of the war was "There'll Be a Hot Time in the Old Town, Tonight." The significant story is told that a French reporter, in preparing for his paper an account of American troops entering Manila, wrote that the bands played two national anthems, "The Star-Spangled Banner" and "There'll Be a Hot Time in the Old Town, Tonight."

There seem to be several stories concerning the origin of "A Hot Time." One of them says that it came from Colorado and that "Old Town" refers to the original mining camp of Cripple Creek. The tune is said to be one sung by an old Negro mammy who lived near the Cripple Creek railway depot. In the boom days of the nineties, one of the actors at this local theater needed a new song and set words to the tune he had heard the old Negress singing. The Cripple Creek company of Colorado National Guards was sent to Manila, and its band took along the tune which had been especially arranged for them.

Song Pluggers. The years from the nineties to well into the twentieth century have been called the "golden age" of popular song writing in this country. New songs appeared in great numbers. Publishing sheet music became a thriving business. In order to sell a large number of copies of a song, it became necessary to make it popular among many people. As soon as a new song came out, singers were employed to boost it in public by singing it in beer parlors, taverns, variety shows, and vaudeville. The singers were called "song pluggers," and their boosting of the song was called "plugging."

Tin Pan Alley. Tin Pan Alley for many years was the main avenue for publishing and popularizing popular songs. The name was given to a neighborhood where a group of song publishers in New York City had their places of business. Just how the name came into existence seems uncertain. One of the most likely explanations is that it came to describe the little rooms in the offices of song publishers in which song pluggers were schooled in the songs they were to sing. Each little room contained a cheap piano with a tin pan sound. As numbers of the publishers tended to establish their businesses in the same neighborhood, the group and the streets they were located on at the time came to be known as Tin Pan Alley.

It is said that the publisher's real work didn't begin until the close of day, when he left his office and set forth to persuade the managers of any of the fifteen hundred or more places of amusement to plug his new songs. This was the only way of creating a market for his wares.

Dance Music

A Typical Dance Program. The volunteer fire department was a leading factor in the social activities of many of the newly formed communities on the advancing frontier. A program for a fireman's ball in the early fifties illustrates the kind of dances popular at the time.

GRAND BALL

given by

Jackson Fire Dept.

July 4th, 1850

Programme of Dances

Plain Quadrille[1]	Plain Quadrille
Waltz	Waltz
Plain Quadrille	Sicilian Circle
Mazurka[2]	Gallop
Lancers[3]	French Four
Polka	Polka
Plain Quadrille	Quadrille (Old Dan Tucker)
Schottische	Waltz
Varsovienne[4]	Virginia Reel
Quadrille (Basket)	Schottische
Danish Polka[5]	Quadrille (Pop Goes the Weasel)
Supper March	Waltz

Tickets, including supper—$5 Ladies Free

"We won't go home 'till morning,

We'll dance 'till break o' day."

1. Quadrille (kwŏ·drĭl′). A square dance having four couples in each set.
2. Mazurka (má·zûr′ká). A Polish dance and music for the dance. 3. Lancers. A set of dances. 4. Varsovienne (vär′sŏ′vyĕn′). A dance similar to a polka. 5. Polka. A lively, hopping dance of Bohemian origin performed by two persons.

The Cake Walk. A little before 1900, a new step called the cake walk appeared on a few dance floors. It immediately became popular, and within the next two years it was being included in nearly all the social dances. It represents the first appearance of a Negro dance movement in ballroom dancing. It created much the same furor among the lovers of the waltz and two step of that day as the Charleston and "big apple" did a generation or two later.

The cake walk was not really a dance; it was a walk. Men and women singly and in couples stepped high to a lively tune, turned corners precisely, carried their heads high, and generally presented as elegant an appearance as possible. The couple which executed the walk most perfectly was awarded the prize of the evening, a large cake.

The introduction of the cake walk step or movement into dancing of course had an influence on the dance music of the day. "The Darktown Strutters' Ball" was a representative dance selection.

Ragtime. Shortly after the beginning of the twentieth century, music called "ragtime" spread like wildfire over the United States. It appeared in 1918-1920 as jazz. By 1935 it had become swing. All this music had the American popular song as the point of beginning.

For a long time Negro minstrels had shuffled and clogged to what were called "coon songs." They had taken Negro work songs, spirituals, or popular songs of the day, and had changed them into an accompaniment for their dances. The main characteristic of all these dances was syncopation, or shifting the rhythmic accent from the usually accented or strong beat (first and third in $\frac{4}{4}$ time) to the unaccented or weak beat (second and fourth in $\frac{4}{4}$ time). Negroes called their syncopations "ragging." It represented boisterousness, gaiety, and escape from things formal or

The cake walk, originally a Negro dance step, became popular at the close of the nineteenth century.

humdrum. Some popular ragtime numbers were "The Georgia Camp Meeting," "Maple Leaf Rag," and "Kitten on the Keys."

Blues. Ragtime and blues are so much alike that it is hard to tell where one leaves off and the other begins. The first blues song to become known was "The Memphis Blues," produced by a Negro, William C. Handy.

Blues had been sung for a long time before Handy ever wrote them down. The old-time blues are as much a characteristic of Negro life as the Negro spiritual. Spirituals were sung in groups and served as an outlet for the religious enthusiasm of the Negro. Blues were sung as a solo and served as a lament for the Negro's misfortunes. There were blues bemoaning hard times, fire, high water, tornadoes, and the like. The blues songs usually expressed a great deal of Negro philosophy. They were simple melodies, sung over and over in three-line stanzas, with a chorus like the following:

> If you ketch fire an dey ain' no water roun'
> If you ketch fire an dey ain' no water roun'
> If you ketch fire an dey ain' no water roun'
> Throw yo' trunk out de window and let de shack
>   buhn down.

They were sung in a melancholy tone of voice and ended in almost a wail. The difference usually given between the original blues and those of today is that the blues started as a form of folk music, and today they exist both as a form of music and as a style of playing any music.

William C. Handy had heard and sung Negro blues when he was a lad in the far South. He was at one time a band leader and soloist with a group of minstrels, and finally organized his own band and moved to Memphis.

Tennessee. During a political campaign, he decided to write a campaign song to help elect a certain man as mayor of Memphis. He selected as a tune a blues song he had heard years before. His band played it over and over during the campaign. The man was elected. Later Handy wrote out the music just as the band had played it and called it "Memphis Blues." Publishers rejected it and Handy had one thousand copies printed at his own expense. These he finally sold to a man who took them north and received a good financial profit from them.

While the "Memphis Blues" was the first of the blues, "St. Louis Blues," also written by Handy, is the most famous. Handy took a street song heard in East St. Louis, and from it wrote the popular selection.

Semi-Popular and Serious Music

Ethelbert Nevin. Two men of this period wrote music which is of a more serious nature, yet some of it has become as well known to American people as the folk song or the so-called popular song. One of these men was Ethelbert Nevin.[6]

Nevin has been compared by some to Stephen C. Foster, for the events in their lives as well as their music have been somewhat similar. When Nevin was a young man he wished to take up piano playing as a profession. In those days music as a profession still did not rank very high; so at the advice of his father he became a bank clerk. He was not happy in this work. His parents finally agreed to a musical career, and he studied in Boston and under some of the best teachers in Europe. He achieved brilliant success as a pianist, but we know him best for his songs. "The

6. Ethelbert Nevin (něv'ĭn). An American composer (1862-1901).

Rosary" is said to be a perfect example of an art song. "O, That We Two Were Maying," a duet frequently heard at lyceum or Chautauqua programs, was first written when Nevin was eighteen years of age. His "Narcissus" was a piano selection known everywhere in the early nineteen hundreds. Next to "The Rosary," his song which attained the greatest success was "Mighty Lak' a Rose." Nevin never saw this song in print, for it was found lying on his desk after his death. Like Foster, he died at an early age.

Edward MacDowell. Edward MacDowell was one of the most important of early American writers of serious music. He is best known for his piano pieces. His "To a Wild Rose" and "To a Water Lily" have probably been played at piano recitals and concerts more often than any other American musical compositions. MacDowell also wrote some songs, including "The Robin Sings in the Apple Tree," "Slumber Song," and "The West Wind Croons in the Cedar Trees." He wrote four sonatas, two piano concertos, several works for orchestra, and three symphonic poems.[7] He made a number of concert tours and became the first head of the music department of Columbia University, New York City.

An interesting story is told in connection with "To a Wild Rose." It was MacDowell's custom to write a few bars of exercises each day for practice. These exercises were crumpled and thrown aside into the fire or in the waste basket. One day, in cleaning his room, Mrs. MacDowell came across a crumpled piece of paper which had missed the waste basket. She picked it up and looked at it. She was interested in the music she saw there and called it to her husband's attention. It became the well-known piano piece "To a Wild Rose."

7. symphonic (sĭm·fŏn′ĭk) poems. Musical compositions based on poetic subjects

MacDowell was greatly interested in nature, and many of his compositions have been on subjects of nature. He bought an estate of forest land at Peterboro, in New Hampshire, where he spent the summers composing music. It was there that he composed his *Woodland Sketches*.

Probably his best-known orchestral work is his *Second*, or *Indian, Suite*. This consists of five movements. The first is "Legend," with its first theme from the Iroquois tribe and second from the Chippewa; the second movement is the "Love Song," with an Iowa Indian love song as the theme; the third, "In War Time," has a Dacota theme and suggestions of the Iroquois scalp dances; the fourth is called "Dirge," with a song of mourning as the theme; the fifth, or "Village Festival," has as its theme the Iroquois women's dance and war song. The music for the suite was suggested for the most part by Indian melodies. MacDowell is reported to have said that of all his music, the "Dirge" in the *Indian Suite* pleased him most.

After MacDowell's death, his widow gave the estate at Peterboro, New Hampshire, to establish a MacDowell Colony as a memorial to her husband. It serves as a summer home for artists, composers, poets, and writers. Recently, those interested in MacDowell's music expressed a desire that the name of the great American composer be further honored. A music festival was held for the purpose of bringing forward works by American composers, particularly the works of present or former members of the MacDowell Colony.

Musical Instruments

Musical Instruments in the Home. There was a tradition among the substantial home-loving people who made up the population during the period of expansion, that every well-brought-up young woman should have certain accomplishments, such as the ability to paint china, recite literary selections, and, most important of all, to play some musical instrument. The piano and organ were the preferred instruments. Nearly every little girl was given music lessons regardless of whether she had talent or not. Music teachers traveled about from house to house or held classes in their homes. After several weeks' struggle with little girls in pig tails, or with their less willing brothers, the teacher would hold a recital for parents and friends. Parents and teacher beamed while the beginners inaudibly counted the one-two-three for "In May," and the more advanced ones triumphantly produced "Poet and Peasant" or "Melody in F." One can see that either a piano or an organ was a necessary part of home-making equipment.

The Parlor Organ. People who could afford pianos bought them; those who had less money bought organs. Many a midwestern farm woman carefully saved money from the sale of chickens, eggs, and butter that she might have the luxury of a parlor organ.

Few of these instruments are now in existence except in isolated farm homes, rural churches, one-room schools, or in antique shops. Although they are frequently ridiculed now, they served a very definite need at a time when the people of a great region were hungry for music of any kind.

The cylinder organ originated at the beginning of the eighteenth century. Since it was small, it could be carried along with other household articles on the long journey westward. Consequently, these instruments were occasionally found in the American homes of the West. They consisted of a small table cabinet with a barrel or cylinder turned with a crank. The barrel had pins which, in turn-

Some years ago, nearly every little girl learned to play the piano.

ing, lowered levers. These in turn played notes. They were at one time widely used in churches and residences.

"Canned" Music. Many people who wished to have music in the home, but who did not have either the opportunity or the talent to learn music, came to be satisfied with a substitute which was known as "canned" music.

The first mechanical piano was patented near the beginning of the twentieth century. It was known as the pianola or player piano. The machinery of the player and the perforated roll of music were on the inside so that at a glance one could scarcely tell this from the ordinary kind of piano.

Even before player pianos came into use, Thomas A. Edison had invented the phonograph. For the first time it was possible to reproduce the human voice and other musical sounds on a musical instrument in one's own home. The market was flooded with records which gave the people an opportunity to hear all kinds of popular songs and dance numbers, as well as selections from operas and other masterpieces. Recordings of orchestra and band selections outsold all others.

The original recordings were made on wax cylinders, dark brown in color, and shaped like a small tin can with both ends cut out. Most of the phonographs had horns which really acted as loud speakers. The machines had to be wound up before playing each record. Later, flat discs came on the market, the phonograph was improved, and sales mounted so rapidly that the machines became serious competitors to pianos.

The radio has broken into the field of the phonograph. There is still a steady demand for dance records, but little for popular songs. The records which sell most readily now are albums of serious music including recordings of entire symphonies, suites, oratorios, and even entire operas.

1. How was music carried into the Northwest?
2. In what ways has the Mormon church promoted music?
3. What type of song was popular during the time of the gold rush? How do you account for its popularity?
4. Why did people who lived in the Rocky Mountain states decide to promote music? What were some of the results of their efforts?
5. Why was the cowboy so greatly interested in music?
6. What musical instruments were considered important among the Indians? What use did they make of these instruments?
7. How did it happen that more people attended concerts during the latter part of the nineteenth and early part of the twentieth century than ever before?
8. Of what importance were the lyceum and the Chautauqua?
9. What did Tony Pastor do to help the development of vaudeville? Why was vaudeville so popular in those days?
10. How was the national folk festival developed?
11. For what type of musical entertainment was Theodore Thomas best known?
12. Why should the name of Walter Damrosch be so well known to school children as well as to adults in the United States?
13. What type of musical compositions did Victor Herbert and Reginald De Koven produce? Name two compositions by each composer.
14. What was Tin Pan Alley? What was its significance?
15. How did ragtime originate?
16. What type of music did William C. Handy introduce? What was the origin of his music?
17. For what type of music is Edward MacDowell best known? What is usually considered his best orchestral work?

Suggested Activities

1. Make a collection of songs which reflect the various kinds of cowboy activities, for example, driving, branding, or telling stories while sitting around camp fires.

2. Find a number of songs which represent the various occupations of the early settlers of the West and learn to sing them.

3. Make up some stanzas of your own for "The Old Chisholm Trail."

4. Draw the old Chisholm Trail on a map of the United States.

5. Write parodies on "Oh, Susannah" and "Camptown Races."

6. Write a story or description in which you contrast the modern migration of Okies to California with that of the forty-niners.

7. Prepare and give an oral report on the life of John Philip Sousa, Edward MacDowell, or Victor Herbert.

8. Write a brief account of the history of opera at the Metropolitan Opera House. Get photographs of opera stars to use or draw illustrations for your story.

9. *Class exercise:* With a group of your classmates, learn to do some square dances. Plan a party or program and do these dances for your own pleasure or for the entertainment of guests.

10. *Class exercise:* Plan an assembly program about the westward movement and mining activities. Prepare several stories or poems for the program about crossing the plains, mining, Indian fights, and famous scouts and sing appropriate songs.

11. *Class exercise:* Write and act out a play, the theme of which represents the experiences of Jenny Lind in her concert tour or of Theodore Thomas in his career.

12. *Class exercise:* With the help of your teacher, invite a local fiddler to come to school and play dance tunes, or invite a square dance caller to show the square dance figures and calls.

PART FOUR

MUSIC IN A FULL-GROWN NATION

In the old days, when a young man became twenty-one years old, he was said to have reached his estate. Frequently his father gave him land or money from which he was expected to make his own living and to establish his own home. He was a full-grown man.

Years ago the United States reached its estate. For a long time this country has been recognized as an independent nation and a world power. Shortly after the Spanish-American War, the United States discovered itself in the midst of world politics. It had become a full-grown nation. Upon the cultures which were brought here from other countries, a new and different culture had been built. The music in this culture had changed and developed as its people had changed and developed. Today, in this mature nation, music is within the reach of nearly every inhabitant, no matter where he lives and no matter whether he is rich or poor.

Each day, as the people of our country go about their daily work, they find music all about them. The housewife turns on the radio to speed up her dishwashing or ironing. The milkman and newsboy whistle at their work. The school day begins with singing. Soothing radio music in a dentist's office relaxes taut nerves. A dance orchestra furnishes the accompaniment for dancing, and the nickel music box in a restaurant grinds out popular tunes. The rhythm of a drum corps proclaims a military drill, and gay marching music keeps up the morale of soldiers. There is music for weddings and music for funerals, music in the classic theater and in the cheap dance hall in a city slum district. There is music in the isolated farm home and the mountain cabin as well as in the apartment home of the city dweller. Music is everywhere.

In Part Four we shall find how music has become such a vital part of American life, and how it has been brought to all our people in so many different ways.

CHAPTER XV

SCIENTIFIC INVENTIONS AND MUSIC

The Radio

The Influence of Scientific Inventions on Music. The part which science and inventions have played in popularizing music, and in taking it even to the remotest sections of the country, is a fascinating story. Erno Rapee,[1] a well-known orchestra conductor, has said that the study of music and an understanding of mechanical instruments are inseparable in this age. In his opinion, each supplements the other. This is true, for it is impossible for us to think of the music of modern times without immediately associating it with the radio, the movies, or the phonograph. The telephone, the telegraph, and modern means of transportation, also, have played supporting roles. All of these inventions have been responsible for an increased interest in music and for bringing it within the reach of every American at a very low cost.

A Joke and a Prophecy. How the people of London must have laughed over a cartoon which appeared in the humorous magazine, *Punch*, over sixty years ago. "Impossible!" you hear them say. The cartoon showed the fireplace in an English drawing room. Above and below the fireplace were several dials or circles resembling clock

1. Erno Rapee (rä·pā′). A conductor of theater orchestras (1891-   ).

faces. Before the fireplace stood the mistress of the house, apparently giving directions to her young servant. "Now recollect, Robert," she was represented as saying, "at a quarter to nine turn on the 'Voi che sapete' from Covent Garden, at ten let in the stringed quartette from Saint James's Hall, and at eleven turn the last quartette from *Rigoletto* on. But mind you, close one tap before opening the other!" The cartoon was evidently intended as ridicule of the telephone which had been invented only two years before. We smile, for it really was a prophecy. In less than a half century the "impossible" events portrayed in the cartoon became an everyday occurrence.

Beginnings of the Radio. Radio had its beginning as a means of communicating wireless telegraphic codes. A quarter of a century ago, David Sarnoff, later president of Radio Corporation of America, outlined a plan for changing radio from a mere means of communication to a household utility in the same sense as the piano or phonograph.

The earliest receiving sets were homemade. Manufacturers of parts for the sets began to transmit a very crude sort of entertainment in order to increase the sale of parts. Then the manufacturers began to sell fully assembled receiving sets. These first sets were very crude. The earliest of them had head phones, a contrivance which fastened over the ears and looked like the receivers used by telephone operators. Only one person could listen at a time. Next, a loud speaker and music box combination was devised. The tubes were in a box, and the sound came out into the room through a large horn similar to the old-fashioned phonograph horn. This was an improvement, for now the whole family could listen at one time, and there were no arguments as to who should use the head phones next.

The Story of the First Broadcast. Doubtless you have turned the dial of your radio to get station KDKA of Pittsburgh. Did you know that this station is credited with being the first commercial broadcasting station in America? This is the story that is told.

Frank Conrad, later assistant chief engineer of Westinghouse Electric Company, had been experimenting with radio receiving sets for several years. He communicated regularly with fellow experimenters but found talking with them tiresome, and so he began using phonograph records for signals. He finally announced he would broadcast records at 7:30 o'clock on Wednesday and Saturday evenings from his station on the upper floor of the garage at his home in Wilkinsburg, Pennsylvania. This was in the days when many people still did not believe that sound could be sent through the air, and the experiment was made partly for the purpose of convincing some of the doubters. Records were borrowed from a local music dealer on condition that the name of the firm furnishing the records should be mentioned. The dealer soon found that records used on the air sold better than others.

Later Frank Conrad conceived the idea of having people drop in for a visit with anyone who cared to tune in for the news, music, entertainment, and possibly a little advertising. The idea was presented to the publicity department of Westinghouse. The result was a new station on the roof of a factory building in East Pittsburgh with the call letters KDKA. The news event selected for the initial broadcast was the result of the election of November 2, 1920, when Warren G. Harding and James M. Cox were candidates for the presidency of the United States.

Some Interesting Changes in Radio. In the beginning, broadcasters had little to spend for talent. Musical programs consisted chiefly of voluntary numbers. However, there were a few excellent programs. Symphony concerts from the stadium in New York City and grand opera from the Civic Opera House in Chicago were sometimes broadcast, but these programs were rare. Two years later, one of the broadcasting stations discovered the commercial sponsor. Large commercial concerns were willing to employ performers to present programs over the radio in order to advertise their products. This solved the problem of financing broadcasting in the United States, and has given us such programs as the Ford Sunday Evening Hour, Cities Service Concerts, the Metropolitan Opera Auditions sponsored by the Radio Corporation of America, and many others.

It has been said that the depression was a blessing in disguise to radio. The type of radio developed at the beginning of the depression was the bulky and quite expensive cabinet model. During the depression few people could afford these costly models. Manufacturers began to develop lightweight, portable sets which could be sold cheaply enough for almost anyone. There was little spending money for theaters, concerts, and night clubs, and so people bought inexpensive radios and spent the long winter evenings at home listening to radio programs.

A third phase of radio development was the organization of networks of broadcasting stations. By combining the resources of many stations, excellent programs, which no single station could afford, were made available to more people. The four well-known organizations now are the National Broadcasting Company, the Columbia Broadcasting System, the Mutual Broadcasting Company, and the Blue Network Company. These organizations, themselves, sponsor such programs as the one given by Walter

Damrosch in the Music Appreciation Hour, and those of
the Metropolitan Opera Company, the New York Philharmonic Orchestra, and the National Broadcasting Company Orchestra. In spite of the fact that these programs

National Broadcasting Company photograph

Broadcasting studios are designed to accommodate an audience, but
give greatest consideration to acoustics and to the exclusion of all
sounds except the words and music of the broadcast.

are broadcast at a time of day and week not ordinarily desired for use by commercial advertisers, surveys indicate
they have a great many listeners. A recent survey showed
that the average sized audience for the Metropolitan Opera
broadcast was somewhat more than ten million persons.

A Glimpse into a Broadcasting Station. Have you ever visited a broadcasting station? Do you know how many people are responsible for the orchestra music which you hear over your radio, or how well trained in music every person in the orchestra must be? The process of producing the program and bringing it to your home is a complex and fascinating one.

The members of the orchestra are not arranged in a regular form such as you would see if you should go to a concert hall to hear a symphony orchestra, but according to the acoustics of the room in which the broadcast takes place and the character of the score to be played. Each person is placed so that in a particular selection the sound of his instrument will reach the microphone in the proper volume in relation to that of other instruments. For example, the violins might be placed nearest the microphone at one time and the flutes at another. The musicians themselves must be perfect in performance because of the sensitiveness of the microphone.

Each member of the orchestra has before him the music for the part he is to play, a separate sheet for each selection. Through symbols and notations on his sheet, the player is informed at every instant what notes to play, how to play them, how long to hold them, and how loudly or with what quality to play them.

The conductor has an orchestral score containing all of the notes for all the players. Each player's part is written on a separate staff. All of these are placed on the page parallel to each other so that the conductor can tell by looking at the score what all of the instruments are to do at a given time.

A system of signals has been devised for communication between the studio and the control room. Care must be taken that no sound except the music be broadcast. If you should see the producer drawing rapid circles in the air with his forefinger, it would likely mean to the conductor that he must speed up his number. If the producer's finger

Courtesy WGN, Mutual Broadcasting Company

In the control room, the engineer controls the complicated electrical equipment while an assistant reads the score of the production being broadcast.

touches his nose, it might indicate that the broadcast was proceeding exactly on time.

The radio engineer must be a trained musician. It is he who controls the complicated electrical equipment which makes the broadcast possible. A helper, also a musician, stands beside him during the broadcast to read the orchestra score and to warn the engineer in advance of changes in volume of sound.

Influence of the Radio. Recently the radio audience in the United States alone was estimated at seventy million listeners. If this number is correct, it means that today more than half of our population listens to the radio. This medium for bringing music to the people exerts a tremendous influence on our nation.

In the days before the phonograph and radio were common, only wealthy people could afford to attend the opera and concerts. People living in the more isolated communities had no opportunity to hear them at all. Today, it is a fact that, no matter where a person lives, what his occupation is, or how much or how little money he has, the most beautiful music of the world is his for the turning of a dial.

In the early nineteen thirties, some people began to be fearful that the radio would replace all other forms of musical entertainment. It seemed that, while radio was arousing a greater interest in music, at the same time it was destroying the desire for other types of musical entertainment and also the aspiration to create music. This fear is proving groundless. In recent years people have come to think of the radio largely as an inexpensive and convenient means of reproducing music. Having developed a taste for more serious music through the radio, Americans are becoming more and more interested in hearing firsthand performances of singers, orchestras, and operas. The desire to create music has increased. More young people than ever before are playing musical instruments. In "The Little Trio," a painting by John Johansen, the young people playing are representative of numerous small groups who get together and play because they enjoy music. Moreover, there is scarcely a high school of any size in the country that does not have its band or orchestra. Radio is credited with stimulating piano sales. The number of pianos sold yearly has been climbing slowly since 1930 until it reached an all-time high ten years later when one

THE LITTLE TRIO, *by John Johansen, courtesy Toledo Museum of Art*

Many groups of young people get together to play for their own enjoyment and for the entertainment of friends.

hundred thousand piano purchases were reported during the first six months of the year.

Television. There is a new invention in connection with radio which has not yet been popularized. In 1935 television became a real part of radio broadcasting instead of a dream. There were few public demonstrations and little discussion about it at the time. The next year the

Radio Corporation of America gave public demonstrations. Pictures were broadcast from the top of the Empire State Building in New York City. A few years later, magazine articles and newspapers carried two interesting announcements. Television sets were on the market, the receiving sets to cost about three hundred and fifty dollars, and the National Broadcasting Company had introduced the first scheduled broadcasting of television. The receiving sets could be purchased, and the entertainment offered by this new invention could be enjoyed at home. As a person tuned in on sound, he would automatically tune in the picture, which was about $7\frac{1}{2}$ by 10 inches in size. Its light or brilliance could be adjusted as the sound of the radio was adjusted. By means of the picture, the action of an opera, a play, a symphony orchestra, or the words of a news flash could be seen as the music or words were produced.

Television is still in the experimental stage. It is impossible now to predict its possibilities or attainments in the field of music.

The Motion Picture

Music in the Movies. The association of music with the motion picture has been very close from the beginning of this modern form of dramatic entertainment. Ask your mother and father to describe for you the first motion picture they remember. If they lived in a small town some thirty-five or forty years ago, they will probably tell you that it appeared on a small screen set up on a high stage in an old "opera house." Just below the screen was a piano played by some home-town boy or girl who could play anything. He was especially fortunate if he could play by ear or improvise. The evening's entertainment consisted of a short feature picture and an illustrated song. The picture, of course, was a silent movie. They were often called "living pictures." Since the characters spoke no words, it was necessary to throw a printed explanation on the screen from time to time so that the audience might keep the thread of the story. About one third of the total footage of the picture consisted of these explanatory subtitles. Appropriate music was played to accompany the picture and to furnish a background for the story. "The Dying Poet" introduced a touching death scene, the "Wedding March" from *Lohengrin*[2] was invariably used for a wedding, "The Fountain" described a babbling brook, and "Melody of Love" made a love scene appear even more romantic. The music used consisted of the familiar classics or the popular song hits of the day. Frequently the pianist purchased a book of miscellaneous compositions and played it through, in one order or another, during the picture. Of course, one would expect to hear different music for the same type of scene at different picture shows. A romantic scene might be accompanied by "Floreine Waltz" at one place, by "Träumerei"[3] at another, and by "Love's Old Sweet Song" at a third. The accompaniment was left largely to the whim or taste of the pianist.

After the feature, a series of colored slides representing the scene of some popular song was shown. The song was sung as the picture appeared on the screen. "Down Lover's Lane We Wandered, Sweetheart, You and I" was sung by a home-town boy as a brilliantly colored picture of a young man and his sweetheart on a flower-bordered lane appeared on the screen. The next two lines would likely bring another scene. Sometimes the showing of the slides was

2. *Lohengrin* (lō′ĕn·grĭn). The hero and title of a medieval German romance and opera. 3. "Träumerei" (troi′mĕ·rī′). Dreaming, revery.

As a home-town boy sang a popular song, a colored slide and the words of the song were shown on the screen in the old-time motion-picture theater.

repeated and the audience joined in singing the song. Through the music of the early motion picture, people became familiar with many tunes.

Today, in the same town, your parents can step into a small but beautifully furnished, air-conditioned theater. Most likely they will see a well-directed production in technicolor, in which the characters sing and speak and dance in a natural manner. The music may have been composed for that particular production. The costumes and setting have been designed with the greatest of care. The entertainment represents the most modern attainment in reproduction of sound, in acting, and in music.

Improvements Made. Motion picture studios began to publish cue sheets[4] which indicated what music was to be used with a particular scene. This did away with the selection of music according to the taste or ability of the pianist. In the city movie houses the piano player was replaced by the pipe organ and the small orchestra. Orchestra leaders began making collections of music particularly suitable for motion pictures. Musicians were soon composing music for special pictures.

Victor Herbert contracted to write the first completely original score ever created directly for a full-length feature film in 1916. The picture was *The Fall of a Nation,* a successor to *The Birth of a Nation*. The picture was not successful, but the music created a great deal of favorable discussion and opened a new field for music in relation to the motion picture. The only melody which we have today from the score for this picture is the "Love Theme," which is considered by some to be one of the loveliest melodies Victor Herbert ever wrote.

4. cue sheets. Lists of the last words of actors which give signals to other actors to speak or come on the stage.

At nearly the same time that radio networks were being formed and better programs were being broadcast, a new era opened for the motion picture also—the sound picture was produced. A musical score was recorded and reproduced from the same film as the picture itself. In the beginning, the actors and actresses of the old silent screen performed the action and merely moved their lips while a double spoke the words or sang the songs. This did not last long, however, for people soon began to detect the same voice for several different actors. It spoiled the effect. Now the person to appear in a movie is chosen for his ability to speak or sing as well as his ability to act. Frequently, all three qualities are necessary.

The music of the first sound pictures was quite realistic. It was thought that every note of the music must be directly related to some object on the screen, that real hoof beats must represent the galloping of horses, a realistic thunder clap should indicate a storm, and so on. This idea, too, changed very soon. Composers arrange music to suggest sounds and action without making the audience too greatly aware of them.

Features of Modern Motion Picture Music. Some people claim that music of the motion picture can never reach a high stage of accomplishment because the ideas of the composer must always be subordinated to those of the dramatic director or producer. A musical pattern or idea may be completely destroyed in the cutting room. Furthermore, they claim that since music of the movie is for the millions (the weekly movie audience is now estimated at eighty million), it must always be of a standard type not conducive to the most artistic composition. In spite of these claims, some very interesting developments are taking place.

The role of music in the sound film has changed from improvisation[5] to composition. Film corporations employ musical directors at enormous salaries to direct the music of the pictures to be filmed. These directors in turn employ some of our best-known composers, such as Virgil Thompson, George Antheil, Mark Blitzstein, Aaron Copland, and others, to write special music for feature pictures.

Aaron Copland's recent remarks in the *New York Times* concerning the music which he composed for *Of Mice and Men* express very well the place of music in the film drama of today.

In composing the score of "Of Mice and Men," however I succeeded, the primary purpose was to write music which somehow suggested the background of the film—the daily life on a California ranch. To do this, I occasionally employed music of a folksong character, though using no direct quotations. . . . . The temper of the music varied . . . . but always I tried to keep away from the overlush harmonies that are so common on the screen.

On the whole, though, the score . . . . is designed to strengthen and underline the emotional content of the entire picture.

Sometimes films are produced to feature music especially. One type of these films is represented by the musical comedy or operetta, such as *Maytime, Rose Marie,* and *Naughty Marietta,* starring Nelson Eddy and Jeanette MacDonald. Another type is the one in which the story is a mere thread of a plot which serves to tie together a variety of vaudeville or night club acts.

Sometimes the story is made to feature a well-known musician, as Jascha Heifetz,[6] who appeared in *And They Shall Have Music,* or one who is particularly popular, as Deanna Durbin, in *One Hundred Men and a Girl.* Films

5. improvisation (ĭm′prŏ·vĭ·zā′shŭn). The art of composing without preparation
    6. Jascha Heifetz (hī′fĕts). A Russian violinist (1901-   ).

Maytime is one of the popular operettas which have been produced as motion pictures.

in which the plot is based on incidents in the life of a musician have pleased many audiences. Among these are *Swanee River,* portraying the life of Stephen Foster, *Lillian Russell,* and *the Great Victor Herbert.*

In some instances, music written for a movie is becoming independent of the movies; that is, the music is something which may be enjoyed apart from the movie, and may continue to be played and sung long after the movie is forgotten. Orchestra leaders are beginning to realize this fact and are using music from motion pictures in their programs. Koussevitzky,[7] of the Boston Symphony Orchestra, has offered motion-picture scores on his programs. Hollywood Bowl has given over entire programs to film music. The radio constantly popularizes song hits of current movies. "Over the Rainbow" and "The Wicked Witch Is Dead," from *The Wizard of Oz,* are excellent examples.

The music used in connection with Walt Disney's productions is particularly interesting in that it has perfect synchronization[8] of music and action arranged by mathematical means. Artists in this studio are chosen for their sense of rhythm and accuracy as well as for their artistic ability.

One of the most interesting recent developments in connection with music and motion pictures is represented by *Fantasia,* a production made possible by the combined efforts of Walt Disney, Leopold Stokowski,[9] Deems Taylor,[10] the Philadelphia Symphony Orchestra, and the Radio Corporation of America. This feature-length color film interprets eight classic musical selections in picture. In

7. Koussevitzky (kōō'sĕ·vĭt'skĕ). A Russian-American conductor (1874-   ).
8. synchronization (sĭng'krô·nĭ·zā'shŭn). Causing to take place at the same time.
9. Leopold Stokowski (stô·kôf'skĕ). An American conductor born in England (1882-   ). 10. Deems Taylor. A music commentator and composer (1885-   ).

The bells of the Washington Memorial National Carillon at Valley Forge, Pennsylvania, ring every hour and at sunset play the national anthem.

it color, sound, and motion are harmonized. In order to
produce the desired effect, a new system of sound recording and reproduction called "fantasound" has been developed. This enables the audience to hear the music as
if a symphony orchestra were actually present. The different sections of orchestral instruments are emphasized at
appropriate times, and the sound appears to come from the
exact location of that particular section of the orchestra.

Other Mechanical Inventions

Electric Musical Instruments. In addition to radio and
recorded music, a number of electric musical instruments
and devices are being developed. By means of electricity
one person can now control the eighteen thousand pipes
found in some of the largest organs. Electrically controlled
attachments of bells, drums, harps, and even colored lights
are modern additions to the organ.

The novachord[11] and Hammond organ are comparatively new electrical instruments. The keyboard of the
novachord is like that of a piano. It produces not only the
tone of the piano but also those of the harpsichord and
other instruments as well. It has no strings, hammers, or
sounding board. The music is produced by a player who
controls the electric mechanism for producing the great
variety of sounds. The Hammond organ operates without
either pipes or reeds, but it is also electrically controlled.
Both of these instruments have been developed by Laurens
Hammond. One of his still more recent inventions is the
solo-vox,[12] which is an auxiliary keyboard of three octaves
that attaches to the underside of a piano keyboard and adds
organ or orchestral tones to the piano.

11. novachord (nō'vȧ·kôrd).   12. solo-vox (sō'lō vŏks).

Carillons. Carillons[13] are mechanically operated chimes. The tones are produced by the striking of bells with small

Courtesy of Dr. Kamiel Lefevere

Dr. Kamiel Lefevere, carillonneur of the Laura Spelman Rockefeller Memorial Carillon of Riverside Church, New York, is shown at the clavier.

hammers which are electrically controlled. The two best-

13. Carillons (kăr′ĭ·lŏnz). Sets of bells, usually with a range of three octaves.

known carillons in the United States are the one in the Bok
Singing Tower at Mountain Lake Sanctuary in Florida
and the Laura Spelman Rockefeller Memorial Carillon of
Riverside Church in New York City. However, there are
many other carillons in the United States. One of the most
interesting ones is at Valley Forge, Pennsylvania.

The carillon in the Bok Tower contains seventy-one
bells with fifty-three tones and a range of four octaves. The
total weight of the bells is 123,164 pounds. The largest bell
weighs eleven tons; the smallest, twelve pounds. From
December 15 to April 15, the carillon is played at three
o'clock in the afternoon on four days of the week.

In the Riverside Church carillon, the bells range in size
and weight from a ten-pound treble bell, not much larger
than an ordinary hand bell, to one which is 123 inches in
diameter and weighs twenty tons. The large bell is called
the Bourdon.[14] It is used mostly on special occasions or
mourning, when it is tolled alone. The Bourdon and the
next four largest bells are swung by electric motors. The
others are stationary and are operated by hand from the
clavier.[15] The chiming or playing of the carillon is done on
a keyboard controlled by levers, by a person called the
carillonneur.[16] Any tune within the octave range of the
bells can be played. It is possible to play the carillon automatically, somewhat like the player piano, but for delicacy
of tone and expression it is best played by hand.

14. Bourdon (bōōr′d'n). A drone bass, an organ stop. 15. clavier (klā′vǐ·ēr).
    The keyboard of the organ or piano. 16. carillonneur (kăr′ǐ·lǒ·nûr′).

CHAPTER XVI

HOW MUSIC IS MADE POSSIBLE FOR ALL THE PEOPLE

Public and Private Support of Music Programs

Aids to Music. Undoubtedly the radio, the motion picture, and the phonograph have been the most successful means of bringing music into our lives. Most music has been arranged primarily for listening. There are also agencies at work whose chief concern is not only to promote an appreciation of music through listening, but to give opportunities for composing to those who wish to participate in making music. These are agencies concerned with what is known as "live music." They are conscious of the fact that there is great social value in having groups make music and enjoy it together. It is impossible to tell about all these agencies, but some account of representative types of the more important and the more interesting ones can be given.

Uncle Sam as a Patron of Music. After the depression which followed the financial crash of 1929, the Works Progress Administration of the federal government undertook to find work for people who were unemployed. In classifying these people according to trades and professions, it was found that there were thousands of composers, singers, orchestral musicians, and music teachers who were out of work.

The Federal Music Project was launched to provide employment for these musicians. It lasted under this name for several years; then the general title of Federal Music Project was discontinued. After that, the various local WPA music projects were named after their communities.

Courtesy Federal Works Agency

The Northern California WPA Symphony Orchestra is one of the many local WPA music projects which give public concerts.

During the first year, a sum of nine million dollars was set aside for the different projects. At the end of that year there were seven hundred and eighty separate projects with a total of 14,109 men and women employed. During the month of August alone in that year, nearly five thousand outdoor concerts were given to audiences of about five million. Within three years over ninety-two million people had been reached through the projects. Music was taken into areas where good music had never been enjoyed before. There were forums, classes for music instruction, concert series, bands, and orchestras. Some of these have become permanent organizations.

Another interesting and valuable phase of the work was the collection of folk songs and folk tunes. Approximately twenty-five hundred of these songs and tunes have been collected and transcribed. In the WPA building at the New York World's Fair, the New York City music project presented twenty-two concerts of works by composers residing in America. Altogether, two hundred and one works by forty-one composers were performed.

Aid from Cities and Towns. More than half the states have laws which permit their cities and towns to levy a tax for the support of music. In some states the law says specifically that the money is to be used for band concerts. Thousands of towns all over the country furnish free band concerts for the people in their trade territories. The members of the band are usually local people. Sometimes, in the small towns, the concerts are sponsored by the merchants as a means of bringing people to town to shop, but large numbers of them are financed through public funds.

Almost every large city has some kind of music for its inhabitants. Municipal aid to bands, orchestras, community choruses, public concerts, and adult music classes is a common practice. The city of Detroit supports concerts by the Detroit Symphony Orchestra. For many years the orchestra has given a free concert every evening for eight weeks during the summer at Belle Isle, a Detroit park. Because of the large number of the foreign population in

Detroit, half of the program of the Wednesday evening concert is given over to songs and dances of foreign countries. San Francisco appropriates money for a series of popular priced symphony concerts. Baltimore pays the amount needed for its orchestra beyond the receipts from the sale of tickets at from twenty-five to seventy-five cents. Some cities, such as New York and Pittsburgh, give public organ recitals. The first of these was held in Portland, Maine, in 1912, when Cyrus H. K. Curtis gave a fine organ to the city, making city-supported organ recitals possible.

A portion of the community chest, created by individual contributions for public use, is set aside by some cities for public concerts or other music activities. The Community Music School of San Francisco is supported in this way. The Young Men's Christian Association and Young Women's Christian Association in many cities provide for music in their programs. Some cities, such as Washington, D. C., have a full-time director of music in these organizations.

Private Support for Civic Music. Several cities have a civic music association financed through membership dues, which are usually about five dollars, and through donations from individuals and organizations. The purpose of these associations is to bring artists to the city for concerts. Concerts are not always free, but the admission price is usually moderate. Concerts arranged especially for children are often sponsored by these organizations.

Aid from Foundations. Many wealthy people, either in their lifetime or through their wills, set aside large sums of money to finance music projects. Amounts of money of this kind with their earnings are called foundations. Music foundations are used in making people more familiar with music, in encouraging the creation of music, and in promoting the work of worthy students.

The Eastman School of Music, at Rochester, New York, with its fine conservatory buildings, its concert hall, and the Rochester Civic Orchestra, were all made possible by George Eastman.

The Carnegie Foundation has given 8,182 pipe organs to churches throughout the country. Grants have been made for the encouragement of music composition. Sets of music

Courtesy Eastman School of Music, the University of Rochester

The students of the Eastman School of Music have their own symphony orchestra.

containing representative scores, books on music, a phonograph, and several hundred records are distributed to certain colleges.

The Julliard[1] Music Foundation was established for the purpose of aiding worthy students to obtain a good music education. The well-known Julliard School of Music in New York City was organized under this foundation.

The Daniel and Florence Guggenheim Foundation supports the concerts given by the Goldman Band in New York City.

1. Julliard (jŭ′lē·àrd). The family name of an American who gave money to further the cause of music.

The Atwater Kent Foundation has been interested largely in giving encouragement to radio singers.

The Elizabeth Sprague Coolidge Foundation serves music entirely through the Library of Congress. This foundation has built an auditorium in the Library of Congress, where concerts of chamber music are given. The income of the trust fund, nearly thirty thousand dollars annually, is set aside for the purpose of helping the music division of the Library of Congress develop the study and appreciation of music. It is used for the purchase of additional musical works for the library, for commissioning musicians to write new works, for prizes, for chamber music festivals, and for concerts.

Women's Organizations. At least two women's organizations have been active in encouraging the growth of music. The General Federation of Women's Clubs has a music division interested in encouraging musical education of students and in the increase of music in the home. The National Federation of Music Clubs has over five thousand clubs which are doing much to foster music in communities.

Opportunities for Training in Music

The Work of the Public Schools. The public schools have been one of the most powerful forces in promoting music. Today millions of children and young people are singing in our public schools, where vocal music is still the most common musical activity. There are few schools in America that do not offer some kind of opportunity for music instruction and enjoyment.

Public school classes in piano playing, as well as in the playing of instruments of the orchestra and band, are increasing. In high schools, particularly in the larger schools, choruses, glee clubs, and a cappella[2] choirs are becoming as common as orchestras.

The world's finest music has been brought to all schools through the Walter Damrosch Music Appreciation Hour. Interest in music appreciation is apparent in the attendance at children's concerts and youth concerts.

An example of the youth concerts is that given at the Philadelphia Academy of Music six times each year for young persons between the ages of thirteen and twenty-five. The large auditorium is always filled. Recently at one performance the balcony was sold out in ten minutes and seats in the entire house were sold within an hour and a half after the ticket sale opened. Committees of young people make all arrangements for the concerts except arranging the program, which is left to the orchestra conductor. The programs are given by the Philadelphia Orchestra and they are similar to those given for adults. Auditions for the youth concerts are held each spring. At that time several young people are selected to appear as soloists in the concerts during the following season.

The training of teachers of public school music has been improved. Colleges and universities offer well-organized courses in this work. The Music Teachers' National Association and the American Music Educators' National Conference are two organizations which have been established for the purpose of improving music instruction.

Home-Study Courses in Colleges. Home-study courses in music are offered by many colleges, and thousands of persons are enrolled in these courses. It is believed the number enrolled has increased steadily during the past ten years. Many adults are enrolled in the evening classes

2. a cappella (ä käp·pĕl'lä). Unaccompanied choral music.

in cities and towns offering work in chorus, orchestra, band, vocal, and instrumental work.

Music in Settlement Schools. One of the first music schools connected with settlement work was that established in 1893 at Hull House, the settlement founded by Jane Addams in Chicago. At about the same time, music began to be used in the settlement centers in New York City. Today the settlement music school has become a definite part of settlement work in many of our large cities. The purpose of these schools is to give music training to children in those districts, where living conditions are crowded and children have no other opportunity for training in music. Thousands of children, many of them of immigrant parentage, who would not otherwise have an opportunity to study and enjoy music, have been taught in these schools. The only requirement for entrance is a desire to study music. Usually the teachers are trained musicians who give voluntary service. Some schools have orchestras of from twenty to forty members. Regular concerts are given. Often singers and players of ability are developed in these schools. They are financed in different ways, in some cities by the community chest, in others by contributions from interested people, and in still others they are helped by a reduction in the tuition fee.

The All-American Youth Orchestra. The National Youth Administration has participated in the organization of the All-American Youth Orchestra. This musical organization of one hundred members, selected from more than fifteen thousand talented young people from every state in the United States, is directed by Leopold Stokowski. Mr. Stokowski's two purposes in his work with the orchestra are: (1) to give talented young Americans an opportunity to develop their talents through playing the greatest music of all times and all countries, and (2) to bring about good will and friendship with our neighboring countries through music. Their first tour was to South America, where the orchestra played in Rio de Janeiro,[3] Sao Paulo,[4] Buenos Aires,[5] Rosario,[6] and Montevideo. Their second year included a complete tour of the United States.

Libraries and Publications. Public libraries are beginning to recognize the importance of circulating music materials as well as books. While music in the libraries of rural areas is still scarce, many of the large city libraries now have a music division. In addition to reading rooms, audition rooms with phonographs and pianos are provided. During concerts, listeners may follow with scores, note by note. Some of the libraries have collections of phonograph records and piano rolls for circulation, as well as music scores and books. The largest and most complete musical collection in America is in Washington, D. C., in the Library of Congress.

In recent years some libraries have conducted a free concert series. Programs featuring symphony orchestras, piano recitals, radio programs, phonograph music, and talks on music appreciation are given. Usually program notes and lists of books and magazine articles prepared by the librarians are distributed. In the Public Library Concert Series in Minneapolis a few years ago, a "Parade of Nations" was conducted from May through September. Singing societies, choruses, and folk dancers representing fifteen different nationalities took part. All were in native costume. Musical instruments characteristic of the nations were used.

3. Rio de Janeiro (rē′ō dā zhá·nā′rō). The capital of Brazil.   4. Saõ Paulo (souN′pou′lŏō). A city in Brazil.   5. Buenos Aires (bwā′nōs ī′rās). The capital of Argentina.   6. Rosario (rō·sä′rĕ·ō). The second largest city in Argentina.

Publishers have aided in bringing music to Americans by publishing music scores, books about music, and music journals. A number of references are listed in the appendix to this book. The best-known music magazines are *Musical Quarterly,* a magazine with professional articles written by musicians for musicians; *Musical Courier,* a review of world music; *Musical America,* a news review of music and musicians in America; and *The Etude,*[7] a magazine containing articles on musical subjects written in an interesting and, for the most part, nontechnical style. *The Etude* also contains musical selections of varying grades of difficulty.

The Music Camp at Interlochen. Joseph E. Maddy, of the School of Music, University of Michigan, was responsible for the founding of a national high school orchestra. His idea was to bring together boys and girls from high school orchestras in different states, combine them into a single, large orchestra, and give them several days of intensive training. For the first two years these meetings took place in April, and the orchestra played before some of the national meetings of educators. Then Maddy conceived the idea of having a summer camp in which these students might come for a month or two for training and playing. The place chosen for the camp was Interlochen, Michigan. Here, every summer, an orchestra of approximately two hundred and a band of one hundred and fifty young men and women rehearse for two hours each day and give popular concerts weekly. Many of their programs are broadcast over national networks. Individual and class instruction, as well as ensemble playing, are directed by artists and trained musicians. Their concerts are at times directed by the leading orchestra conductors in the country. The camp

7. *The Etude* (ā'tüd').

is situated in a beautiful location. The young people live
in cottages. There are club houses, assembly halls, buildings for class rooms, and the Interlochen Bowl. Now there
is a similar camp in Maine.

Courtesy Joseph E. Maddy, President, National Music Camp

Frederick Stock, as guest conductor, directs the orchestra
in Interlochen Bowl at the National Music Camp.

National Music Week. The first week in May has been
chosen as National Music Week. The purpose of the ob-
servance is to increase community interest in music. It is
directed by a National Music Week committee, whose ex-
ecutive secretary is C. M. Tremaine. The committee is
composed of the presidents of thirty-four leading national
organizations, including musical, educational, religious,
civic, and service organizations. There is also an honorary

committee, which is headed by the President of the United States. The governor of every state and territory in the United States is a member of the honorary committee. Forty-five governors have issued a formal proclamation or some similar type of statement through the newspapers, asking their people to participate in National Music Week.

The idea for a national music week was probably first expressed by Mr. Tremaine through an article in the *Music Trade Review* some years ago. He advocated making a drive to spread the enjoyment of music more widely among people as a whole. He thought that music should have the center of the stage in public thought for a seven-day period each year, when individuals and groups could enjoy various types of music through listening or participation.

Nearly twenty-five years ago, Boise, Dallas, St. Louis, and Sharon, Pennsylvania, held celebrations of this nature. Also, under the leadership of Mr. Tremaine, the New York City Music Week was organized. This was used as a model for music weeks all over the country. Within four years, about one hundred and fifty cities and towns had organized local music weeks held at various times during the year. These served as a nucleus; later, eight hundred and forty cities and towns joined in the first national celebration. It is believed that the number of communities now featuring National Music Week has increased to three times that number. National Music Week undoubtedly represents one of the most democratic and far-reaching efforts in the country to increase public interest in music.

I HEAR AMERICA SINGING

By Walt Whitman

I hear America singing, the varied carols I hear;
Those of mechanics—each one singing his, as it should be, blithe
and strong;
The carpenter singing his, as he measures his plank or beam,
The mason singing his, as he makes ready for work, or leaves off
work;
The boatman singing what belongs to him in his boat—the deck-
hand singing on the steamboat deck;
The shoemaker singing as he sits on his bench—the hatter singing
as he stands;
The wood-cutter's song—the ploughboy's, on his way in the morn-
ing, or at the noon intermission, or at sundown;
The delicious singing of the mother—or of the young wife at work
—or of the girl sewing or washing—Each singing what belongs to
her, and to none else;
The day what belongs to the day—At night, the party of young
fellows, robust, friendly,
Singing, with open mouths, their strong melodious songs.

From LEAVES OF GRASS; *courtesy of Columbia University Press.*

CHAPTER XVII

MUSIC IN THE EVERYDAY LIFE OF THE NATION

Music in Industry

Early Uses of Music in Industry. Music has been used as a help to workers for many years. Singing was regularly practiced by seamen, both on fishing boats while drawing in their nets of fish and on freighters when loading or unloading cargo. The "Song of the Volga Boatmen" is a song used to help oarsmen pull their boat along. We have already mentioned the songs of the cotton pickers and of workers on railroads as an aid in producing more efficient work.

Increase in Production by Means of Music. While the work songs of earlier days do not always fit into the machine age and the tempo of our modern industrial life, the practice of using music as an aid in speeding up production still continues. One of the regulations of the United States Navy relating to bands is that the band shall play while a ship is being coaled. It has been found that about thirty per cent more coal is put in when music is played than when men work without it. A postmaster in a Minnesota city installed a phonograph in the post office to enliven the mail clerks who worked on the night shift. Special radio programs are broadcast through the night and early hours of the morning for the benefit of scrubwomen and other night workers in large office buildings in cities. Printing plants, garment factories where piece work is done, canneries, and many other industries have installed phonographs and radios. They have found that people work faster when a stirring piece of music is played. One frequently hears a radio or phonograph in large dairy barns at milking time, for the amount of milk given by cows is said to be increased when the cows hear music.

Music as a Friend of Labor. Music has other uses in large industrial plants than that of increasing the rate and amount of human effort and production. The noise of machinery, the monotony of the work, the speed at which factory work must be done, all produce nervous strain and fatigue. Music has proved to be helpful in relieving this fatigue and in producing a happier working mood. William Green, president of the American Federation of Labor, has said that music is a friend of labor, for it lightens the task by refreshing the nerves and spirit of the worker and makes work pleasant as well as profitable.

Some large factories arrange for a ten- or fifteen-minute rest period at ten o'clock in the morning and at three o'clock in the afternoon. During this period, music is played. Workers listen, hold brief sings, or dance. In these factories it is claimed that work runs more smoothly, workers are much happier, fatigue is lessened, and production is increased.

At first, when the officials of a Connecticut brass factory were asked to give a fifteen-minute recreation period for singing every day, they said that shutting down the factory for this length of time would cost hundreds of dollars. However, they finally consented to try the experiment. Workers were noticeably refreshed, more work was done on every day than before, and the number of accidents was cut down. Eighty-five to ninety per cent of the accidents had been attributed to afternoon fatigue and carelessness. The rest period with music relieved that situation.

Courtesy Federal Works Agency

Many industrial plants encourage their workers to organize company orchestras.

Another interesting experiment was carried on in the Insurance Building in Oakland, California. At the Christmas holiday season, the building manager installed sound equipment throughout the entire office building. It was so arranged that the sound could be regulated on each floor. The music could be heard in the halls and lobby, but not in the offices if the doors were closed. Varied programs of phonograph records were played in the morning, at noon, and in the evening. Groups were frequently found listening in the lobby. The tenants of the building liked the music and soon began sending requests for special numbers to be played. At one checkup it was found that twenty-five out of twenty-seven office doors were propped open so that the music could be heard in the offices as well as in the halls. At that time of year, when work was usually heaviest, it was found that when music was played there was less strain, more work was accomplished, and organizations ran more smoothly and efficiently than ever before.

In one of the department stores in a city in Mississippi, community singing is held in the store for thirty minutes every Tuesday morning. The Larkin Company of Buffalo, New York, at one time had community singing one day a week with from three hundred to one thousand participating. A daily organ recital and the organization of an orchestra and a ukelele club were reported as a part of their music program.

Encouragement of Music as a Hobby. Many industrial concerns, by providing money for the expenses of such organizations as orchestras, glee clubs, and bands, encourage their workers to engage in musical activities as a hobby and recreation. Frequently rehearsals are held on the company's time and the money for instruments, leaders, instructors, uniforms, and the like is furnished by the company. Officials believe that, in addition to providing relaxation, musical organizations create a more friendly feeling among workers. After all, it is a good advertisement for the industry. Many of these musical organizations broadcast programs over the radio and furnish music for numerous civic affairs.

Value of Music in Industry. Numerous other examples of encouragement of music in industry might be given, for it is no longer an experiment. Its value has been proved many times in nearly every field of industry. The most important values are as follows: (1) it increases production; (2) it relieves fatigue; (3) it improves the morale of the workers; (4) it provides a common meeting ground for executives and laborers; (5) it creates good will advertising; (6) it gives opportunity for self expression; and (7) it brings wider friendship and greater happiness to the workers.

Music and Health

Music in Modern Hospitals. One does not usually think of anything as pleasant as music in connection with hospitals; yet in one year nearly a thousand concerts were given for the benefit of nearly forty-five thousand patients in thirty-seven of our large hospitals. For the most part the music was furnished by volunteer, visiting musicians. Regularly the Junior League Glee Club of New York City sings in concerts in the buildings of Medical Center. Frequently one finds a radio in a hospital room. Some hospitals have radio pillows, through which the patient gets his music without raising his head. A radio is sometimes used in an operating room where the patient is given a local anesthetic.[1] Although he feels no pain, he may be uncomfortably nervous at the thought of an operation. The music of the radio is believed to reduce the nervous tension and to make the patient more comfortable. Some hospitals are equipped with ear phones so that the music will not disturb the surgeon in his operation. Music is filling an important place in restoring health to the sick.

1. anesthetic (ăn′ĕs·thĕt′ĭk). Something which produces loss of feeling.

Use of Music in Curing Diseases. It has been said that when the therapeutic[2] value of music is understood and appreciated, it will be considered as necessary in the treatment of disease as air, water, and food. Tests given at Temple University have shown that music has a direct effect on pulse, respiration, and blood pressure. One report states that "Rhapsody[3] in Blue," for example, raised all three, and that "The Invitation to the Dance" lowered them. The report also shows that "Hungarian Rhapsody" tended to give one a pickup, and that "Stars and Stripes Forever" would almost race one's motor.

The use of music as an instrument of healing is not altogether new. You will remember that Florence Nightingale brought music to the hospitals during the Crimean War.[4] Thirty years ago the psychologist, William James, was using music as a treatment in a mental hospital in Boston. During the First World War the relaxing effect of music in treating shell shock was well known. About twenty-five years ago, the Russell Sage Foundation commissioned a psychologist to test the healing effect of music in the state institutions of Pennsylvania and New York. In making his test, the psychologist carried his folding organ or his phonograph into hundreds of hospitals and prisons. The results of the experiment indicated that music has a definite healing effect upon those who are ill and that it improves morale in prisons.

Today music is accepted more and more as standard treatment in progressive institutions for the insane and criminal. In jails and prisons it has been found that hearing good music, studying it, and taking part in it relieve

2. therapeutic (thĕr′á·pū′tĭk). Healing or curative. 3. Rhapsody (răp′sŏ·dĭ). An instrumental composition which is irregular in form as if improvised. 4. Crimean (krī·mē′án) War. A war fought on a peninsula in southern Russia (1854-56).

the nervous tension brought on by the repression and confinement of prison life. Better behavior has resulted even in the case of the most rebellious prisoners. In the United States penitentiary at Atlanta, a musical director has been employed as an officer. The organization of an orchestra there has proved to be one of the best methods for establishing good conduct. In tests of music as a cure for insanity, it has been found that music lessens the fury of even the most violent. Music is useful in the treatment of amnesia,[5] for the sound of a familiar tune will often bring a flood of memories that the patient has associated with it.

In one hospital, where a twilight musicale was tried for three months, the use of medicine to produce sleep fell off a third. Nocturnes,[6] lullabies, and serenades replaced the sleeping pills. Music is reported to bring a marked improvement in the temperature and respiration of tubercular patients by providing brief rest periods.

Musical Selections Prescribed for Certain Diseases. In a recent article in the *American Magazine,* the work of Mrs. Harriet Ayer Seymour in connection with music and disease is described. Mrs. Seymour has found that certain musical selections tend to decrease certain ailments. For example, she recommends for paralysis and joint diseases such selections as "The Anvil Chorus," Sousa's marches, Brahms's[7] "Hungarian Dances," Lieurance's "By the Waters of Minnetonka," and light folk dance music; for tuberculosis, "La Paloma," "Over the Rainbow," Beethoven's "Minuet in G," Schubert's[8] "Serenade," and Strauss's waltzes; for heart disease, the "Song of India," and the "Barcarole" from *Tales of Hoffman.*

5. amnesia (ăm·nē′zhĭ·à). Loss of memory.   6. Nocturnes (nŏk′tûrnz). Night pieces, dreamy compositions.   7. Brahms's (brämz). Brahms was a German composer (1833-1897).   8. Schubert's (shŏo′bĕrts). Schubert was an Austrian composer (1797-1828).

She has found that just any kind of music played by any musician will not produce the desired results. Modern swing and syncopated music are not effective in healing. The best combination of voices or instruments is a trio of voices or a trio composed of violin, cello, and piano. A sympathetic quality of voice is more necessary than a highly trained voice.

Other Uses of Music in Health. Music is used not only as an aid in curing certain diseases but also as an aid in building and in maintaining health. It is one of the essentials in any physical education program. Recreation leaders on playgrounds make extensive use of music in singing games, rhythmic games, and folk dances. Instructors in physical education use music for skipping, marching, swaying, running, and other rhythmic activities. Music is an essential accompaniment to the modern dance, to folk dancing, or to social dancing.

In summer camps, many of the activities call for music. All camps have periods for singing, and almost all of them have periods for listening to music. Playing of taps, grace at mealtime, campfire songs, folk dancing, devotions, plays and festivals, acting out old ballads, singing games, team songs, minstrel shows, song contests, and singing in camp choirs are examples of the use of music in summer camps.

Music in Religion

Religious Music of Modern Times. In three centuries, music as a part of religious worship has come a long way from the lining out of psalm tunes by the early settlers. Today, hymn tunes are more familiar to the American people as a whole than any other group of melodies. This is not strange when one finds that the churches of America,

including Protestant, Jewish, and Catholic, have more than
fifty-four million members, and that on Sunday morning
more people sing together than at any other time.

The kind of religious music and frequently the selections
themselves vary according to the church denomination or
the locality. All over our country may be heard many types
of religious music—hymns, gospel songs, masses, cantatas,[9]
oratorios, solos, duets, trios, quartettes, and instrumental
music, chiefly for organ or orchestra.

Some Important Changes. Most of the hymns used in
church today represent good poetry and good music. Many
of the cheap gospel songs, popular a generation ago, have
been discarded. Sentimental hymns have been replaced by
those which express a calmer type of worship. The hymns
that told of a longing for Heaven have given way to those
that express the ideals of everyday living here and now.

There still is a difference of opinion among church people as to whether the music at church services should be
sung by the entire congregation or by a choir of specially
trained singers. A great number of churches, however, use
both types of singing. Many churches employ trained musicians to sing in their choirs, and congregational singing,
itself, has been greatly improved.

Choral Music in the Modern Church. There is a tendency toward a revival of great choral music. At Christmas
and at Easter throughout the country, people may hear
such stirring and inspiring productions as Handel's *Messiah* or Stainer's[10] *The Crucifixion*.

A cappella singing is becoming well known in churches.
This type of singing is reviving an interest in the polyphonic[11] music of the old masters.

9. cantatas (kăn·tä′tȧz). Sacred or secular music sung by choirs. 10. Stainer's
(stān′ẽrz). Stainer was an English composer (1840-1901). 11. polyphonic
(pŏl′ĭ·fŏn′ĭk). Having many sounds or voices.

The anthems and cantatas by Dudley Buck, written some fifty years ago, continue to be sung by church choirs. However, the compositions of modern composers of lofty church music are received with great favor by many churches. Among these composers are F. Melius Christiansen of St. Olaf College in Northfield, Minnesota; Leo Sowerby, Eric De Lamarter, and Nobel Cain of Chicago; John Finley Williamson of Princeton, New Jersey; Father William J. Finn, and Father Eugene O'Malley.

The tours of college and church choirs such as the St. Olaf College Choir, the Northwestern a Cappella Choir, and the Westminster Choir, have greatly influenced public opinion with regard to church music. Their excellent performances of the best religious music have led to an appreciation of music of this type and to a desire that it be given regularly in churches.

Radio broadcasts have also increased the demand for church music of the highest type.

Instrumental Music in Church Services. Orchestras have been used in the Sunday school service for some time. The use of stringed instruments and the small orchestra in the church service, however, is a comparatively recent one, but it is increasing in favor. Organ music is most frequently heard in the larger churches. Selections representing the most beautiful and sublime music are used for this part of the church service.

The Ministry of Music. In the modern church, music as well as the gospel is recognized as a spiritual agency. In keeping with this recognition, many churches are now employing a minister of music in addition to the regular minister. He is a person highly trained in music and he devotes his full time to training musical organizations and to directing the musical activities of the church.

These musical activities of the church frequently extend throughout the week. Riverside Church, one of the large churches of New York City, listed on its calendar for one week more than twenty musical affairs, including tower sings, rehearsals and performances of the orchestra, various choirs, men's choruses, and instrumental trios.

Music in Leisure Time

Leisure-Time Activities. The pursuit of some pleasant activity of one's own choosing occupies a place in modern life never before experienced. Modern labor legislation has shortened the working day. Modern interpretation of education recognizes the value of recreation in mental and physical health. Numerous other social forces have combined to give leisure an important place in modern American life. Every day, hours are occupied by outdoor sports, by reading in the library, by attending movie theaters, by listening to the radio, or by pursuing hundreds of other individual interests and hobbies.

Millions of people choose to participate in music in some way during their leisure time each day. This participation may be through listening, through performance with voice or instrument, through dancing, or through composing music. It is interesting to note that these same activities in turn furnish a means of livelihood for many people.

As one reviews all of the leisure-time activities in which music plays a part, one immediately discovers that the music itself naturally falls into two groupings—serious and popular music. The paragraphs that follow are intended to give a clearer understanding of each of these phases of music and its relation to life in America today.

The United States as a Music Center. There is increasing evidence that the United States is becoming an important music center. Formerly our young musicians had to go to European music centers for their training. Today they can attend excellent schools for music education in our own country. In the United States they have the privilege of hearing the best music of all times played by talented musicians. They have the opportunity to hear skilled performers play their own compositions. Here, too, everyone is given increased opportunities to become familiar with the music of American composers.

The conditions in Europe brought about by the Second World War have contributed toward making America a world center for serious music. Many European musicians —composers, conductors, and performers—have either left their native country voluntarily or have been driven out, and have come to the United States to become a part of the musical life here.

The training now offered in the public schools and colleges has helped many young people to participate in orchestras and choral organizations. This training and the work of music groups under the Federal Works Progress Administration and the National Youth Administration have been responsible for much of the interest shown in serious music.

The Symphony Orchestra in a Grown-up Nation. The musical organization which gives the most universal pleasure in the field of serious music is the symphony orchestra. The following clipping from Eleanor Roosevelt's daily newspaper column points out something of the achievement of our country in the field of serious orchestral music. It is noteworthy that it is a youth orchestra which she praises so highly.

MY DAY

Wednesday night we attended the concert at Carnegie Hall, conducted by Leopold Stokowski, in which the All-American Youth orchestra gave a program of Bach which was completely enchanting. It was so beautifully conducted and played, that I felt as though I were hearing this music for the first time.

The second half of the program, Symphony Number Five, by Shostakovich,[12] I had never heard before, and because it was unfamiliar, I enjoyed certain parts more than I did others. But taken all in all, it was an unforgettable evening, and one in which you were proud of the achievements of young America in music.

They say no young country can produce great artists or great musicians. Then we must be growing up, for we did hear a great all-American symphony orchestra last night.

Growth of the Symphony Orchestra. At the opening of the twentieth century there were only a few important symphony orchestras. Among them were the New York Philharmonic (1842), the Boston Symphony Orchestra (1881), the Chicago Symphony Orchestra (1891), the Cincinnati Orchestra (1895), and the Los Angeles Orchestra (1897). Since 1900 these orchestras have become more and more important, and other large cities have organized orchestras of their own. Among the cities now having these musical organizations are Philadelphia, Minneapolis, St. Louis, Cleveland, Seattle, Pittsburgh, Kansas City, and Rochester.

The early orchestras were supported largely by endowments from wealthy individuals. The newer organizations are usually supported through subscriptions. That is, individuals wishing to attend the concerts subscribe a certain amount for one or more seats in the concert hall for the season.

12. Shostakovich (shŭs·tá′kŭ·vĭtch). A Russian composer (1906-   ).

The outdoor concerts given during the summer at Grant Park, on the lake shore in Chicago, are popular with many people.

For many years the programs of symphony concerts were
dominated by compositions of European musicians such as
Bach, Beethoven, Brahms, and Tchaikovsky. While these
compositions are still important, there is a growing ten
dency to perform more works of American composers
Now one may attend symphony concerts and hear programs
which include one number or more by an American com
poser.

Symphonic music has become so popular that there is a
great demand for concerts given out of doors in the sum
mer time. Some of the better-known places for these
summer concerts are Lewisohn Stadium in New York
Hollywood Bowl in California, Grant Park in Chicago
Fairmount Park in Philadelphia, and Forest Park in St
Louis.

The broadcasting of concerts by leading symphony
orchestras, such as the New York Philharmonic, and the
organization of orchestras specifically for radio use, such
as the National Broadcasting Company's Symphony Or
chestra, are among the important developments of today
The increased interest in symphony orchestras and sym
phonic music has in many cases lengthened the season for
concerts. A few years ago an orchestra usually played about
thirty concerts during a season. Now that number is often
doubled. This makes a difficult task for the conductor of
the orchestra, and in many cases guest conductors are used
for some of the concerts.

Musicians in Symphony Orchestras. The musicians
playing in these large symphony orchestras are employed
for pay as in any other business or profession. Most of them
belong to unions which dictate the pay and the hours of
work. The players receive a minimum fee for rehearsals
two and one-half hours long. If the practice is longer, extra

pay is received. A single rehearsal for the New York Philharmonic Orchestra costs about one thousand dollars. Since expense is such an important item, only very skilled musicians are hired. These players must be all-round musicians and excellent sight readers. The Boston Symphony has established a pension system for members of its orchestra. For years it was the only important nonunion orchestra in the nation. It has recently become unionized.

Orchestra Leaders. A consideration of the modern symphony orchestra would be incomplete without recognizing the importance of some well-known leaders of today. Among them are Damrosch, Toscanini, Stokowski, Stock, Barbirolli,[13] Koussevitzky, Rodzinski,[14] and others. Two of these have for a long time played such an important part in the music of America that they are given special mention here.

Toscanini. Arturo Toscanini has been called the "first musician of the world," and is probably the world's most famous orchestra leader. He first came to the public notice when he was a young man of nineteen. At that time he was a cello player in a touring opera company. While the company was playing in Rio de Janeiro, the orchestra leader refused to conduct at a performance because of a dispute. Toscanini was asked to conduct the opera *Aïda*[15] by Verdi.[16] He had never conducted before, but he did so then, going through the whole performance without the musical score. The audience and the whole opera company as well were amazed.

In 1908, Toscanini became orchestra conductor for the Metropolitan Opera Company in New York. He remained

13. Barbirolli (bär·bē·rôl′ē). A conductor of symphony orchestras (1899-   ).
14. Rodzinski (rō·jĭn′skĭ). The conductor of the Cleveland Symphony Orchestra (1894-   ). 15. *Aïda* (ä·ē′dä). 16. Verdi (vâr′dē). An Italian composer (1813-1901).

Courtesy National Broadcasting Compan

Arturo Toscanini, one of the most famous orchestra leaders in the world, has conducted many of the leading orchestras in the United States.

in this position for seven years. Later he was conductor of the New York Philharmonic Orchestra for ten years. In 1936, he left America and planned to remain away permanently. The National Broadcasting Company, realizing that his going from America would create a gap which could never be filled by any other conductor, made every effort to bring him back to America the following year.

They provided him with working conditions to satisfy his most fastidious[17] requirements as an artist: a sufficient number of rehearsals, full liberty in the planning of the programs, complete control of the artistic policies of the orchestra, and a promise that the concerts would never be commercialized. They gave him a fabulous salary, and (the medium of radio being what it is) a weekly audience of several million listeners.

Toscanini finally yielded, consenting to conduct ten consecutive weeks of radio concerts. It was costing the National Broadcasting System a quarter of a million dollars to restore Toscanini to American music lovers.

His remarkable memory is one of the Toscanini traditions. He conducts entire symphonic and orchestral scores from memory. He has been known to learn a new symphony in three hours and conduct it without looking at the score. He played from memory all of Mendelssohn's *Songs without Words* when he had not seen the scores for more than fifty years.

There are many interesting and humorous stories told about Toscanini. One of them is particularly amusing. When he relaxes he likes to listen to the radio. He often criticizes the performance, scolding a bad performer or commending a particularly good one. Once he tuned in on the middle of a symphony. "Not bad," he observed to those in the room listening with him. "That fellow has a

17. fastidious (făs·tĭd′ĭ·ŭs). Difficult to please.

feeling for tempo. The phrasing is good." When the symphony ended, the announcer said, "You have been listening to a recording of the *Pastoral Symphony* conducted by Arturo Toscanini." It is said the old maestro[18] snapped off the radio furiously and stormed out of the room. He was greatly chagrined[19] not to have recognized his own recording.

Damrosch. Walter Damrosch is a name familiar to both children and grownups in all parts of the United States. He has always been interested in giving many people an opportunity to know music, for he feels that music belongs to all of the people, not to a few. He has probably done more to mold the musical taste of Americans than any other one person. One of his greatest services has been his interpretation of music for children.

More than fifty years ago, when many people felt that serious music would not appeal to children, Mr. Damrosch thought he could lead them to understand and love it. With this purpose in mind, he gave the first concert for children in New York at Carnegie Hall. An unusual opportunity to present music to a great many people came to him about fifteen years ago, when he was asked by the National Broadcasting Company to conduct a radio concert and to say a few words before each number. This program proved so popular that a series of concerts for adults was given. Its success led to the organization of a series of radio concerts for children.

He was one of the first to realize the importance and to see the possibility of radio as a means of bringing music to millions of children who had had no opportunity to hear good music. His Music Appreciation Hour, broadcast

18. maestro (mä·ĕs′trŏ). Teacher.   19. chagrined (shȧ·grĭnd′). Humiliated, mentally distressed.

weekly during the school year, has not only given children a chance to hear and to understand better music, but it has also increased the study of music.

A New Interest in Opera. Opera was once popular with comparatively few people—the wealthy people who were patrons and considered attendance at the opera the fashionable thing to do, and the people who were outstanding in the musical world. The place of opera in the opinion of the average person only a few years ago is illustrated by the following story. During the early nineteen hundreds, a grand opera company was to play in Marion, Ohio. The director was eager to have a good attendance so he went to see the editor of the paper to get some publicity. He gave the editor two complimentary tickets for the first night's performance and noticed with surprise that the editor did not appear enthusiastic. In fact, the editor announced that, since he did not know anything about grand opera, he did not wish to attend. The director discovered that the editor enjoyed concerts and showed him that in many cases concert numbers were taken from operas. Here he would have an opportunity to see the whole thing and find out the setting for many of the concert selections he liked. The editor finally agreed to attend the opera and, after the performance, said to the manager, "You know, grand opera isn't so bad when you know how it fits together and what it is all about." The editor attended all the other performances that week. He was Warren G. Harding, later President of the United States.

During this century a keen and more universal interest in opera has developed. Large cities, realizing the value of opera, are encouraging this form of art. Opera study clubs and opera societies have been organized. New opera companies are successfully giving performances. Some of them are in the cities of Chicago, Los Angeles, San Francisco, Cincinnati, and Portland, Oregon.

Outdoor opera is popular in many localities. The operas given each summer at Chautauqua, New York, and at the Municipal Stadium in St. Louis, are typical. Frequently students and local musicians of talent have an opportunity to participate in these operas, although the leading roles are taken by those especially trained for grand opera.

The Saturday afternoon opera broadcasts of the Metropolitan Opera Company succeeded in winning a great interest in opera. The interest was so great that, when it appeared as though the Metropolitan Opera would have to close because of lack of funds, one hundred and fifty thousand people sent contributions of money. Nearly one-third of the total fund of one million dollars was raised by the radio audience. The radio had created a new and larger audience for opera, one so enthusiastic about it that when the time came to help support it, they were willing to pay for the privilege of hearing it. Now the Metropolitan Opera Association owns the opera house and has done considerable work in renovating and improving it. Prior to this, opera depended upon the support of the wealthy; now it is supported by the public. This is a symbol of American democracy.

From the beginning of opera in the United States, the greater number produced have been popular German and Italian operas. Today many leaders are advocating reform—that opera be given in the English language, that singers be employed who can act as well as sing, and that new shorter operas be written by our American composers. Some such operas have already been written and are receiving favorable recognition. They are shorter than the usual grand opera and more nearly resemble the musical comedy. Some of them are *Of Thee I Sing* and *Porgy and Bess,* by George Gershwin, *Face the Music,* by Irving Berlin, *Show Boat,* by Jerome Kern, and *Emperor Jones,* by Louis Gruenberg.[20]

Opera for Children. Operas given in English and performed primarily for children and young people are becoming popular. These have been made possible largely through the work of the Junior Programs Opera Company. The movement was started by the National Music League about ten years ago, and three years later was taken over by the Junior Programs, Incorporated. This is a new commercial organization which has three groups presenting programs in the fields of opera, ballet, drama, concerts, and other cultural entertainment for children. One of the operas they have presented is *Jack and the Beanstalk.* The music is written by Louis Gruenberg and the text by John Erskine. Both are American composers. Another favorite is "The Bumblebee Prince," from *The Tsar Sultan,* by Rimski-Korsakov.[21]

America's Composers of Serious Music. Not only has the public interest in opera and symphony orchestras emphasized the importance of music in America, but it has given American composers an opportunity such as they have never had before to have their compositions produced. Leading orchestra conductors have shown an interest in producing the works of American composers. WPA orchestras, in particular, feature the performance of the work of American composers. Important music schools, such as the Julliard School of Music in New York, the Curtis Institute in Philadelphia, and the Eastman School at Rochester, pro-

20. Louis Gruenberg (grün'bûrg). A Russian-American composer known for his symphonic and operatic treatment of jazz tunes (1884-   ).   21. Rimski-Korsakov (rĭm'skê kôr'så·kôf). A Russian composer (1844-1908).

vide opportunity for the works of American composers to
be heard.

It would be impossible in these short accounts to mention all of the American composers who are producing good
music at the present time. One group is accomplishing
some interesting results in the use of folk songs, particularly the Indian, Negro, and mountain music. The inspiration of this group can probably be traced to Anton
Dvořák[22] (1841-1904), a Bohemian composer, who was invited to come to New York City as a guest teacher at the
National Conservatory of Music. He was greatly interested
in the use of folk melodies and had made extensive use of
them in his own compositions. While in this country, he
attempted to show his pupils how to use the folk music
found here. He wrote a part of his *New World Symphony*
while he was in America, staying in Spillville, Iowa. One
of his students, Henry T. Burleigh, has since made extensive use of the music of the Negro in his compositions.
Others who have emphasized Negro music are Nathaniel
Dett, David Guion, and John Powell.

Arthur Farwell was another composer to follow the suggestions of Dvořák to take folk music as a basis for compositions. He has used the music of the Indian and, to
some extent, mountain music. Charles Wakefield Cadman
has also successfully used Indian melodies in his compositions. Henry Gilbert, who produced an orchestral work
based on three minstrel tunes, "Zip Coon," "Dearest May,"
and "Don't Be Foolish, Joe," is another of the group making use of American folk music.

Another group of composers is experimenting with jazz
as the basis for their serious compositions. This may be
illustrated by John Alden Carpenter's "Skyscrapers" and

22. Anton Dvořák (dvôr′zhäk).

"Krazy Kat." Still others are attempting to work out entirely new ideas such as using many keys at the same time, using new scales, and writing without form.

American composition is encouraged in a number of ways. Music publishers are becoming more interested in printing the works of American composers. Numerous fellowships, some of them providing from fifteen hundred to twenty-five hundred dollars annually, are available. The American Society of Composers, Authors, and Publishers (ASCAP) protects copyrighted works and enables composers to collect royalties on works performed on radio or stage. In this way the composer's improved financial status enables him to pursue his work without interruption.

Contributions of Popular Music. If one could jump upon a magic carpet some night and peep into all of the restaurants and cafes with juke boxes and swing bands, into all of the dance halls, into all of the homes with radios, one would think that all the world was listening to popular music. Indeed it has been said that "the one outstanding contribution which America has made to twentieth-century music has been in the field of popular activities—jazz, swing, or whatever name we may wish to give it. . . . . The popular music of America has had a far-reaching effect on the world, for it has been as eagerly sought in Europe, in Australia, and even in the Far East as it has been in the land of its birth."

Changes in Popular Music. There has been much change in the character of popular music since the early nineteen hundreds. At that time the songs had simple tunes with their success depending upon either the appeal of the melody or the sentiment expressed in their words. These songs were written to be sung, and reached popularity by way of Tin Pan Alley and the song pluggers.

Their financial profit came from the sale of sheet music and phonograph records. Every dime store had its sheet music department with a pianist obligingly ready to play any number one wanted to hear. Parents and grandparents of today can tell you of how groups of young people used to gather about the piano and sing "My Little Georgia Rose," "On the Banks of the Wabash," "Hello Central, Give Me Heaven," "Cheyenne," "School Days," and "When You Wore a Tulip and I Wore a Big Red Rose," or listened to these same songs played on the phonograph. Now a few of the old songs have been revived, but they are jazzed or swung until they can scarcely be recognized.

Song hits of the modern time are short-lived. If they last for a period of two or three months they are considered successful. They are popularized by means of radio hit parades or the motion picture. A person goes to see a new movie and comes out humming a catchy tune; the next week he notices that it has reached first place in the hit parade of the week, and the following week he can drop his nickels in a restaurant juke box and dance to the music again and again. It has in that very short time become a hit and one of the modern popular songs. Six months from that time it will have given place to half a dozen others.

The modern popular song is used for dancing rather than for singing. Tunes have to be danceable to be successful. Little attention is given to the words or their meaning. Silly little ditties with words adapted from nursery rhymes, such as "A Tisket a Tasket" and "Three Little Fishes," have attained tremendous popularity even though the words are as meaningless as a child's nonsense rhyme.

Irving Berlin. The change from the sentimental song written for singing to the modern jazz song intended primarily for dancing seems to date back to "Alexander's Rag-

Courtesy Twentieth Century-Fox Film Corporation

Irving Berlin rehearsed with members of the cast of *Alexander's Ragtime Band* when that motion picture was in production.

time Band" written by Irving Berlin, one of America's best-known popular song writers. He is credited with having written some eight hundred tunes.

Berlin, whose real name is Izzy Baline, is an interesting character and represents the possibilities America offers for achievement. He was born in Russia and came to this country with his parents at about the age of four. When still a young boy he became a singing waiter in a restaurant in New York's Chinatown. He says he became a song writer by accident. He enjoyed writing jingles for songs and one day took one of them to a publisher. The publisher, glancing up from reading the rhymes said, "I suppose you have a tune to this?" The young man, after some quick thinking, hummed a tune which he made up as he went along. Thus his first song, for which he was paid twenty-five dollars, was created.

The next year he wrote "Alexander and His Ragtime Clarinet," but publishers were not interested in it because the number appeared to be purely instrumental and the form was not that of the usual popular song. Berlin, however, did not forget the song and, when the Friars Club was preparing for an entertainment and asked him to provide a dance song, he produced his former melody, and "Alexander's Ragtime Band" made song history.

Some of his best-known songs are "Oh! How I Hate to Get Up in the Morning," "Call Me Up Some Rainy Afternoon," "My Wife's Gone to the Country," "All Alone," "The Song Is Ended, but the Melody Lingers On," and "God Bless America." His songs seem to be the bridge between the popular sentimental songs of the nineties and the modern jazz song. One of our modern writers of music history places Irving Berlin in line with Stephen Collins Foster as a writer of American folk songs. He says that ragtime was the form chosen because it happened to be popular at the time.

Berlin now owns a publishing house, is a theatrical producer, and is classed as one of America's millionaires. He is not a trained musician, but is able to pick out his tunes in one key. He is said to have a gearshift piano which will play in any key if the player merely twists a crank. This mechanical device helps to make up for his lack of musical training.

Serious and Popular Music. Jerome Kern, whose *Show Boat* has been mentioned previously, represents the composers of popular music which is on a somewhat higher scale. He has succeeded in using ragtime and jazz without placing it in the ranks of cheap music. His "Ol' Man River" and "I Can't Help Lovin' Dat Man" are general favorites of which the public never seems to tire.

Jazz Music. Jazz is said to be the most typically American thing we have yet produced. It has developed in various stages from its reported origin with the old Negro, Stale Bread, and his Spasm Band which played along the New Orleans water front, to Paul Whiteman's band playing in a New York concert hall.

It is exceedingly difficult to define jazz because it is not a particular kind of music, but rather a language of music, a means of communicating ideas and moods. It is characterized by the syncopated beat of ragtime, by improvising variations of the melody and adding parts to it, and by strange effects made by the instruments, such as laughing, moaning, and squealing. Jazz seems to be definitely related to the Negro spiritual, where each singer takes his turn at improvising while the others harmonize with him. In jazz the instruments instead of the voice do the improvising. In its early stages, the pianist or cornetist played the melodies while the counter melodies were played on the clarinet or saxophone. The modern jazz band or orchestra employs more instruments. There is much freedom in jazz, the players preferring to be free to improvise on any theme they choose, whether it be a march, blues, popular song, or folk song. The word "jazz" is probably of Creole origin and means "to speed up."

The Rapid Growth of Jazz. Jazz is said to have originated among the Negroes in the South, probably in New Orleans. The popularity of it, however, dates back nearly thirty years to the time when Joseph K. Gorham brought one of the southern jazz bands to play in a cafe in Chicago.

In the beginning, the music of these bands was very crude. One of the early jazz bands consisted of a piano player, a cornetist, a trombonist, and a drummer, who also had a collection of tin pans, cow bells, and whistles. The cornetist and pianist played the tune while the trombonist and drummer were busy with all the fancy touches.

Following the close of the First World War, jazz spread over the country rapidly. It was used primarily for dancing and was frowned upon by most lovers of serious music.

Paul Whiteman, however, had a vision of the possibilities of jazz. Nearly twenty years ago, at the Aeolian Music Hall in New York City, he gave a concert in which he attempted to show the possibilities of this kind of music. He called the program "An Experiment in Modern Music." He tried to show the effect created by producing melodies of serious music as jazz, and also the effect of a symphonic treatment of popular tunes. A special feature of the program was a number by George Gershwin called "A Rhapsody in Blue," a piano concert number which was based on a jazz theme. The audience showed keen delight in the whole performance and the newspapers immediately gave to Paul Whiteman the title of "jazz king," which he has continued to hold.

The program of the first Whiteman concert is of particular interest, for it marked a definite step in the musical history of America. From that time, jazz has developed along several lines, three of which are especially worthy of mention here.

George Gershwin. One direction which jazz has taken is that represented by the music of George Gershwin, who was a leader in the movement to make jazz the basis of serious music. Gershwin's career is that of another poor boy rising to fame. He first studied piano in his father's ghetto[23] restaurant, becoming a brilliant performer. Later he became a song plugger for a publisher of popular sheet music. At that time his first successful tunes were written. After his "Rhapsody in Blue" made such a hit on the Whiteman program, Walter Damrosch, then conductor of the New York Symphony Society, commissioned him to write a piano concerto. It was quite an unusual commission, for Damrosch always maintained the highest musical standards and this showed his recognition of Gershwin and his work.

PROGRAM OF THE FIRST WHITEMAN CONCERT
An Experiment in Modern Music

TRUE FORM OF JAZZ
    a. Ten Years Ago—Livery Stable Blues..............*La Rocca*
    b. With Modern Embellishment[24]—
       Mama Loves Papa................................*Baer*
COMEDY SELECTIONS
    a. Origin of Yes, We Have No Bananas...............*Silver*
    b. Instrumental Comedy—
       So This Is Venice...............................*Thomas*
       Adapted from the Carnival of Venice
CONTRAST—LEGITIMATE VS. JAZZING
    a. Selection in True Form—
       Whispering ....*Schonberger*
    b. Same Selection with Jazz Treatment
RECENT COMPOSITIONS WITH MODERN SCORE
    a. Limehouse Blues...............................*Braham*
    b. I Love You.....................................*Archer*
    c. Raggedy Ann....................................*Kern*
FLAVORING A SELECTION WITH BORROWED TUNES
    Russian Rose......................................*Grofé*
      Based on the Song of the Volga Boatman

23. ghetto (gĕt'ō). The quarter of a city in which Jews live. 24. Embellishment (ĕm·bĕl'ĭsh·mĕnt). That which adds beauty or elegance.

SEMI-SYMPHONIC ARRANGEMENT OF POPULAR MELODIES
  Consisting of
    Alexander's Ragtime Band
    A Pretty Girl Is Like a Melody ⎬ ....*Berlin*
    Orange Blossoms in California
A SUITE OF SERENADES..............................*Herbert*
  a. Spanish; b. Chinese; c. Cuban; d. Oriental
ADAPTATION OF STANDARD SELECTIONS TO DANCE RHYTHM
  a. Pale Moon.......................................*Logan*
  b. To a Wild Rose............................*MacDowell*
  c. Chansonnette[25] ....*Friml*
GEORGE GERSHWIN—PIANO—
  A Rhapsody in Blue...........................*Gershwin*
    Accompanied by the Orchestra
IN THE FIELD OF CLASSICS
  Pomp and Circumstance.............................*Elgar*

Sweet Jazz. A second course of development was that which is known as sweet jazz. One usually hears it over the radio or in a softly lighted night club or hotel dining room. It is a type of popular jazz which introduces the voice in crooning parts. The players sometimes lay down their instruments and croon alone or in harmony, or the crooning may be accompanied by an instrument. The music is played much more softly than other jazz and with muted instruments. Rudy Vallee is largely responsible for the crooning idea. Other leaders of orchestras and bands which play sweet jazz are Wayne King, Fred Waring, and Vincent Lopez. The bands which these men direct are frequently spoken of as "name bands."

Swing Music. A third development of jazz is swing music. Swing music is smoother than jazz, is played with even more freedom, but is basically the same. Its develop-

25. Chansonnette (shăn′sŏn·ĕt′). A little song.

ment came about partly as a reaction against the commercialization of jazz. Music publishers had commercialized jazz by having arrangements of certain popular numbers written down and printed so that they might be sold. This was contrary to the original idea of jazz. Players of swing music maintain the privilege of freedom in interpretations and in improvisations.

Swing has been defined as improvised variations on a popular tune. The arranger of the music is one of the most important members of the swing band. He lays out the general plan and makes suggestions as to the treatment of the parts. Usually these parts are not even printed. Each player receives his suggestions from the arranger, works out his own variations, and never plays from written music. The more important swing bands have their own arrangements which they guard jealously.

The swing band usually makes use of four saxophones (two tenor and two alto) and five brass instruments (three trumpets and two trombones) for melody and variations. A piano, drums, string bass, or guitar furnish the rhythm.

The players, many of whom are Negroes, frequently have little background of musical education. They play swing because they love it and because of a natural talent. Many have learned all they know by carefully observing others play and by working out their own ideas. The player in the swing band, however, must not be thought of as an unskilled musician, for he reaches a very high degree of skill with his own instrument.

In 1938 an important event in the development of swing music occurred. Benny Goodman and his swing orchestra gave a concert at Carnegie Hall in New York City. This was a recognition of swing music equal to that given to Paul Whiteman and his jazz music fourteen years before.

A Swing Vocabulary. Swing music is said to have developed a vocabulary all its own. You may be interested and amused to know some of the words in the "swing dictionary."

agony pipe—clarinet
barrel house—free improvisation
canary—a girl singer
dog house—bass fiddle
front man—the leader
frisking their whiskers—getting warmed up to swing
get off man—one who plays a solo part
go to town—get hot
groan box—the accordion
grunt iron—tuba
hides—the drum
hot star—creator of a swing style
jam—to swing freely
jam session—an informal meeting of musicians playing for their
    own amusement without score
jitter bugs—swing fanatics
long hair—classical musicians
long underwear gang—a term of contempt for a "sweet" band
nitery—night club
paper man—man who plays with written music (a term of contempt)
platter—phonograph record
plumber—the trumpeter
push pipes—the slide trombone
squeak box—the violin
wheat bender—term of contempt for one who doesn't like swing
wood pile—the xylophone
woodshed—to experiment in private with a new tune

CHAPTER XVIII

MUSIC OF THE WORLD WARS

Music of the First World War

Characteristics of War Songs. War, like many other important national events, presents an occasion for the composition of new songs and for the revival of old ones. For the most part, the music of each war America has participated in seems to have certain features which are characteristic of the time of its origin. Some of the songs of the Revolution and the War of 1812 seem absurd and clumsy to us now. Those of the War between the States were, on the whole, sad and sentimental. Songs of the Spanish-American War were definitely sentimental. The First World War gave us songs with a dash of bravado[1] and gaiety. Those which were sung in this country at the beginning of the Second World War were, for the most part, of a serious nature.

A few songs of each of the earlier wars have lived and are still sung on patriotic occasions. For example, "Yankee Doodle," with many new versions and parodies, has survived several wars. "The Old Gray Mare" was sung during the War between the States, again in the Spanish-American War, and in the First World War. Each time, however, there were different words to the tune.

1. bravado (brȧ·vä′dō). Great show of boldness.

Songs Sung. While there has not been enough time since the First World War to determine which of its songs, if any, will really live, already some of them are being revived in the modern military training camps. For example, "K-K-K-Katy, Beautiful Katy," a First World War favorite, has become

> K-K-K-K-P
> Dirty old K-P
> That's the only army job that I abhor, etc.

A great deal of singing occurred during the First World War. There was singing in camps, at patriotic rallies, and at home. Everybody sang to keep up his courage. Many songs were of a humorous and somewhat boisterous nature. Among these were "Where Do We Go from Here, Boys?" "How You Gonna Keep 'em Down on the Farm?" "Goodbye Broadway, Hello France," "They're All Out of Step but Jim," "Oh! How I Hate to Get Up in the Morning," and "K-K-K-Katy, Beautiful Katy." There were others, such as "Keep the Home Fires Burning" and "Till We Meet Again," which were intended to keep up the morale at home. There were songs which reflected the philosophy and cheerful spirit of the boys who went across. Examples of this type were "Smiles," "Pack Up Your Troubles," "Over There," and "Tipperary." Songs such as "There's a Long, Long Trail" and "Rose of No Man's Land" were of the more sentimental type.

Some of the most popular songs were borrowed from the allies. "Keep the Home Fires Burning" and "Tipperary" were from England; "Madelon," from France.

Stories of World War Songs. "Smiles" is a First World War song which has been sung thousands of times and in all sorts of places. There is scarcely a song sheet for group singing that does not contain the words of "Smiles." The words for the song were written by J. Will Calahan and the music by Lee S. Roberts. The melody was written before the words. At one time Roberts heard a speaker stress the importance of a smile. This suggested to him the title for a song and he wrote the melody in a few minutes. The lyric followed almost immediately, and the song became one that the soldiers, as well as those at home, loved to sing. The sales of the song for the first six months were said to have reached 1,800,000 copies.

"There's a Long, Long Trail," a popular song, had a sale of five million copies. It was originally written not as a war song but for a fraternity banquet at Yale. Its melody was composed by Zo Elliott and its words were written by Stoddard King. When the song was sung at the banquet, the young men present demanded to hear it again and again.

During the six months which followed the banquet, the composers submitted the song to practically every music publisher in New York, but all of them turned it down. After graduation from Yale, Zo Elliott went to England to attend college. One day he went to a music shop to see about renting a piano for use while at school. In trying out a piano he played the melody of his "Long, Long Trail." It happened that the proprietor of the shop was a song scout for a large publishing house in England. He liked the melody which Elliott played and sent for his London publisher. The song was accepted and published in 1913, but received little attention until after the outbreak of the war. Then it became one of the most popular songs of the allies.

In the original song the verse was written in a minor key. However, when the song was published in the

United States, the publisher required that the verse be rewritten in a major key. And so the English sing "Days are growing very lonely" in a minor key, while Americans sing it in a major key.

"Over There," with its melody representing a bugle call, was written by George M. Cohan. It became another of the popular war songs. The secretary to President Wilson at the time sent Cohan this note: "The President considers your song, 'Over There,' a genuine inspiration to all American manhood." In May, 1940, Cohan received a gold medal for this song from President Roosevelt, a recognition which had been authorized by Congress four years before.

Music in the Camps. Everyone agreed that the boys in camp must have music. The Y. M. C. A. did much to provide them with materials and entertainers. Famous singers went from camp to camp to sing for the boys. Caruso and Schumann-Heink sang for gatherings all over the United States. Irving Berlin wrote *Yip, Yip, Yaphank,* a musical comedy with songs about the routine of army life, to be given by the enlisted men at Camp Upton, Long Island. "Oh! How I Hate to Get Up in the Morning" was one of its hit songs. All publishing houses sent music free for the use of the soldiers. Even though there was a shortage of paper and printing rates advanced, music still had to be provided for the boys, for army officials ruled that music was essential to win the war. Sheet music was printed in a smaller size than customary in order to conserve paper. This form was found to be more convenient and still continues in use.

An Aid to Army Morale. The appreciation of music for army men is shown in an article in *The Etude* about the late Major General Smedley D. Butler. "Old Gimlet

Eye,"[2] as Butler was called, was in command of a detachment of United States soldiers sent to France. The reception camp at Brest, France, was in a miserable place. "Acres and acres of mud flats with dripping, dejected, khaki-colored tents. Beyond, a cheerless steel sea half hid-

Courtesy Twentieth Century-Fox Film Corporation

Irving Berlin and Jack Haley sing "Oh! How I Hate to Get Up in the Morning."

den in fog. Shivering cold, bleak, death-stricken—a hell of a place," is the description in the major general's own words. One hundred men had died of influenza on the way over. Many others were ill. General Butler himself was ill, but when he saw the dismal place and looked into

2. "Old Gimlet Eye." A sharp eye boring like a gimlet, which is a small tool used for boring holes.

the white, drawn faces of his troops as they came from the boat he shouted, "Do you suppose you could sing?" The whole crowd broke out in "Sweet Adeline." You can imagine the cheers with which they were greeted by their buddies who were already over there.

General Butler was placed in command of this same reception camp with the orders to clean it up. With twelve thousand cases of influenza among sixty-five thousand men in camp, it became a battle of saving men's lives from disease rather than from battle wounds. The general appreciated the great value of music in keeping up the spirits of his men. He said, "Our regimental band of sixty pieces was a knockout. It was composed of Italians, musical to the fingertips, who had been recruited and trained by a band leader. . . . . He marched his Italians up and down the hill day and night. They played, until their drums were soggy, to give courage to those poor devils flattened out by the epidemic. I soon had more than thirty regimental bands in different sections of the camp, playing jazz, one-steps, stirring military marches, in continuous shifts. The doughboys, miserable as they were, were soon shuffling their feet in the mud to keep time to the lively airs."

A More Serious Type of Music. "The Victory Ball," a symphonic poem, is another musical selection of particular interest. It was not a song of the First World War, but came about as a result of the war. After the signing of the armistice, November 11, 1918, people went wild with joy. Every type of celebration imaginable was held to express the relief from the worries and horrors of war. In London a ball was given in celebration of the close of the war. Alfred Noyes, a prominent British poet, was present at the ball and, as a result of his thoughts during the celebration, wrote the poem "The Victory Dance." This poem expresses the resentment which he thought the dead soldiers felt at such gaiety and frivolity so soon after their sacrifices. It represents the shadows of the dead men looking on at the celebration and discussing the occasion among themselves.

Ernest Schelling, a modern American composer, was inspired by the poem to write an orchestral composition expressing its feeling. The introduction begins very softly, then abruptly changes to bring out the atmosphere and motion of a crowded ballroom. Then one hears the tuning of instruments and the dance is ready to begin. Dance music with a military note is built to a climax, when the call to arms from the ghostly legions is heard. A soft march brings the imaginary troops gradually nearer and nearer. This march is interrupted by the sound of an approaching airplane. Following a tremendous climax of sound come the solemn strains of the hymn of death. The music is an exceedingly strong representation of the feeling of the poem.

Patriotic Music after the War. Little patriotic music appeared during the years between the First World War and the second great struggle for democracy.

During the depression which followed the crash of the stock markets in 1929, there were some attempts to write songs to keep up the spirits of the American people. On the whole, however, these songs were unsuccessful.

Music of the Second World War

Music during the Period of National Emergency. With the beginning of the Second World War, the people of the United States came to realize that the First World

War had not been a war to end wars, that the world had not been made safe for democracy, and that no permanent peace had been found. Our own freedom and safety seemed to be threatened. Measures were taken to build up our defenses and to extend aid to the countries which were being attacked by the aggressor nations. It was a period of national emergency.

Patriotic fervor was aroused. The American flag was displayed at the close of movie films, on motor cars, and in shop windows. Women's dresses and jewelry displayed red, white, and blue colors and military emblems. The national anthem was sung or played at every public gathering. School curriculums emphasized the ideals of democracy more sharply.

An outburst of patriotic songs resulted. The majority of these songs were serious in nature and lacked the gaiety and humor of the First World War songs. Some of them were "God Bless America," "We Like It over Here," "This Is Our Side of the Ocean," "Our Nation's Prayer," and three songs with the title "I Am an American." Song publishers held in readiness a large number of songs for immediate release if an occasion arose which demanded them. "Any Bonds Today," written by Irving Berlin, was brought out to urge people to buy bonds to help finance the defense program and later the war effort.

Many old songs were revived. Among them were "Madelon," "My Buddy," "Joan of Arc," and "How You Gonna Keep 'em Down on the Farm?" Several new songs from England received recognition here. Undoubtedly the favorites were "There'll Always Be an England" and "The White Cliffs of Dover." Ivor Novello, who wrote "Keep the Home Fires Burning," composed a new song, "We'll Remember the Meadows." Some others were

"Even Hitler Had a Mother," "Run, Rabbit, Run," and "We Must All Stick Together." American music in turn was used in England. The popular "Beer Barrel Polka" became a favorite marching song of the British troops. One song, "The Tears of an Angel," brought together the two world wars in its text. The angel is a mother who, during the First World War, waved good-bye to Dad and in the Second waved good-bye to their lad.

It is interesting to note that the song which attained the greatest popularity, "God Bless America," was really written at the time of the First World War, but had been discarded at the time. Irving Berlin had written it to be sung in the finale of *Yip, Yip, Yaphank,* but it was replaced by "We're on Our Way to France," which seemed more appropriate at the time. Kate Smith, a well-known radio singer, wanted a patriotic selection to sing in an Armistice Day broadcast. She appealed to Irving Berlin, who remembered the old song he had written twenty years before. He spent two weeks in revising it. The song as sung by Miss Smith immediately became a favorite, and soon everybody was singing it. Irving Berlin announced that all royalties from the sale of the song were to be given to the Boy Scouts and Girl Scouts of America. These organizations received eight cents for every copy sold, and the money was spent in promoting their activities. By the summer of 1940, five hundred thousand copies had been sold.

A New Army Songbook. When the young men of the United States were drafted for training in army camps as a part of the national defense program, it was said that soldiers must sing, no matter what. A new soldier's songbook was published to encourage singing in camps. This *Army Song Book* was small enough to be carried in the soldier's blouse pocket. It contained the words of sixty-seven favorite songs which were chosen by the soldiers themselves. "The Star-Spangled Banner" received the most votes when soldiers were given an opportunity to check their choices from a list given them. Among the other ten first choices were "America," "God Bless America," "Home on the Range," "I Am an American," "My Buddy," "Caisson[3] Song," "The Last Roundup," "You're in the Army Now," and "Carry Me Back to Ol' Virginny."

A Ballad for Americans. In 1935 a young American poet in Columbia University, New York City, became concerned about the intolerance and persecution which seemed to be spreading through the whole civilized world at the time, and expressed his feeling in a poem. He sketched the history of the United States and, in its stirring climax, emphasized America as the symbol of freedom and democracy. The poet was John Latouche.

A few years later he met a young musician, Earl Robinson. Together they arranged the poem to a musical setting for *Sing for Your Supper*, a musical review given as a Federal Theater Project in New York City. The show ran for only a few weeks and the song, which had already received much favor, was offered to the Columbia Broadcasting System. The famous Negro bass, Paul Robeson, sang it over the radio on the Pursuit of Happiness program. The reception was amazing. The magazine *Time*, in its issue of November 20, 1939, gave the following report:

In the studio an audience of 600 stamped, shouted, bravoed for two minutes while the show was still on the air, for 15 minutes after. In the next half-hour 150 telephone calls managed to get through CBS's jammed Manhattan switchboard. The Hollywood

3. Caisson (kă′sŏn). An ammunition wagon for movable artillery.

switchboard was jammed for two hours. In the next few days bales of letters demanded words, music, recordings.

The song received unusual recognition when it was sung at the opening of the Republican National Convention in Philadelphia. The music is exquisitely adapted to the words and sentiment of the poem.

Both the words and music of this "Ballad for Americans" have the power to thrill and inspire one with the importance, privilege, and obligation of being an American. It truly presents, through the combination of words and music, a vision of America's heritage. Robinson and Latouche have recently written another ballad called "Battle Hymn." This ballad tells the story of the events leading up to the entrance of the United States in the Second World War.

After Pearl Harbor. Pearl Harbor in Hawaii was attacked by the Japanese on December 7, 1941, and the United States became actively engaged in the Second World War. A host of new popular songs sprang up almost over night. Daily, over the radio and from restaurant juke boxes, were heard such songs as "Remember Pearl Harbor," "We Did It Before, We Can Do It Again," and "Keep Them Flying." The words for songs praising the work of General Douglas MacArthur in the Philippines, which were under attack, appeared in magazines and daily newspapers. Among them were "Just Fightin' Along," sung to the tune of "Old Man River," and "Old Doug MacArthur."

It has been estimated that, within the twenty-four hours after the first radio announcement of the attack on Pearl Harbor, one thousand songs were written. Probably within one half-hour as many songs were written as during the whole of the Revolutionary War. It is said that

"You're a Sap, Mister Jap," thirty thousand copies of which were sold in three weeks, was put into publication three hours before war was declared on Japan by the United States.

Of course, many of these hastily written songs were not good music. Many of the selections which did reach publication did not last. In general, most of the songs were sentimental ballads about the soldier's home, mother, or sweetheart, such as "Dear Mom," or "We'll Meet Again, Don't Know Where, Don't Know When," or a humorous type of song intended to amuse and cheer up the people.

A definite trend toward the writing of serious and dignified music was noted, however. Tin Pan Alley and the radio did much to promote such music as "American's Creed" by Hugo Frey and William Tyler Page, "Freedom's Land" by Archibald MacLeish and Roy Harris, and a "Songs of Democracy" series, with music by Roy Harris.

Changes and Adjustments Brought On by the War. The months immediately following the entrance of the United States into the Second World War brought many changes and adjustments in the pattern of musical life in America. Some of these changes tended to encourage and to promote greater effort in musical affairs; others seemed to discourage or retard advancement. The rapidity and willingness with which adjustments were made, however, indicated the democratic spirit and the true patriotism of Americans.

Many talented musicians—concert and opera singers, members of orchestras, composers, students, and members of church choirs—were called into war service. Plans for concerts and music festivals had to be cancelled or changed in some instances because of new situations. There might be occasions for blackouts. There was need to conserve tires and gasoline. Moreover, many people spent every possible minute in some kind of war work.

Musical instruments were hard to obtain because materials such as steel, copper, and brass, which had been used in their manufacture, were needed to make implements of war. The few instruments which were available became more expensive because of a federal tax placed upon all articles not considered necessities.

The business of making phonograph records, which had reached an all-time high in 1941, one hundred million records having been produced and distributed, was halted because of a lack of shellac which was needed in their manufacture. Shellac had been obtained largely from India, and the limited amount which could be obtained was needed for war articles.

A Music Program for Men in Service. A definite program for music in the training camps was arranged. It was planned for the most part by the War Department, the Joint Army and Navy Committee on Welfare and Recreation and its Music Sub-committee, and by representatives of national music organizations. Numbers of new army bands were organized. In order to provide directors for these bands, an Army Band Leader School, with a two months' course for training musicians to lead military bands, was provided. In addition to these specially organized bands which were a part of the regular military forces, there were many volunteer organizations within soldier groups, such as dance bands, radio orchestras, orchestras for dramatic productions by army men, small instrumental ensembles, and even symphony orchestras. Soldiers talented in music had an opportunity to use their talents in concerts and in entertainments staged by the soldiers themselves. Soldier artists were frequently invited to near-by cities to be soloists in symphony orchestra or radio programs.

For the entertainment of the boys in the more isolated camps, music kits were furnished. Some contained sets of

U. S. Army Signal Corps photograph

Regimental bands are provided in the army camps.

musical instruments and collections of music for dance orchestras; others had guitars, ocarinas,[4] ukuleles, and collections of popular songs for singing. Lists of band music suitable for military bands and vocal music for use by song leaders were furnished to each camp.

4. ocarinas (ŏk′á·rē′náz). Simple wind instruments with mouthpiece and finger holes; give soft, whistlelike tones.

An elaborate program of radio and other forms of mechanical music was provided for the army camps. As a special means of maintaining the morale of our armed forces in foreign countries, a number of popular sponsored radio programs, through the facilities of the Columbia and National Broadcasting systems, were transmitted by short wave to the four corners of the earth. Someone gave these broadcasts the fitting name of "global entertainment." An American stationed in Australia, Iceland, Ireland, or Egypt could hear the same programs heard by his family in the United States, for these programs were broadcast from recordings made when the selections went on the air in the United States.

The Camp Shows, Incorporated, an organization which served as a clearing house for professional talent for army and navy programs, provided excellent musical entertainment for the boys in camp. Practically every concert artist in the country volunteered to give performances for the soldiers. Well-known vocal and instrumental organizations made tours which included a large number of camps. Frequently their programs were broadcast from the camp which they were visiting.

A special type of contribution by individual musicians is illustrated by the work of Irving Berlin. Mr. Berlin returned to Camp Upton in the Second World War as a volunteer to write another military show. The production, *This Is the Army,* was prepared to be presented on Broadway in New York City for the purpose of adding to the Army Emergency Relief Fund. Irving Berlin felt a need for living in camp while he was composing the music for the show. He wanted to live as one of the soldiers, to talk with them and share their experiences in barracks, canteen, church, and infirmary. In this way he thought, he would be better able to express the thoughts and feelings of the men in the army.

A Music Program for Civilians. Music in camps was not the only concern of national planning agencies. Music as a vital force in keeping up the morale of the people back

U. S. Naval Official Photograph, courtesy Columbia Broadcasting Company

Many radio artists are making appearances at training camps
to entertain the sailors and soldiers.

home was considered also. The National Music Council, an organization composed of thirty-seven musical organizations representing practically every phase of musical activity in America, was formed and it worked with the War Department on a wartime program in music. The program for civilians during wartime included the following features:

1. Promoting noontime concerts in war industry plants and encouraging other musical activities such as glee clubs, choruses, bands, and group singing for defense workers and their families.

2. Establishing a series of free concerts for the general public in museums, libraries, and other institutions, and promoting community singing.

3. Stimulating the activities of all musical organizations so that high standards of musical excellence could be maintained.

4. Encouraging the composition of music for all purposes, including music for propaganda.

5. Encouraging study and musical performance by young people and others so that the art of music should not suffer after the close of the war.

6. Encouraging an increased use of music in the churches.

Music as a Stimulus in the Sale of War Stamps and Bonds. Music was frequently used to stimulate the sale of war stamps and bonds, one means of helping to finance the war. The Michigan WPA Symphony Orchestra is said to have originated the idea of war stamp concerts whose proceeds were used for the purchase of war stamps and bonds. During the first six months of the war, this organization was responsible for the sale of three hundred thousand dollars worth of stamps and bonds. Units of the New York City WPA Music Project gave concerts at the Brooklyn museum. While they were not permitted to charge admission to concerts given in a public building, during the programs the audience was urged to show patriotism and appreciation of the concert by buying war stamps at booths provided in the building for that purpose. Individual artists frequently gave the proceeds from a concert to the purchase of war stamps and bonds or to some branch of war relief. A special series of radio opera broadcasts was arranged to stimulate the sale of these stamps and bonds.

A New Arrangement of Our National Anthem. The war brought about increased opportunities for singing and playing "The Star-Spangled Banner." In trying to find a suitable arrangement for use by army bands, it was discovered that the Library of Congress possessed no fewer than fifty different arrangements. It appeared that our national anthem was standard in title and words only. To correct this situation, Dr. George S. Howard and Major Howard C. Bronson worked out a simple arrangement which provided a good accompaniment for singing. It was written in the key of A-flat, a tone lower than the music is usually written. The arrangement was intended to be used for bands and instrumental performance and for group singing by adults.

STUDY EXERCISES

Questions and Problems

1. Of what importance is an understanding of mechanical musical instruments today?
2. Of what significance has the organization of networks of broadcasting stations been?
3. What influence has the radio had on the study of music?
4. How does the music of motion pictures of today compare with that of early motion pictures?
5. Name two of the best-known carillons in the United States. How is a carillon played?
6. How has Uncle Sam promoted music?
7. What provisions do many cities and towns make for music in their own communities?
8. In what way do music foundations promote music and give aid to musicians?
9. How is music used in industry? What benefits are derived from it?
10. In what way is music used in promoting health? in curing disease?
11. What is the place of music in church services today?
12. How important is music in the everyday life of Americans today? Give examples.
13. How do you account for the increased interest in opera today?
14. Where do some modern composers get inspirations for their music?
15. For what type of music is Irving Berlin famous? Name some of his compositions that have been most popular.
16. What did Paul Whiteman do to bring jazz music to the attention of the public? What influence did he have on its development?
17. What songs were popular during the First World War? Where did some of them originate?

Suggested Activities

1. Collect newspaper articles and illustrations of modern musical instruments. Make a folder or display of the material you find.

2. Write an account comparing and contrasting the work of Gottlieb Graupner and Theodore Thomas with that of Leopold Stokowski and Walter Damrosch.

3. For a week, listen to radio programs of serious music and make a list of the selections heard. Note if some are played more frequently than others. Study the life and work of the composers whose numbers you like best.

4. Write a brief account of the development of dance music from the blues to the swing of today. List important composers and orchestra leaders who play this music.

5. Study the poems "Ballad for Americans," by John Latouche and "I Hear America Singing," by Walt Whitman. Listen to the records with the musical arrangements by Earl Robinson and George Kleinsinger, respectively. Be prepared to tell how, in your opinion, the music adds to the effectiveness of the poems.

6. Keep a record for a month of the music used in church services together with the names of the composers.

7. Attend theater productions or moving pictures based on some operas or operettas.

8. Make a study of the importance of Tin Pan Alley and Hollywood in the development of popular music in this country since 1890.

9. Keep a scrapbook or clipping file of articles on music in the Second World War.

10. *Class exercise:* Work with a class committee to prepare a chart showing in what ways the members of your class have participated in music training or music organizations.

11. *Class exercise:* Under the guidance of your teacher, make a frieze or series of drawings representing the various phases of music in American life today.

REFERENCES FOR PUPILS AND TEACHERS

Pupils' References

Song Collections:

The Golden Book of Favorite Songs, by John Walter Beattie and Others. Hall & McCreary Co., 1923.

The Gray Book of Favorite Songs, by John Walter Beattie and Others. Hall & McCreary Co., 1924.

A Treasury of American Song, by Olin Downes and Elie Siegmeister. Howell, Soskin & Co., 1940.

Famous Songs and Their Stories, by James J. Geller. Garden City Publishing Co., 1940.

A Century of Progress in American Song, compiled by Marx E. Oberndorfer and Anne S. Faulkner. Hall & McCreary, 1933.

The American Songbag, compiled by Carl Sandburg. Harcourt, Brace & Co., 1927.

Singing America, edited by Augustus D. Zanzig. C. C. Birchard & Co., 1941.

Books:

How Music Grew, by Marion Bauer and Ethel R. Peyser. G. P. Putnam's Sons, 1939.

The Story of Our National Ballads, by C. A. Browne. Thomas Y. Crowell Co., 1919.

Child Life in Colonial Days, by Alice M. Earle. The Macmillan Co., 1927.

The Sabbath in Puritan New England, by Alice M. Earle. Charles Scribner's Sons, 1891.

What We Hear in Music, by Anne Shaw Faulkner. RCA Manufacturing Co., 1939.

The Music That Washington Knew, by William Arms Fisher. Oliver Ditson Co., 1931.

The Music of George Washington's Time, by John Tasker Howard. United States George Washington Bicentennial Commission, 1931.

History Sings, by Hazel Gertrude Kinscella. University Publishing Co., 1940.

Music and Romance for Youth, by Hazel Gertrude Kinscella. RCA Manufacturing Co., 1930.

Tales of Olden Days, by Hazel Gertrude Kinscella. Kinscella Readers; Stories in Music Appreciation, Book 5. University Publishing Co., 1930.

Our Singing Country, compiled by John A. Lomax and Alan Lomax. The Macmillan Co., 1941.

People and Music, by Thomasine C. McGehee. Allyn & Bacon, 1929.

Opera Cavalcade; The Story of the Metropolitan. The Metropolitan Opera Guild, Inc., 1938.

The Singin' Gatherin', compiled by Jeannette Thomas and Joseph A. Leeder. Silver, Burdett Co., 1939.

Teachers' References

History of Public School Music in the United States, by E. B. Birge. Oliver Ditson Co., 1937.

Music in Everyday Life, by Eric T. Clarke. W. W. Norton Co., 1935.

The History of American Music, by Louis C. Elson; revised by Arthur Elson. The Macmillan Co., 1925.

The National Music of America, by Louis C. Elson; revised by Arthur Elson. L. C. Page & Co., 1924.

Our American Music; Three Hundred Years of It, by John Tasker Howard. Thomas Y. Crowell Co., 1939.

History of American Music, edited by W. L. Hubbard. American History and Encyclopedia of Music, Vol. VIII. Irving Square, 1908.

Spiritual Folk-Songs of Early America, by George P. Jackson. J. J. Augustin Co., 1937.

Songs of Yesterday; A Song Anthology of American Life, compiled by Philip D. Jordan and Lillian Kessler. Doubleday, Doran & Co., 1941.

From Jehovah to Jazz, by Helen Kaufmann. Dodd, Mead & Co., 1937.

Music in History; The Evolution of an Art, by Howard D. Kinney and W. R. Anderson. American Book Co., 1940.

They All Sang, by Edward B. Marks. Viking Press, 1934.

Gentlemen, Be Seated; A Parade of the Old-time Minstrels, by Dailey Paskman and Sigmund G. Spaeth. Doubleday, Doran & Co., 1928.

The House That Music Built, by Ethel R. Peyser. Robert M. McBride & Co., 1936.

SUPPLEMENTARY MUSIC MATERIALS

Music for Part One

Music in the Colonial Period

Chapter I. Early Music in the New England Colonies

Songs:
  "Confess Jehovah" (Puritan hymn); "Dundee" (psalm tune); "Old Hundred" (psalm tune)

Song Collection:
  Ye Olde New-England Psalm-Tunes, 1620-1820, edited by W. A. Fisher. Oliver Ditson Co., 1930.

Chapter II. Music in the Southern Colonies

Songs:
  "Auld Lang Syne" (Scotch); "Comin' thro' the Rye" (Scotch); "Oh! Dear, What Can the Matter Be?" (English); "Sally in Our Alley," from *The Beggar's Opera* (English)

Records:
  "Green Sleeves" (English), Victor 21619; "Sailor's Hornpipe" (English), Victor 21685; "Virginia Reels" (English), Victor 20447

Chapter III. Early Music in New York and Pennsylvania

Songs:
"Captain Kidd" (Early American); "The Little Dustman" (Dutch); "O Sacred Head"—Passion Chorale (Moravian); "Rosa" (Dutch)

Record:
"Songs of Old New York (1650-1906)," Decca Album 47

Chapter IV. The Influence of the French and Spanish Colonists

Songs:
"Alabado" (Spanish); "Alouette" (French); "At the Gate of Heaven" (Spanish); "At Pierrot's Door" (French); "Going through Lorraine" (French)

Song Collections:
Folk-Songs of the West and South, edited by Arthur Farwell. Schirmer.
Spanish Songs of Old California, edited by Arthur Farwell. Schirmer.

Records:
"Bridge of Avignon" (French), Victor 22178; "Farandole" (French), Victor 21685; "Fricassee" (French folk dance), Columbia 299-M

Chapter V. Instruments and Instrumental Music in Colonial Days

Records:
"Galliard," by William Byrd, Victor 7873; "First Harpsichord Suite in G," by Henry Purcell, Columbia DB-502; "Cat's Fugue," by D. Scarlatti, Victor 1664; "Sonata in A Major," by D. Scarlatti, Victor 1942

Music for Part Two

Music in the Struggle to Become a Nation

Chapter VI. Music of War and Patriotism

Songs:
"Dixie," by Daniel Emmett; "The Star-Spangled Banner" (to "Anacreon in Heaven"), by Francis Scott Key; "Tenting Tonight," by Walter Kittredge; "When Johnny Comes Marching Home," by Louis Lambert; "Hail, Columbia," attributed to Philip Phile; "Tramp! Tramp! Tramp!" by George F. Root; "Battle Hymn of the Republic," by William Steffe; "Columbia, the Gem of the Ocean," (uncertain origin)

Records:
"American Song Album," Columbia Set M-329; "Ballads of American Revolution and War of 1812," Victor Album P-11; "Liberty Bell March," by John Philip Sousa, Columbia 366-M; "National and Patriotic Airs," Decca Album 139; "Patriotic March Medley," Victor 22013; "Songs of the North in the War between the States, 1861-1865," Decca Album 46; "Songs of the South in the War between the States, 1861-1865," Decca Album 45

Chapter VII. American Statesmen as Patrons of Music

Song Collection:
Colonial Love Lyrics, by Francis Hopkinson. A. P. Schmidt Co.

Collections of Piano Music:
Music from the Days of George Washington, compiled by George Engel. United States George Washington Bicentennial Commission.
A Program of Early American Piano Music, edited by John Tasker Howard. J. Fischer & Bro., 1931.

Chapter VIII. Music of the Folk

Negro
  Songs:
    "Li'l Liza Jane"; "Listen to de Lambs"; "Steal Away"

  Records:
    "Ezekiel Saw de Wheel," Victor 20604; "De Glory Road,"
    Victor 7486; "Juba Dance," by R. N. Dett, Victor 21750;
    "Trampin'," Victor 1896

  Piano Music:
    "Plantation Melody," by Arthur Farwell. G. Schirmer.
    "Pickanniny Dance," by David Guion. G. Schirmer.

Creole
  Songs:
    "Caroline"; "Mah Lindy Lou," by Lily Strickland.

  Song Collections:
    Bayou Ballads, edited by Mina Monroe and Kurt Schindler.
    G. Schirmer.
    Bayou Songs, by Lily Strickland.

  Piano Music:
    "Bamboula," and "Creole Eyes," by L. M. Gottschalk. G.
    Schirmer.

Mountain
  Songs:
    "Barbara Allen"; "Billy Boy"; "Down in the Valley"; "Frog
    Went A-Courting"; "Skip to M'Lou"

  Song Collection:
    Lonesome Tunes, by Loraine Wyman and Howard Brockway.
    H. W. Gray Co.

  Records:
    "Early American Ballads," Victor Album M-604; "Sourwood
    Mountain," Victor 21751

Lumberjacks
  Songs:
    "Flat River Girl"; "The Shanty Man's Life"

Cowboys
  Songs:
    "Good-bye, Old Paint"; "Night-Herding Song"

  Song Collections:
    The Singing Cowboy, edited by Margaret Larkin. Alfred A. Knopf, 1931.
    Cowboy Songs and Other Frontier Ballads, edited by John A. Lomax and Alan Lomax. The Macmillan Co., 1938.

  Records:
    "Sheep and Goat," by David Guion, Victor 24532; "Turkey in the Straw," by David Guion, Victor 22131

Canalmen, Sailors, and Rivermen
  Songs:
    "Blow the Man Down"; "The Erie Canal"; "Rio Grande"; "The Wide Mizzoura"

Composed Popular Songs, Early Nineteenth Century
  Songs:
    "When You and I Were Young, Maggie," by James A. Butterfield; "Ben Bolt," by Nelson Kneass; "The Old Oaken Bucket," by Samuel Woodworth; "Grandfather's Clock," by Henry C. Work

Composed Popular Songs, Time of War Between the States
  Songs:
    "Darling Nellie Gray," by B. R. Hanby; "Listen to the Mockingbird," by Alice Hawthorne

  Song Collection:
    A Program of Early and Mid-Nineteenth Century American Songs, collected and arranged by John Tasker Howard. J. Fischer & Bro., 1931.

Composed Popular Songs of Stephen Collins Foster

Songs:
"Beautiful Dreamer"; "Jeannie with the Light Brown Hair"; "Old Black Joe"; "Old Folks at Home"; "Uncle Ned"

Sound movie:
Stephen Collins Foster, Famous Music Master Series. Fitzpatrick Pictures, Inc., New York, N. Y.

Operetta:
Way Down South (based on Foster melodies), by Frederick Martens. C. C. Birchard & Co.

Chapter IX. Religious Music

Songs:
"What a Friend We Have in Jesus," by Charles C. Converse; "Rescue the Perishing," by William H. Doane; "Holy Ghost, with Light Divine," by L. M. Gottschalk; "All Hail the Power of Jesus' Name!" by Oliver Holden; "Work, for the Night Is Coming," by Lowell Mason; "Stand Up, Stand Up for Jesus," by G. J. Webb; "Sweet By-and-By," by Joseph P. Webster

Record:
"The Lonesome Road," Decca Album 224

Chapter X. Music Education

Singing Schools:
Songs:
"El-a-noy" (pioneer song); "Red River Valley" (American)

Public Schools
Songs:
"The Blue Alsatian Mountains," by Stephen Adams; "Wildwood Flowers," by Lowell Mason

Chapter XI. Music Organizations and Their Struggle to Bring Music to a New Nation

Oratorios
  Records:
    "Hallelujah Chorus," from *The Messiah*, by Georg Handel, Victor 11825; "The Heavens Are Telling," from *The Creation*, by Josef Haydn, Victor 11960

Operas
  Records:
    "Largo," from *Xerxes*, by Georg Handel, Columbia 7331-M; "Largo al Factotum," from *The Barber of Seville*, by Rossini, Columbia 7299-M

Instrumental Music
  Records:
    "Eighth Harpsichord Suite," by Georg Handel, Columbia DB-502; "Symphony No. 4" (The Clock), by Josef Haydn, Victor M-57; "Symphony No. 45" (The Farewell), by Josef Haydn, Columbia M-205

Violin and Piano Music
  Record:
    "Herd Girl's Sunday," by Ole Bull, Victor 35885

Music for Part Three

Music in the Period of Expansion

Chapter XII. Music on the Advancing Frontier

Songs:
    "America, the Beautiful" (homeland song), by S. A. Ward; "Bury Me Not on the Lone Prairie" (cowboy song); "Goin' Down the Road Feelin' Bad" (Okie ballad), by Woody Guthrie; "Her Blanket" (Navajo Indian air), by Thurlow Lieurance; "Casey Jones" (railroad song), by Eddie Newton;

"Pat on the Railway" (railroad song); "Sacramento" (sea chantey); "Sweet Betsy from Pike" (song of the forty-niners)

Records:
"Cowboy Songs," Decca Album 65; "Turkey in the Straw," by David Guion, Victor 4390; "By the Waters of the Minnetonka," by Thurlow Lieurance, Victor 1198; "Suite Number 2" (The Indian), by Edward MacDowell, Columbia M-373; "Santa Fe Trail," from *Symphony No. 1,* by Harl McDonald, Victor Album M-754; "Deer Dance," by Charles Skilton, Victor 22174; "Songs of Old California," Decca Album 49

Chapter XIII. Musical Entertainment

Songs:
"In the Evening by the Moonlight," by James A. Bland; "Kentucky Babe," words by Richard H. Buck; "Oh, Promise Me," from *Robin Hood,* by Reginald De Koven; *Robin Hood,* by Reginald De Koven, adapted by Lois von Haupt as a children's opera story; *Katinka* (musical play), by Rudolph Friml; "Darling Nellie Gray," by B. R. Hanby; "Sippin' Cider through a Straw," by Terry Morgan and Lee David; "Little Annie Rooney," by Michael Nolan; "Sweet Genevieve," by Henry Tucker

Song Collection:
Album of Songs by Victor Herbert. M. Witmark & Sons, 1927.

Records:
"Oh, Promise Me," by Reginald De Koven, Victor 1295; "Donkey Serenade," from *The Firefly,* by Rudolph Friml, Columbia 384-M; "Indian Love Call," from *Rose Marie,* by Rudolph Friml, Victor 9652; "Friml's Melodies," Vol. I, Victor Album P-58; "Ah! Sweet Mystery of Life," by Victor Herbert, Columbia 4107-M; "Dagger Dance" (Natoma), by Victor Herbert, Victor 11932; "Victor Herbert Melodies," Vol. II and III, Decca Albums 72 and 73; "Favorite Melodies of Sigmund Romberg," Decca Album 98; "Student Prince" (selections), by Sigmund Romberg, Columbia 7350-M

Chapter XIV. Popular Music

Songs:

"Sweet Adeline," by Harry Armstrong; "De Blues Ain' Nothin' " (Negro blues); "Silver Threads among the Gold," by H. P. Danks; "In the Good Old Summer Time," by George Evans; "Friendless Blues," by W. C. Handy; "After the Ball," by Charles K. Harris; "In the Gloaming," by Annie F. Harrison; "A Hot Time in the Old Town," by Theodore A. Metz; "Love's Old Sweet Song," by J. L. Molloy

Records:

"Alexander's Ragtime Band," by Irving Berlin, Victor 25445; "Blues," Decca Album 59; "Missouri Waltz," by T. K. Logan, Victor 20973; "American Patrol," by F. W. Meacham, Victor 22061; "Cakewalk" (scherzo from *Third Symphony*), by Harl McDonald, Victor 15377; "Old Time Dance Music," Decca Album 19; "The Whistler and His Dog," by Arthur Pryor, Columbia 325-M; "Marches by John Philip Sousa," Decca Album 22; "Semper Fidelis," by John Philip Sousa, Victor 4392; "Stars and Stripes Forever," by John Philip Sousa, Victor 4392; "Anchor's Aweigh," by Charles A. Zimmerman, Victor 21296

Music for Part Four

Music in a Full-Grown Nation

Chapter XV. Scientific Inventions and Music

Records:

"The Cradle Will Rock," by Marc Blitzstein, Musicraft 18; "When Johnny Comes Marching Home," by Roy Harris, Victor 8629; "The Magic of the Novachord," Victor Album P-57; "Modern American Music" (ten short works commissioned for radio programs), Decca Album 219; "Pinocchio," Victor Album P-18; "The Wizard of Oz," Decca Album 74

Chapter XVII. Music in the Everyday Life of the Nation

Music in Industry
Records:
"Skyscrapers," by J. A. Carpenter, Victor Album M-130;
"Pacific 231," by Arthur Honneger, Victor 9276; "The Steel
Foundry" (*Symphony of Machines*), by Alexander Mossolov,
Columbia M-347

Music in Health
Records:
"From the Land of Sky Blue Water," by Charles Wakefield
Cadman, Victor 1115; "By the Waters of the Minnetonka,"
by Thurlow Lieurance, Victor 1198; "El Capitan March," by
John Philip Sousa, Victor 1441

Music in Leisure Time—Serious Music
Records:
"Adventures in a Perambulator," by J. A. Carpenter, Victor
Album M-238; "Danny Deever," by Walter Damrosch, Victor
6638; "Standin' in the Need of Prayer," by Louis Gruenberg,
Victor 17911; "Merry Mount" (orchestral suite), by Howard
Hanson, Victor Album M-781; "Rhumba," by Harl McDon-
ald, Victor 8919; "A Victory Ball," by Ernest Schelling, Victor
1127 and 1128; "Through the Looking Glass," by Deems
Taylor, Columbia Set M-350

Music in Leisure Time—Popular Music
Records:
"Dixieland Jazz," Decca Album 132; "Creole Rhapsody," by
Duke Ellington, Victor 36049; "Rhapsody in Blue," by
George Gershwin, Columbia 7192-M; "I Got Rhythm," by
George Gershwin, Columbia 4268-M; "Porgy and Bess," by
George Gershwin, Victor Album C-25; "Grand Canyon
Suite," by Ferde Grofé, Victor Album C-18; "Smoke Gets in
Your Eyes," by Jerome Kern, Columbia 292-M; "Showboat"
(medley), by Jerome Kern, Victor 26043

Music in Religion
  Records:
    "Festival Te Deum," by Dudley Buck, Victor 35994; "67th Psalm," by Charles Ives, Columbia 17139-D

Chapter XVIII. Music of the World Wars

Songs:
  "God Bless America," by Irving Berlin; "Over There," by George M. Cohan; "There's a Long, Long Trail A-Winding," by Zo Elliott; "Hinkey Dinkey Parlee-Voo" (World War); "Keep the Home Fires Burning," by Ivor Novello; "Ballad for Americans," by Earl Robinson; "Battle Hymn," by Earl Robinson.

Records:
  "Ballad of the Leatherneck Corps," Victor 36404; "On the Mall," by E. F. Goldman, Victor 26292; "I Hear America Singing," by George Kleinsinger, Victor Album M-777; "Ballad for Americans," by Earl Robinson, Victor Album P-20; "Stars and Stripes Forever," by John Philip Sousa, Victor 1441

Song Collections:
  Legion Airs. Leo Feist Co.
  Songs for America. Robbins Music Co.

Collection of Piano Music:
  Marches in the American Way. Sam Fox Publishing Co.

INDEX